Read this book online today:

With SAP PRESS BooksOnline we offer you online access to knowledge from the leading SAP experts. Whether you use it as a beneficial supplement or as an alternative to the printed book, with SAP PRESS BooksOnline you can:

- Access your book anywhere, at any time. All you need is an Internet connection.
- Perform full text searches on your book and on the entire SAP PRESS library.
- Build your own personalized SAP library.

The SAP PRESS customer advantage:

Register this book today at *www.sap-press.com* and obtain exclusive free trial access to its online version. If you like it (and we think you will), you can choose to purchase permanent, unrestricted access to the online edition at a very special price!

Here's how to get started:

1. Visit *www.sap-press.com.*
2. Click on the link for SAP PRESS BooksOnline and login (or create an account).
3. Enter your free trial license key, shown below in the corner of the page.
4. Try out your online book with full, unrestricted access for a limited time!

Your personal free trial license key
for this online book is:

nm3s-te5h-uxpz-y982

Account Determination in SAP®

 PRESS

SAP® Essentials

Expert SAP knowledge for your day-to-day work

Whether you wish to expand your SAP knowledge, deepen it, or master a use case, SAP Essentials provide you with targeted expert knowledge that helps support you in your day-to-day work. To the point, detailed, and ready to use.

SAP PRESS is a joint initiative of SAP and Galileo Press. The know-how offered by SAP specialists combined with the expertise of the Galileo Press publishing house offers the reader expert books in the field. SAP PRESS features first-hand information and expert advice, and provides useful skills for professional decision-making.

SAP PRESS offers a variety of books on technical and business related topics for the SAP user. For further information, please visit our website: *www.sap-press.com.*

Naeem Arif and Sheikh Mohammed Tauseef
SAP ERP Financials: Configuration and Design, Second Edition
2011, 664 pp., hardcover
978-1-59229-393-3

Paul Ovigele
100 Things You Should Know About Financial Accounting with SAP
2011, 343 pp., hardcover
978-1-59229-364-3

Manish Patel
Discover SAP ERP Financials
2008, 544 pp., paperback
978-1-59229-184-7

Faisal Mahboob
Integration of Materials Management with Financial Accounting in SAP
2010, 429 pp., hardcover
978-1-59229-337-7

Manish Patel

Account Determination in SAP®

Bonn • Boston

Galileo Press is named after the Italian physicist, mathematician and philosopher Galileo Galilei (1564–1642). He is known as one of the founders of modern science and an advocate of our contemporary, heliocentric worldview. His words *Eppur si muove* (And yet it moves) have become legendary. The Galileo Press logo depicts Jupiter orbited by the four Galilean moons, which were discovered by Galileo in 1610.

Editor Meg Dunkerley
Copyeditor Julie McNamee
Cover Design Graham Geary
Photo Credit Image Copyright tommiphoto. Used under license from Shutterstock.com.
Layout Design Vera Brauner
Production Graham Geary
Typesetting Publishers' Design and Production Services, Inc.
Printed and bound in the United States of America

ISBN 978-1-59229-382-7

© 2012 by Galileo Press Inc., Boston (MA)

2nd edition 2012

Library of Congress Cataloging-in-Publication Data
Patel, Manish.
Account determination in SAP / Manish Patel. — 2nd ed.
p. cm.
Includes bibliographical references and index.
ISBN 978-1-59229-382-7 (alk. paper) — ISBN 1 59229-382-4
(alk. paper)
1. SAP ERP. 2. Accounting—Computer programs. 3. Accounting—
Data processing. 4. Financial statements. I. Title.
HF5679.P317 2011
658.15'244—dc23
2011041668

FSC
www.fsc.org
MIX
Paper from
responsible sources
FSC® C014174

Contents at a Glance

Dear Reader,

If you are using or need to get up to speed on account determination in SAP ERP, this is your must-have guide. In this second edition of one of our best-selling books, Manish Patel will help you master account determination techniques in each component for generating General Ledger postings, including areas such as AR/AP, tax transactions, bank transactions, human capital management, and materials management. Each chapter provides step-by-step instructions, real-world examples, business processes, useful screenshots, and practical tips to help readers understand and master account determination.

I welcomed the opportunity to work with Manish — it was a pleasure to witness such expertise and proficiency. I'm confident that you will find his most recent book with SAP PRESS up to the same standard as his previous books.

We appreciate your business, and welcome your feedback. Your comments and suggestions are the most useful tools to help us improve our books for you, the reader. We encourage you to visit our website at *www.sap-press.com* and share your feedback about this work.

Thank you for purchasing a book from SAP PRESS!

Meg Dunkerley
Editor, SAP PRESS

Galileo Press
Boston, MA

meg.dunkerley@galileo-press.com
www.sap-press.com

Contents

4   Tax Transactions   83

5   Bank Transactions   103

9   Inventory Transactions   193

1 Overview

One of the major goals of any SAP installation is to improve efficiency by automating as many manual, cross-departmental activities as possible.

General Ledger (GL) account determination in the SAP ERP Financials component assists in reaching this goal by providing a structured framework and methodology. Using GL account determination, business transactions originating in different SAP ERP components automatically determine the appropriate GL account for posting—therefore eliminating manual intervention for the most part.

By design, SAP uses different techniques for GL account determination in different SAP ERP components. This Essentials guide provides you with an overview of the GL account determination techniques used in some of the major SAP components. This Essentials guide is relevant up to SAP ECC 6.0.

Chapter 1 begins by explaining the GL account setup in the SAP ERP system. This is primarily for the benefit of readers who are familiar with the setup of GL accounts in SAP but are not necessarily experts in SAP ERP Financials. Even if SAP ERP Financials is your primary area of expertise, the section in Chapter 1 on different types of account determination techniques used in SAP ERP will be useful to you.

You do not have to read this guide in any particular sequence, although it helps if you read the chapters that form the basis of the discussion first. You should definitely read this first chapter before proceeding through the remainder of this guide in the order you choose. Section 1.3 is particularly important because it explains the three techniques discussed in this guide on a conceptual level.

1.1 Chart of Accounts

GL accounts master data is maintained in SAP ERP at two levels: the chart of accounts level and the company code level. This type of master data maintenance enables the same chart of accounts to be shared by multiple company codes. The chart of accounts assigned to a company code is its operating chart of accounts.

1.1.1 Operating Chart of Accounts

Every operative company code in SAP ERP is assigned an operating chart of accounts. This chart of accounts contains GL accounts to which transactional postings are made for the business transactions posted to the company code. Primary financial statements and most of the operational reports of the company code are generated using GL accounts from the operating chart of accounts.

The operating chart of accounts (see Figure 1.1) is assigned to the company code as part of the global parameters for the company code via the menu path FINANCIAL ACCOUNTING IMG • FINANCIAL ACCOUNTING GLOBAL SETTINGS • GLOBAL COMPANY CODE • ENTER GLOBAL PARAMETERS.

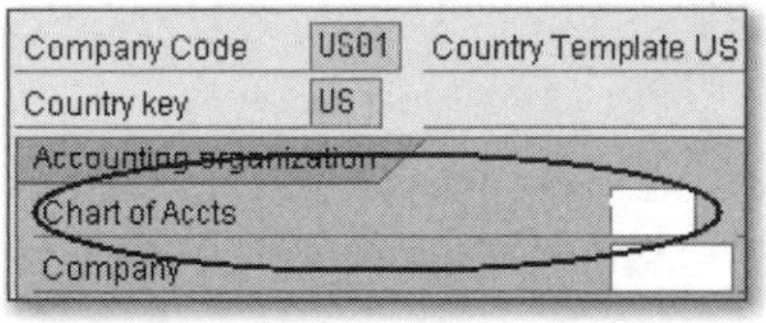

Figure 1.1   Operating Chart of Accounts

However, consider SAP installations for a large company, with multiple company codes in multiple countries. In such an implementation, business, management, or statutory requirements make it difficult to use a single, common worldwide chart of accounts. Each company must be able to generate financial statements that meet local statutory requirements. At the same time, if companies start using different charts of accounts, it becomes difficult to obtain a consolidated financial picture at the head office. Such requirements can be broadly classified into the following two groups:

▶ Requirements to generate consolidated financial statements across all companies at the head office

▶ Requirements of individual companies to generate financial statements that meet their local management and statutory requirements

To handle these requirements, SAP ERP provides two charts of accounts that can optionally be set up for a company in addition to the operating chart of accounts:

- ▶ Country chart of accounts
- ▶ Group chart of accounts

Let's take a look at these two charts of accounts.

1.1.2 Country Chart of Accounts

This chart of accounts contains country-specific GL accounts to enable preparation of financial statements per local statutory requirements. If you choose to use the country chart of accounts for your implementation, you can also include GL accounts that meet your unique local management requirements.

The country chart of accounts is useful, (e.g., if all company codes in a group are set up with the same operating chart of accounts). In this type of setup, consolidated reports across company codes are prepared with relative ease because all company codes use the same chart of accounts. At the same time, local statutory financial statement requirements are met by the country-specific chart of accounts.

The country chart of accounts is assigned to the company code along with other global parameters maintained for the company code (see Figure 1.2) via the menu path FINANCIAL ACCOUNTING IMG • FINANCIAL ACCOUNTING GLOBAL SETTINGS • COMPANY CODE • ENTER GLOBAL PARAMETERS.

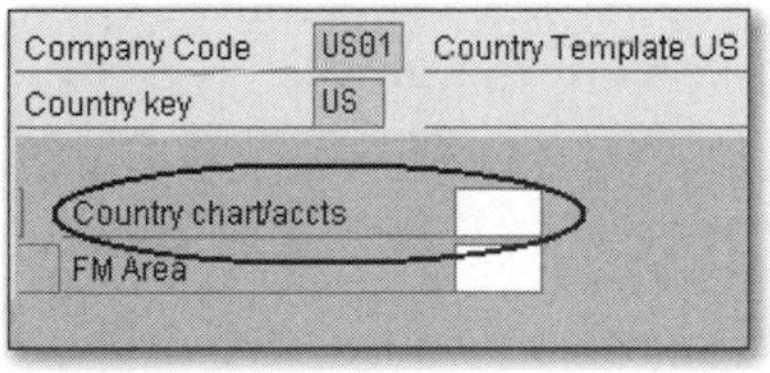

Figure 1.2 Country Chart of Accounts Assignment

In the GL account master data, the GL account corresponding to the country chart of accounts is maintained in the ALTERNATIVE ACCOUNT NO. field. If the country chart of accounts is assigned to a company code, then this alternative account number provides a link between the operating chart of accounts and the country chart of accounts. The ALTERNATIVE ACCOUNT NO. field is available on the CONTROL DATA tab of the company code GL account master data (Figure 1.3).

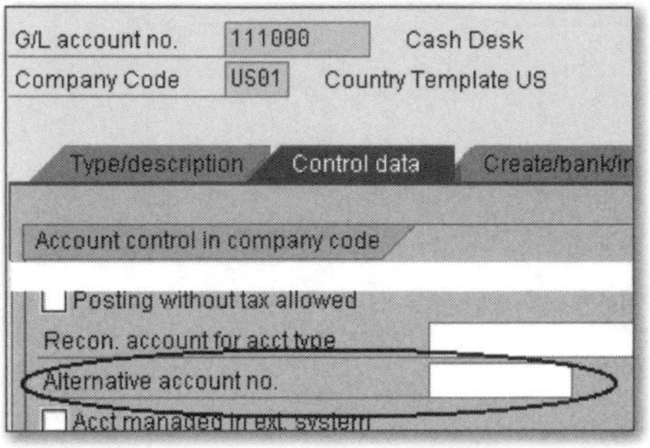

Figure 1.3 Country Chart of Accounts—Account Number

1.1.3 Group Chart of Accounts

The group chart of accounts consists of GL accounts relevant for consolidation purposes. This chart of accounts is useful; for example, if each company code in a group is set up with its own localized operating chart of accounts. In this type of setup, it is relatively easy to prepare local statutory financial statements.

However, it becomes difficult to generate consolidated financial statements because the same information can be in different accounts in different company codes. You can use the group chart of accounts in such a scenario to meet the requirements of group consolidation.

The group chart of accounts is assigned to the operating chart of accounts in the configuration activity for the chart of accounts (see Figure 1.4) via the menu path FINANCIAL ACCOUNTING IMG • GENERAL LEDGER ACCOUNTING • G/L ACCOUNTS • MASTER DATA • PREPARATIONS • EDIT CHART OF ACCOUNTS LIST.

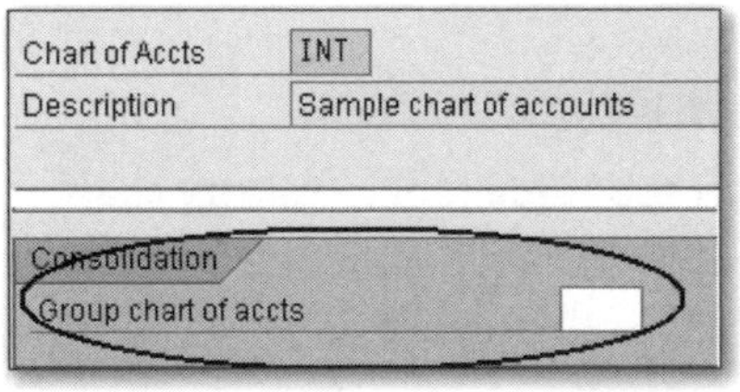

Figure 1.4 Group Chart of Accounts Assignment

In the GL account master data, the GL account corresponding to the group chart of accounts is maintained in the GROUP ACCOUNT NUMBER field (Figure 1.5). This field forms a link between the operating chart of accounts and the group chart of accounts, and is maintained on the TYPE/DESCRIPTION tab of the GL master data at the chart of accounts level.

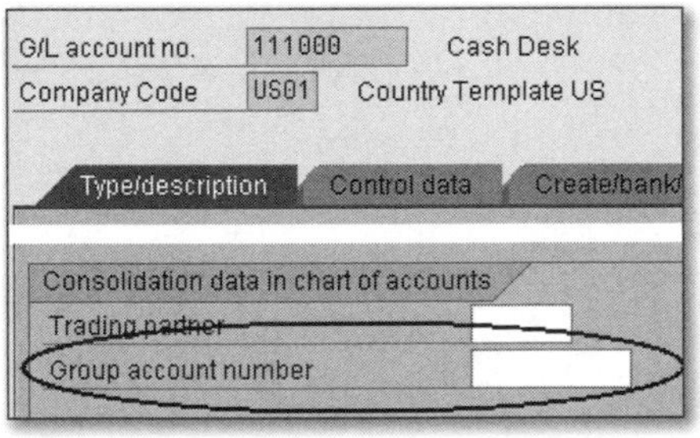

Figure 1.5 Group Chart of Accounts—Account Number

Whether to implement either of these charts of accounts depends on the business requirements of the individual implementation. You can implement these charts of accounts after an SAP ERP system has already become productive. However, it is strongly advisable to implement these charts of accounts during the original implementation of an SAP ERP system.

You can also use other functionalities or approaches to meet the business requirements of unique local reporting combined with the ease of worldwide consolidation. For example, you can use an additional set of accounts in your operating chart of accounts to meet any local requirements of individual company codes. Another option is to use an operating chart of accounts for consolidation purposes, and then use the special purpose ledger component to prepare ledgers for individual countries. Yet another option is to use SAP ERP's consolidation component that has its own financial statement definition. GL accounts from the operating chart of accounts of individual company codes are directly mapped to the financial statement items to generate consolidated statements.

The country chart of accounts and the group chart of accounts were introduced in this section so that you are aware of their existence in SAP ERP, and, if required, you can trace an automatic posting while carrying out top-down or bottom-up analysis from a report. These charts of accounts will not be mentioned any further. All references to GL accounts from this point on will be to the operating chart of accounts, unless explicitly noted. Using the links described in this section, you can arrive at the corresponding GL account in the country chart of accounts and the group chart of accounts.

1.2 General Ledger Account Master

We will now look at some of the important fields in the GL account master that are relevant for automatic GL account determination. This list also includes fields that are not directly used in automatic GL account determination but which have an indirect influence on which GL account can or cannot be used in automatic GL account determination.

1.2.1 Account Group

Even though it is not directly linked to GL account determination, the account group (SKA1-KTOKS) controls which fields are available for maintenance in the GL account master data.

A chart of accounts consists of multiple account groups that arrange different types of GL accounts and also determine a valid number range for those GL accounts. At the very minimum, you'll have two account groups: Balance Sheet accounts and Income Statement accounts. The field status group associated with an account group controls the fields that are available in GL account master maintenance. This is important because unless a field is enabled or made available in GL account master maintenance, you won't be able to maintain it to influence account determination.

Figure 1.6 shows an example of a field status group setup for the account GROUP PL for P&L STATEMENT ACCOUNTS. You can reach this configuration activity via menu path FINANCIAL ACCOUNTING IMG • GENERAL LEDGER ACCOUNTING • G/L ACCOUNTS • MASTER DATA • PREPARATIONS • DEFINE ACCOUNT GROUP • FIELD STATUS.

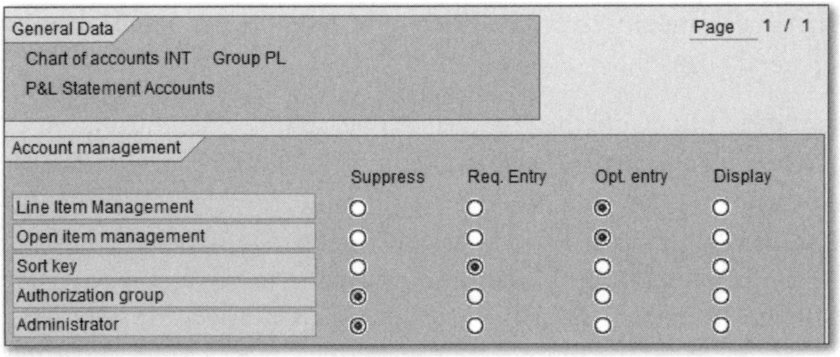

Figure 1.6 Field Status Group Definition

1.2.2 P&L Statement Account or Balance Sheet Account

Now let's see the relevance of the P&L STATEMENT ACCOUNT (SKA1-GVTYP) or BALANCE SHEET ACCOUNT (SKA1-XBILK) fields.

For example, in Asset Accounting (AA) (see Chapter 6), depreciation expenses can be posted only to a P&L type of GL account, whereas accumulated depreciation can be posted only to a balance sheet type of GL account. Similarly, in the revenue recognition process (see Chapter 8), recognized revenue is posted only to a P&L type of GL account, whereas deferred revenue is posted only to a balance sheet type of GL account.

Many configuration transactions for GL account determination have built-in validations to expect only one of these types of accounts. If you try to assign the incorrect type of GL account in those configuration activities, you'll get an immediate error.

1.2.3 Group Account Number

As already discussed, this field is relevant only if your implementation uses group chart of accounts. In such an implementation, this field (SKA1-BILTK) contains the GL account number from the group chart of accounts.

1.2.4 Reconciliation Account for Account Type

The reconciliation account for the account type (SKB1-MITKZ) field determines whether the GL account is a reconciliation account. You can indicate an account as a reconciliation account for customers, vendors, assets, and others.

There are few automatic account determination configuration activities where you have to enter a reconciliation GL account. For example, you can specify alternate reconciliation accounts for special GL transactions (see Chapter 3), or you have to use asset reconciliation accounts in configuration activities of AA (see Chapter 6). However, where applicable, it is usually intuitively obvious whether the reconciliation GL account is for assets, for customers, or for vendors.

1.2.5 Alternative Account Number

As already discussed, this account is relevant only if a country chart of accounts is used in an implementation. In such an implementation, this field (SKB1-ALTKT) contains the GL account number from the country chart of accounts.

1.2.6 Open Item Management

This flag (SKB1-XOPVW) in the GL account master is relevant only for balance sheet types of GL accounts. This flag determines whether an account is maintained as an ending balance account or whether debit and credit postings on the account have to be cleared. If a GL account is maintained as an ending balance account, then this flag is not selected. These types of GL accounts include bank accounts, cash accounts, most tax accounts, equity accounts, and so on.

On the other hand, if GL account determination posts to an account that requires subsequent clearing between debit and credit entries, then this flag should be selected for the corresponding GL account. For example, consider a goods receipt/ invoice receipt (GR/IR) account in a purchase-to-pay business process. In this type of account, you must be able to match individual credits and debits of goods receipts and invoice receipts by purchase order. Similarly, for an accrual account, you would like to match credits and debits of individual accruals with actual expense entries. If this flag is not set, then that reconciliation can be a laborious manual process. Whereas if this flag is set, you can use automatic clearing transactions and processes in SAP ERP to match debit and credit entries posted to a GL account.

Please carefully consider this flag before making postings to a GL account in a productive environment. Changing this flag is typically not an easy process after a GL account already has transaction postings.

1.2.7 Sort Key

This field (SKB1-ZUAWA) determines how, and with what value, the allocation field in the document posted to this account is filled. The sort key for a GL account should be selected judiciously to assist in account clearing for open item managed accounts or to assist in easy grouping and reporting of documents posted in other accounts.

Even though it is advisable to select the appropriate sort key during the initial setup of GL accounts, this field in the GL account master can be changed easily. Any change will impact all subsequent document entries posted to that account. For existing documents, you can simply override allocation field values as necessary. For example, you can set the sort key for the GR/IR account to a purchase order + line item number. This will enable you to easily group together all goods receipts and invoice receipts for the same purchase order item, thereby assisting in easy clearing or reporting of any discrepancies.

You configure sort keys in SAP ERP via menu path Financial Accounting IMG • General Ledger Accounting • G/L Accounts • Line Items • Display Line Items • Determine Standard Sorting for Line Items. Because the sort key can be configured to derive values even from a line item text entered in a document, you can create your own rules for what should be updated in the allocation field. By combining this feature with the automatic clearing processes discussed in the previous section, you can considerably automate month-end reconciliation and clearing processes.

1.2.8 Field Status Group

This field (SKB1-FSTAG) also indirectly impacts GL account determination postings. It controls fields that are available while posting transactions to a GL account. This field is so important to automatic account postings generated by SAP ERP that Appendix A discusses its configuration in detail.

Carry out settings for Field Status using the menu path: Financial Accounting IMG • General Ledger Accounting • Business Transactions • G/L Account Posting • Make and Check Document Settings • Define Field Status Variants.

1.2.9 Post Automatically Only

Most of the GL accounts set up in automatic GL account determination have this field (SKB1-XINTB) selected, though very few GL account determination configuration transactions explicitly check for this flag. Separating automatic postings from manual adjustment postings usually translate into easier account reconciliation and troubleshooting of any problems. If there is a business requirement to make manual adjustments, you should create a separate GL account to post manual adjustments.

1.2.10 Tax Category

The tax category field value (SKB1-MWSKZ) indirectly influences automatic account determination in SAP ERP. As we will discuss in the chapter on tax accounting (see Chapter 4), taxes can be either input tax (in the procure-to-pay cycle) or output tax (in the order-to-cash cycle). Depending on the business transaction, only a specific type of tax is allowed.

The value in this field determines the types of taxes that can be posted to a GL account. It is possible to use a field value so that any type of taxes can be posted to the corresponding GL account. However, if you happen to run into a "tax type not allowed" error while posting a transaction in SAP ERP, you should check the value in this field for a corresponding GL account.

1.2.11 Only Balances in Local Currency

This flag (SKB1-XSALH) controls whether balances for a GL account are updated only in the local currency (the operative currency of the company code). This field value indirectly influences automatic account determination and, in particular, account determination for clearing transactions.

If this flag is not selected, SAP ERP translates any foreign currency transactions into local currency at the time of posting a clearing entry. For example, you may want to look at this flag for relevant GL accounts if you run into any error about local currency posting or local currency balance not being zero.

1.2.12 Authorization Group

The authorization group (SKB1-BEGRU) is used to extend SAP ERP's authorization protection to specific accounts. This functionality allows you to provide authorization to only specific groups of individuals who can post to certain accounts. If those accounts are used in automatic account determination, then this is another field value in the GL account master that you will need to keep an eye on.

Even though it may appear that the field values are freely definable, you will need to coordinate with your authorization and securities team to decide on valid values for this GL account field.

Now that we have discussed the relevant fields in the GL account master, let's shift to the main subject of this Essentials guide: account determination techniques.

1.3 Account Determination Techniques

This section describes the concepts related to the GL account determination techniques used in different SAP ERP components. This section, and by extension, this whole guide — concentrates on three GL account determination techniques that are most commonly used for automatic GL account determination.

The conventions used in all the figures throughout this Essentials guide are shown in Figure 1.7.

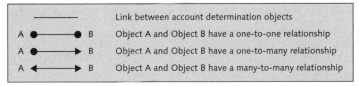

Figure 1.7 Conventions Used for Account Determination Diagrams in This Guide

Keep an eye on these relationships because they play a crucial role in the approach you take, whether you are implementing a new component or troubleshooting some pesky production environment problem. The next section provides a high-level overview of the three main account determination techniques.

1.3.1 Transaction Key Technique

Figure 1.8 illustrates the account determination objects that are directly or indirectly involved in GL account determination using this technique. This is a fairly simple configuration technique, so GL account assignment, configuration, and troubleshooting are also relatively simple. The transaction key technique is used in several areas, such as GL accounting (Chapter 2), Accounts Receivable (AR)/Accounts Payable (AP) (Chapter 3), and Inventory Management (Chapter 9).

In transaction key techniques, a business transaction is associated with a three-character transaction key that uniquely identifies the business transaction. Account determination is carried out by assigning one or more GL accounts to the transaction key.

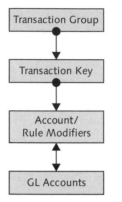

Figure 1.8 Transaction Key Technique

Some transaction keys (particularly for Inventory Management transactions) have one or more account modifiers (rules) associated with them. These modifiers allow the assignment of GL accounts based on multiple criteria.

For example, if a configuration activity supports only a transaction key, you can assign only one GL account for the corresponding business transaction, and that's the end of it.

However, if a transaction key has an associated debit/credit account modifier, you can assign two GL accounts: one if the business transaction generates a debit posting and another if the business transaction generates a credit posting.

Similarly, if a transaction key has a tax code as an account modifier, then you can assign multiple GL accounts to the same transaction key—one for each tax code.

If a transaction key has both (debit/credit and tax code) as account modifiers, you can assign two GL accounts (for debit posting and for credit posting) for each tax code. As is evident, the number of account modifiers available for a transaction key increases the number of GL account assignment positions to create. This will become clearer as you read through this guide.

It is important to note that account modifiers are assigned to a specific transaction key, and whether or not they can be modified is set by SAP ERP. Therefore, there are two possible scenarios with respect to their influence on the configuration of GL account determination:

▶ The account modifier is enabled by default for a transaction key, and it cannot be modified. If you cannot modify configuration, then there isn't much flexibility. If you don't want to assign different accounts for debit and credit transactions, then just assign the same account for both values.

▶ The account modifier is available and can be modified. In this case, it depends on business requirements as to whether or not you want to enable the modifier and maintain different GL accounts for each combination value.

A third, less common, scenario combines both of the above, in which one transaction key has more than one account modifier—some that cannot be modified, and others that can. In this case, you will use a combination of the methods described previously for GL account determination.

For example, consider configuration Transaction OBYC. This GL account determination used in inventory management (see Chapter 9) beautifully illustrates the concept of account modifiers:

▶ The transaction key for unplanned delivery costs (UPF) doesn't provide any account modifiers. So even if you wanted to, you can't assign different GL accounts to this business transaction using this configuration activity. In such a scenario, you have to evaluate whether you can use any other functionality, such as a substitution technique (discussed in Appendix B), to achieve the desired solution.

▶ The transaction key for the GR/IR clearing process (WRX) provides four account modifiers (debit/credit indicator, general modification, valuation modifier, and valuation class), which can all be enabled as required.

▶ The transaction key for posting external activity costs (FRL) provides three account modifiers (debit/credit indicator, valuation modifier, and valuation class). The debit/credit indicator cannot be enabled.

The transaction keys for (conceptually) related business transactions are grouped into a transaction group. As far as GL account determination is concerned, this transaction group is only used for informational purposes. Usually, you only need to know the transaction key to identify and decide on GL account determination.

It is relatively easy to identify the GL account determined using this technique. However, it is important to know the transaction key associated with the corresponding business transactions that generate the posting. Transaction FBKP provides a single source for configuring GL accounts for transactions that use the transaction key technique.

1.3.2 Symbolic Account Technique

The symbolic account technique (see Figure 1.9) consists of two parts:

▶ The derivation of a symbolic account

▶ The substitution of a symbolic account with an actual GL account

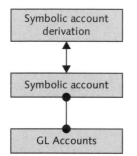

Figure 1.9 Symbolic Account Technique

This GL account determination technique is used in bank transactions (Chapter 5), travel expense transactions (Chapter 7), and payroll transactions (Chapter 10).

The derivation of a symbolic account can vary in complexity. For example, in GL account determination for bank transactions, you can assign a symbolic account directly in place of an actual GL account. On the other hand, payroll transactions use a fairly complex combination of multiple techniques discussed in this guide for symbolic account assignment. (And this is just the assignment of a symbolic account. You still have to assign an actual GL account to the symbolic account. We will cover this complexity in later chapters.)

It should be noted that symbolic account derivation logic in SAP ERP is not always configurable, meaning that you cannot always configure the criteria by which you want to derive a symbolic account. In some components, SAP ERP sets the structure and the format of a symbolic account, which cannot be modified. You will encounter these scenarios as you go through the rest of this Essentials guide.

Now let's look at the third account determination technique called the condition technique.

1.3.3 Condition Technique

The condition technique provides considerable flexibility in terms of configuring GL account determination. Most, if not all, objects used in this technique are configurable, although some require greater technical skills than others.

Figure 1.10 shows the different objects involved in this GL account determination technique. At the highest level, the field catalog provides the list of table fields that can be used as parameters for GL account determination. Each business scenario that uses the condition technique is associated with a field catalog. For some business scenarios, you are allowed to add new fields to the corresponding field catalog. Otherwise, the only fields available to you are the ones provided as default in SAP ERP.

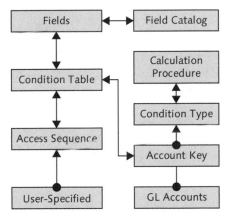

Figure 1.10 Condition Technique

Fields from the field catalog are used to create condition tables. Condition tables provide a combination of characteristics (fields) for which you would like to assign a GL account.

For example, a condition table with a customer group and material group as its characteristic fields allows different GL accounts to be assigned to combinations of customer group and material group values.

You can create another condition table for the same business scenario, with the sales organization and customer group as its characteristic fields. This condition table will allow you to assign different GL accounts for different combinations of sales organization and customer group values. Standard SAP ERP provides some condition tables for each scenario, but if required, you can create additional condition tables.

In condition tables, for every combination of characteristic field values, one or more account keys are assigned. Therefore, GL accounts in condition tables are assigned to a combination of characteristic field values *and* an account key. An account key indicates the specific purpose for which the associated GL account will be used.

For example, in SAP Sales and Distribution (SD) (Chapter 8) you can have separate account keys for revenue, freight expense, custom duty, discount, and accruals.

Therefore, in the condition table example discussed earlier, for the same combination of customer group and material group values, you can assign different GL accounts for revenue, freight, and discount, using different account keys. SAP ERP allows the creation of additional account keys with relative ease.

We discussed that you can have more than one condition table, each with different fields as characteristics, referring to the same business scenario. So how does SAP ERP know in which sequence it should access these tables to determine the required GL account? This is where the concept of access sequence comes into play.

The access sequence determines the sequence in which SAP ERP searches through condition tables to find the required GL account. SAP ERP provides standard access sequences for each scenario; however, you can create additional access sequences if necessary and as required.

A fairly common use of the condition technique is in calculation procedures. A business scenario requires the configuration of corresponding calculation procedures. These procedures (e.g., the pricing procedure in sales or calculation schema in purchasing) provide the structure for calculating prices or desired amounts.

Calculation procedures carry out the required calculations using one or more condition types. Condition types represent the different factors that need to be calculated or considered for calculation of the end result. The amounts calculated by each condition may impact the end result or could be part of the procedure only for reference purposes. Each condition type is assigned an access sequence.

Finally, in the calculation procedure, each condition type that is expected to post to accounting is assigned one or more account keys. The following process list links all the objects we have discussed so far:

▸ SAP ERP determines the calculation procedure to use for a business scenario.

▸ The calculation procedure consists of multiple conditions.

▸ Every condition in the procedure is associated with a condition type.

  ▸ A condition type is associated with an access sequence.

  ▸ The access sequence is used to go through condition tables.

  ▸ Depending on the characteristic values, the access sequence determines a GL account.

▸ A condition relevant for the GL account posting is also associated with an account key.

▸ SAP ERP assigns the GL account determined by the access sequence to the account key.

As you may have observed, the account key in this technique serves a similar purpose as the symbolic account described in the previous section.

Now that we've covered the concepts related to the different account determination techniques, let's review what we've discussed so far before continuing with the next chapter.

1.4   Summary

When reading this guide, you may sometimes find that the information you need is scattered across multiple chapters. This is bound to happen when dealing with an integrated system such as SAP ERP. However, all the information about a specific topic is contained within a single chapter, irrespective of where it resides in the configuration guide.

Another point to keep in mind is that it is possible to override GL accounts determined from the configuration by using the user exits or enhancements available for each SAP ERP component.

In addition, you can use Transaction OBBH to set up substitution rules that can change the GL account to which the posting is made.

You should keep this in mind when you are trying to diagnose a problem or you are deciding on the available functionality related to the GL account determination.

1.5   Reference

All chapters in this guide conclude with a Reference section that provides you with a technical reference for the objects discussed in the chapter. As applicable, a Reference section in each chapter consists of three lists relevant to the discussion in the chapter. The general structure of the Reference section is as follows:

- ▶ List of configuration transactions
- ▶ List of relevant tables and structures
- ▶ List of any available enhancement routines

Considering the breadth and depth of the topics being discussed in this guide, these lists are not totally complete. However, they do provide a good starting point for exploring the subject matter.

1.5.1   Configuration Transactions

Table 1.1 provides a list of the configuration transactions for the account determination objects discussed in this chapter.

Transaction Code	Description
OB13	Maintain chart of accounts
FS00	Maintain GL accounts centrally
FSP0	Maintain GL accounts in chart of accounts
FSS0	Maintain GL accounts in company code
OBD4	Maintain GL account group

Table 1.1 Configuration Transactions

1.5.2   Tables and Structures

Table 1.2 contains a list of the tables and structures used to store data relevant for GL account determination discussed in this chapter.

Table/Structure	Description
T001	Company code data—with global parameters
T004	Chart of accounts directory
SKA1	GL accounts in chart of accounts
SKB1	GL accounts in company code
T030	Accounts table based on the transaction technique

Table 1.2 Tables and Structures

The symbolic account technique and the condition technique use different sets of tables and structures for different business scenarios. Corresponding lists of tables and structures are provided in later chapters.

2 General Ledger Transactions

General ledger (GL) accounting is a central component in SAP ERP Financials where monetary values corresponding to all business transactions are recorded.

Throughout the month, GL accounting is often at the receiving end of postings generated in other SAP ERP components. For example, a goods receipt posted in Inventory Management creates a GL entry to debit an inventory and credit a clearing account. Similarly, an expense report posted in Accounts Payable (AP) creates a GL entry to debit a travel expense account and credit a payables account.

As part of month-end processing, quarter-end processing, or year-end processing (collectively called period-end processing), you must carry out several activities in the GL component of SAP ERP to prepare financial statements that are in statutory compliance and reflect the state of the business as accurately as possible.

These activities typically include the reconciliation of numbers, the reversal of accrual entries from prior months, the creation of new accrual entries based on the current month's business, valuation of foreign currency transactions, adjustment postings for errors or for the purpose of reclassification of GL entries that are already posted, and so on.

Some of these activities must be done manually, such as adjustment postings to correct errors. However, for some other activities, such as valuation of foreign currency and accrual processing, some level of automation can be introduced.

As you will see in this chapter, the account determination process in the GL component of SAP ERP mostly uses the transaction key technique to obtain the required GL accounts for business transactions.

2.1 Foreign Currency Transactions

In today's marketplace, at least some part of your procure-to-pay process or order-to-cash process or both processes likely involve business transactions and accounting entries in foreign currency. In this context, foreign currency means any currency other than the operating currency assigned to a company code. Operating currency for a company code is the currency in which the company does most of its business and prepares its financial statements, such as balance sheets and income statements.

To prepare accurate financial statements, you must first convert foreign currency transactions to your operating currency using the currency valuation process. These transactions could represent entries posted to accounts maintained on an open item basis but denominated in operating currency (such as receivables and payables accounts), or they could represent transactions in an account that is denominated in foreign currency (such as bank accounts maintained in a foreign currency).

Figure 2.1 shows the IMG menu path that takes you to the activity for currency valuation configuration. Currency valuation uses the transaction key technique for GL account determination. Transaction keys corresponding to currency valuation are grouped under transaction group FWA (exchange rate differences).

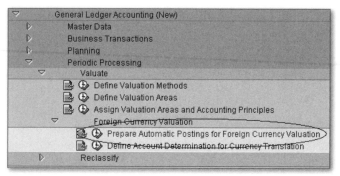

Figure 2.1 Currency Valuation in the Implementation Guide

How currency valuation of a transaction is carried out, and how corresponding accounting entries are posted, depends on the OPEN ITEM MANAGEMENT flag in the GL account master data (see Chapter 1, Section 1.2.6). As you may recall, this flag in the GL account master controls whether a GL account is maintained as an ending balance account or as an open item managed account. Depending on the setting of this flag, you can configure GL account determination for foreign currency revaluation in two different ways.

2.1.1 Open Item General Ledger Accounts

If a GL account is maintained as an open item managed account, GL account determination is configured under transaction key KDF (exchange rate dif.: open items/ GL acct). This transaction key has two optional rule modifiers:

▶ **Currency**
If most of your business transactions are dominated by a couple of foreign currencies, you can use this rule modifier to record exchange gain/loss due to different currencies into separate GL accounts.

▶ **Currency type**
This rule modifier can be used to separate postings of exchange gain/loss to different GL accounts based on the currency type specified at the time of the currency valuation. You carry out the configuration of currency types for a company code in FINANCIAL ACCOUNTING GLOBAL SETTINGS IMG • LEDGERS • LEDGER • DEFINE CURRENCIES OF LEADING LEDGER.

Both of these rule modifiers enable you to carry out GL account determination for foreign currency valuation at a lower level of classification.

Figure 2.2 shows an example of GL account configuration for G/L ACCOUNT (00), maintained on an open item basis. Other accounts in Figure 2.2 are posted when valuation of this GL account is carried out. When an open receivable or payable item in foreign currency is cleared (paid or adjusted with an offsetting entry), any loss or gain due to the exchange rate difference is posted to the EXCHANGE RATE DIFFERENCE REALIZED—LOSS (01) or EXCHANGE RATE DIFFERENCE REALIZED—GAIN (02) account.

Any gain or loss due to exchange rate fluctuations at the time of the currency valuation in open receivable or payable items in foreign currency (essentially, those that are not yet cleared) is considered unrealized. For the financial statement reporting purpose, you want to account for these gains or losses, but you would want to separate the GL accounts for realized gains and losses from unrealized gains or losses.

During the currency valuation process, such unrealized loss is posted to the VAL. LOSS 1 (03) account, and unrealized gain is posted to the VAL.GAIN 1 (04) account. The offsetting entry for both of these accounts is posted to the BAL.SHEET ADJ.1 (05) account.

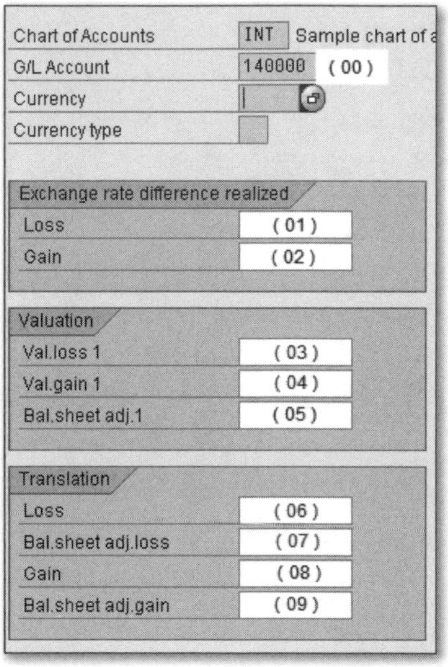

Figure 2.2 Foreign Currency Open Item Accounts

If your corporate group currency is different from your operating currency, you may be required to submit your financial data in the group currency. You can do this by translating the entire financial statement from the operating currency to the group currency. If currency translation is carried out, SAP ERP uses the following GL accounts for posting exchange rate differences:

▶ TRANSLATION LOSS (06)

▶ TRANSLATION LOSS — OFFSETTING (07)

▶ TRANSLATION GAIN (08)

▶ TRANSLATION GAIN — OFFSETTING (09)

Compared to configuration activities discussed in this section, account determination for GL accounts maintained as ending balance accounts is simpler.

2.1.2 Ending Balance General Ledger Accounts

If a GL account is maintained as an ending balance account, the OPEN ITEM MANAGEMENT setting in the GL account master is not set. For these types of accounts, GL account determination is configured under transaction key KDB (Exch. Rate Diff. using Exch. Rate Key).

The rule modifier available for this transaction key is the exchange rate key. This is freely definable code that is maintained in the GL account master (see Chapter 1).

Figure 2.3 shows GL account determination using the exchange rate key. In the figure, the exchange rate key corresponds to different currencies; however, it can refer to any user-defined criterion.

Chart of Accounts	INT	Sample chart of accounts
Transaction	KDB	Exch. Rate Diff. using Exch. Rate Key

Account assignment				
Exchange r...	Expense a...	E/R gains ...	Rolling Val...	Rolling Val...
	(10)	(11)	(12)	(13)
FRF				
INR				
USD				

Figure 2.3 Foreign Currency Ending Balance Accounts

In this case, GL account determination is fairly simple. At the time of the currency valuation, any loss or gain due to the exchange rate difference is posted to the Expense account (10) or E/R gains account (11), respectively.

If your business uses rolling valuation methodology, SAP ERP uses GL accounts Expense account—rolling valuation (12) and Revenue account—rolling valuation (13) to post exchange rate loss or gain, respectively.

2.1.3   Other Accounts Relevant to Foreign Currency

A few other accounts are relevant for foreign currency valuation, if the corresponding functionality has been activated and is being used:

▶ **Document split functionality**
Document splitting functionality in SAP ERP enables you to split an accounting line item by user-defined characteristics, such as profit center, segment, or business area. This, in turn, enables you to generate financial statements by those characteristics without having to go through detailed and cumbersome allocation of accounting entries.

If the document split functionality is active, configure GL accounts for balancing entries under transaction key CEX (document split for currency exchange).

This transaction key is configured using the same menu path shown in Figure 2.1. The only rule modifier available for this transaction key is debit/credit.

▶ **Rounding differences**
If any rounding differences must be posted due to foreign currency transactions, these differences are posted to GL accounts determined using transaction key RDF (internal currencies rounding differences).

This transaction key is also configured using the menu path shown in Figure 2.1, and again, the only rule modifier available for this transaction key is debit/credit.

▶ **Payments in alternate currency**
Business transactions in which payment currency is different from the invoice currency present an interesting scenario for recording exchange gain or loss. The gain or loss that you have to recognize in such a scenario can be attributed to two parts: (1) exchange rate fluctuations between payment currency and invoice currency, and (2) exchange rate fluctuations between the payment currency and local currency of the company code.

Using transaction key KDW, you configure GL accounts for payment differences in alternate currency. Using transaction key KDZ, you configure an offsetting account for the payment differences. This transaction key is also configured using the menu path shown in Figure 2.1, and rule modifier debit/credit is available for both of these transaction keys. Also, because GL accounts for which such exchange gains/losses have to be calculated may be subject to taxes, you can use tax code as the rule modifier for transaction key KDW.

▶ **Financial statement versions**
A relatively new functionality in SAP ERP allows foreign currency GL account determination based on financial statement versions. This configuration is carried out via the menu path FINANCIAL ACCOUNTING IMG • GENERAL LEDGER ACCOUNTING • PERIODIC PROCESSING • VALUATE • FOREIGN CURRENCY VALUATION • DEFINE ACCOUNT DETERMINATION FOR CURRENCY TRANSLATION.

Figure 2.4 shows the maintenance of these GL accounts. Fields (14) and (15) provide the exchange rate type that should be used to determine the effective exchange rate.

Chart of Accts	INT
Valuation Area	🔘
Fin.Stmt Vers.	INT

Account Determination for Translation of Balances					
Fin.statemt itm	Debit bal. E/R type	Credit bal. E/R type	Bal.sheet adj.	Val.loss 1	Val.gain 1
1031000	(14)	(15)	(16)	(17)	(18)

Figure 2.4 Foreign Currency General Ledger Account Determination by Financial Statement Versions

For each financial statement item, any valuation loss or gain due to an exchange rate difference is posted to the VAL.LOSS 1 (17) and VAL.GAIN 1 (18) accounts, respectively. The offsetting entry for these accounts is posted to the BAL.SHEET ADJ. (16) account.

This GL account determination is maintained for a combination of charts of accounts, valuation area (optional), and financial statement version. Even though this configuration is relatively simple, it provides you with the ability to control, at a very detailed level, how exchange rate gains/losses are posted and presented in financial statements.

2.2   Other General Ledger Transactions

This section covers automatic GL account determination for other commonly used GL transactions in SAP ERP.

2.2.1   Retained Earnings

One of the accounting activities performed at the end of a fiscal year is to carry forward GL account balances to the next fiscal year.

For balance sheet accounts, balances are carried forward to the same GL accounts in the next fiscal year. For income statement accounts, net gain or loss is calculated based on all income statement accounts, and that amount is carried forward to a retained earnings account in the next fiscal year.

SAP ERP determines a retained earnings account based on the income statement account type maintained in the GL account master data (see Chapter 1). It is most common to use only one income statement account type for all income statement accounts in a chart of accounts. However, if necessary, it is possible to set up more than one income statement account type. You can choose to carry forward the net balance of all income statement accounts with the same income statement account type to a retained earnings account. This level of abstraction enables you to maintain more than one retained earning account in your chart of accounts.

As the configuration in Figure 2.5 shows, the balance of all income statement accounts of type "T1" will be carried forward to retained earnings account "330000", whereas the balance of all income statement accounts of type "T2" will be carried forward to retained earnings account "330001".

Chart of Accounts	CANA
Transaction	BIL

Account assignment

P&L statmt ...	Account
T1	330000
T2	330001

Figure 2.5 Retained Earnings Account

This configuration activity is carried out via the menu path FINANCIAL ACCOUNTING IMG • GENERAL LEDGER ACCOUNTING • BUSINESS TRANSACTIONS • CLOSING • CARRY FORWARD • DEFINE RETAINED EARNINGS ACCOUNT.

2.2.2 Intercompany Transactions

SAP ERP can post intercompany accounting documents by the direct or indirect specification of other company codes. For example, you can enter a different company code in a line item when posting a manual journal entry in another company code. This is a direct specification of other company code. On the other hand, if a vendor invoice is posted in one company code, but you pay for that invoice from a different company code, then you have indirectly specified the other company code

In either scenario, SAP ERP can automatically generate or clear entries in the other company code. However, the system needs to know which GL accounts to use for posting intercompany receivables and payables. These GL accounts are configured under the menu path FINANCIAL ACCOUNTING IMG • GENERAL LEDGER ACCOUNTING • BUSINESS TRANSACTIONS • PREPARE CROSS-COMPANY CODE TRANSACTIONS. SAP

ERP uses transaction key BUV (clearing between company codes) for determining these GL accounts.

Figure 2.6 shows the maintenance of intercompany GL clearing accounts. In this figure, GL accounts "(01)" and "(02)" are posted in company code "US01" for receivables from company code "CA01" and payables to company code "CA01". Similarly, GL accounts "(03)" and "(04)" are posted in company code "CA01" for receivables from company code "US01" and payables to company code "US01".

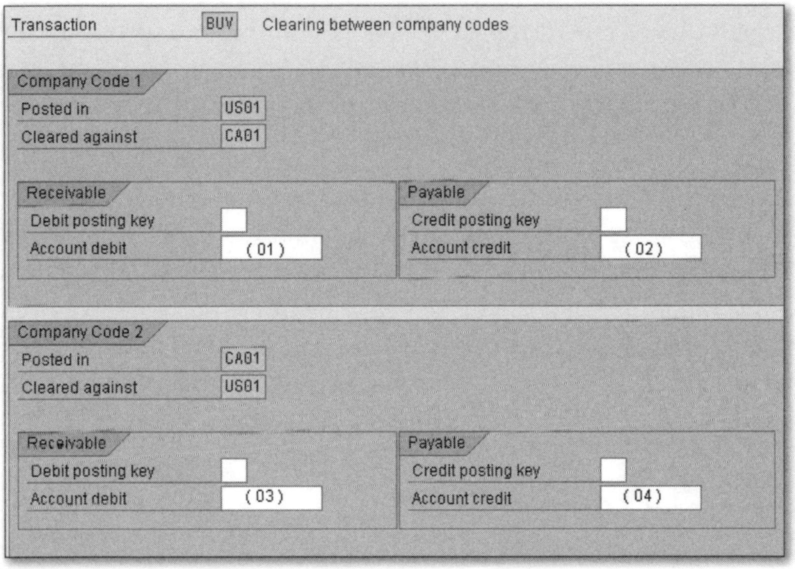

Figure 2.6 Cross-Company Code Clearing Accounts

> **Note**
>
> It is important to note, however, that configuring these GL accounts is only one of the ways to post intercompany transactions in SAP ERP. For example, to process intercompany stock and inventory transfers, it is fairly common to set up customer accounts and vendor accounts corresponding to each company code.

2.2.3 Account Receivable/Accounts Payable Reclassification

This activity refers to configuration of GL accounts for Accounts Receivable (AR) and Accounts Payable (AP) documents. However, it is included in this chapter on

GL transactions because it is primarily used at the time of preparing financial statements, which is definitely a GL accounting activity.

The purpose of AR and AP reclassification is to group receivables and payables based on their due date. For example, you can use this functionality to separate receivables and payables that are due in the short term and those that have due date more than a year away. This is a fairly common balance sheet supplement report.

Before you carry out this GL account determination activity, you must create different time frames by which you would like to group your receivables and payables. This configuration is carried out via the menu path FINANCIAL ACCOUNTING IMG • GENERAL LEDGER ACCOUNTING • PERIODIC PROCESSING • RECLASSIFY • TRANSFER AND SORT RECEIVABLES AND PAYABLES • DEFINE SORT METHOD AND ADJUSTMENT ACCOUNTS.

Figure 2.7 shows you three time frames defined for payables. You can select whether the time frames defined are applicable for customers, vendors, or both. Even though the example shows time frames in years, you can define them for months or days also. For each time frame, SAP ERP automatically generates a transaction key Vxx under Transaction Group BI2 (receivables/payables sorting). It is interesting to note that this is one of the few configuration activities in which transaction keys are automatically generated.

D...	Time unit	Name
0	Year	Payables within 1 year
1	Year	Payables due between 1 - 5 yea
5	Year	Payables due after 5 years

Figure 2.7 Sort Method Definition

Subsequently, you can assign GL account determination for each combination of AR/AP reconciliation account and transaction key generated in the previous step. This configuration activity is carried out under FINANCIAL ACCOUNTING IMG • GENERAL LEDGER ACCOUNTING • PERIODIC PROCESSING • RECLASSIFY • TRANSFER AND SORT RECEIVABLES AND PAYABLES • DEFINE ADJUSTMENT ACCOUNTS FOR RECEIVABLES/PAYABLES BY MATURITY. Figure 2.8 shows the assignment of GL accounts.

In the figure, GL account "140000" corresponds to the reconciliation account for which this configuration is done. The target account "(02)" specifies the GL account to which the balance per the specified time frame is posted. The adjustment account

"(01)" specifies the GL account to which the corresponding offsetting entry is posted.

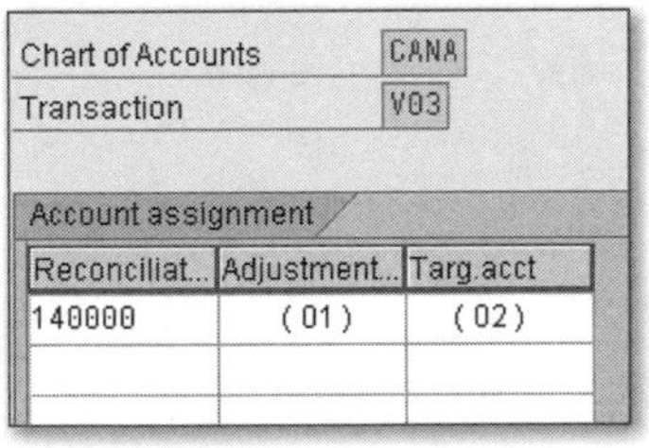

Figure 2.8 Reclassification Account Assignment

Subsequently, and in order to prepare this balance sheet supplement, you run the reclassification transaction available under the menu path SAP MENU • ACCOUNTING • ACCOUNTS RECEIVABLE/PAYABLE • PERIODIC PROCESSING • CLOSING • RECLASSIFY.

2.2.4 Bad Debt Reserve

This activity also refers to receivables in the AR subcomponent of SAP ERP, but because it is used during the preparation of financial statements, it is included in this chapter. The purpose of this activity is to analyze open accounts receivables and then, based on assumptions, logic, and experience, determine what portion of the receivables you may not be able to collect. Based on this, you can create a reserve to use in the future if indeed you are unable to collect those receivables. In its simplest form, the bad debt can be calculated as a percentage of the total accounts receivables, and you can manually post the corresponding accounting entry to GL. However, if your business requirements are more complex than that, it may be useful to automate the bad debt reserve functionality.

Before you can set up GL account determination for bad debt, you have to set up provision methods. Provision methods let you specify the period after which an open receivable is moved to a special GL account. A bucket consisting of the number of months and percentage is assigned to a provision method. If a receivable is due at least for that many months, then a specific percentage of that receivable is put in the bad debt reserve.

As Figure 2.9 shows, you can assign four such buckets for each provision method. In the example shown, bad debt reserve consists of 15% of all receivables due in two months, 25% of all receivables due in three months, and so on. The fairly high percentage may indicate a company with a lot of collection issues, a lot of defaulting customers, or both.

Prov.	Per.	Mo	Perc 1	Mo	Perc.2	Mo	Perc.3	Mo	Perc.4
CNS	1	2	15	3	25	4	50	6	100

Figure 2.9 Bad Debt Provision Method

SAP ERP uses transaction key ACC (provision for doubtful receivables) for this GL account determination. It can be configured via menu path FINANCIAL ACCOUNTING IMG • ACCOUNTS RECEIVABLE AND ACCOUNTS PAYABLE • BUSINESS TRANSACTIONS • CLOSING • VALUATE • RESERVE FOR BAD DEBT • DEFINE ACCOUNTS FOR RESERVE FOR BAD DEBT.

2.2.5 Clearing Differences for GL Accounts

We've already discussed clearing open debit and open credit items posted to a GL account. Using standard clearing transactions available in SAP ERP (e.g., Transaction F.13 or F13E), you can post clearing entries to match these debit and credit entries in a GL account. However, what if these debit and credit entries do not net to exactly zero?

SAP ERP provides the functionality of TOLERANCE GROUPS to clear out debits and credits for the scenarios where the net difference is within acceptable tolerance limits. You can specify the tolerance groups for GL accounts by clicking FINANCIAL ACCOUNTING IMG • GENERAL LEDGER ACCOUNTING • BUSINESS TRANSACTIONS • OPEN ITEM CLEARING • CLEARING DIFFERENCES • DEFINE TOLERANCE GROUPS FOR G/L ACCOUNTS. In the GL account master, you maintain a tolerance group on the control data tab.

The SAP system uses transaction key DSA to determine GL accounts to which any GL account clearing differences should be posted. Figure 2.10 shows an example of automatic account determination configuration for GL accounts clearing differences.

Figure 2.10 also shows how you can set account modifiers for the transaction key DSA. This transaction key offers two account modifiers: debit/credit indicator and tax codes. You use a similar user interface (UI) for setting account modifiers for other transaction keys. You can set the account modifiers of a transaction key by clicking RULES. Subsequently, you click on the ACCOUNTS button to go back to the GL accounts configuration screen. Configure this transaction key by clicking FINANCIAL ACCOUNTING IMG • GENERAL LEDGER ACCOUNTING • BUSINESS TRANSACTIONS • OPEN ITEM CLEARING • CLEARING DIFFERENCES • CREATE ACCOUNTS FOR CLEARING DIFFERENCES.

Group	GAU	Financial statement readjustment		

Procedures

Description	Transaction	Account determ.
Clearing account	GA0	☑
Adjustment accts for reconciliatn accts	GA1	☑
Adjustment accounts for tax accounts	GA2	☑
Adjustment accts for cash discount accts	GA3	☑
Adjustment accts for ex.rate diff.accts	GA4	☑
Adjustment accounts for other G/L accts	GA5	☑

Chart of Accounts	INT	Sample chart of accounts
Transaction	GA1	Adjustment accts for reconciliatn accts

Account assignment

Reconciliati	Adjustment
140000	140098
141000	141098
144000	144098
145000	145098

Figure 2.10 GL Account Clearing Differences

2.2.6 Subsequent Balance Sheet Adjustments

This GL account determination configuration is only relevant if your SAP ERP system is set to prepare balance sheets by business area or balance sheets by profit centers. To understand this functionality at a high level, consider an AR posting to a customer account. If the line item entry for the AR balance sheet account does not carry a profit center, SAP ERP needs to know how to distribute the receivables amount to appropriate profit centers. This and similar types of postings need to be identified, calculated, and distributed to different profit centers to prepare accurate balance sheets. You carry out these functions using SAP ERP transactions under the menu path ACCOUNTING SAP MENU • FINANCIAL ACCOUNTING • GENERAL LEDGER • PERIODIC PROCESSING • CLOSING • RECLASSIFY • BALANCE SHEET ADJUSTMENT.

These accounts are configured using FINANCIAL ACCOUNTING IMG • GENERAL LEDGER ACCOUNTING • BUSINESS TRANSACTIONS • CLOSING • RECLASSIFY • DEFINE ACCOUNTS FOR SUBSEQUENT ADJUSTMENT. All transaction keys for balance sheet adjustments are grouped under transaction GROUP GAU. Figure 2.11 shows an example of GL account determination for adjustment accounts for reconciliation accounts, as well as the different transaction keys associated with transaction group GAU. As you can see, such adjustments are calculated and posted for the following types of GL accounts.

- Reconciliation accounts (transaction key GA1)
- Tax accounts (transaction key GA2)
- Discount accounts (transaction key GA3)
- Exchange rate difference accounts (transaction key GA4)
- Other GL accounts (transaction key GA5)

Group	GAU	Financial statement readjustment	
Procedures			
Description		Transaction	Account determ.
Clearing account		GA0	☑
Adjustment accts for reconciliatn accts		GA1	☑
Adjustment accounts for tax accounts		GA2	☑
Adjustment accts for cash discount accts		GA3	☑
Adjustment accts for ex.rate diff.accts		GA4	☑
Adjustment accounts for other G/L accts		GA5	☑

Chart of Accounts	INT	Sample chart of accounts
Transaction	GA1	Adjustment accts for reconciliatn accts

Account assignment	
Reconciliati	Adjustment
140000	140098
141000	141098
144000	144098
145000	145098

Figure 2.11 Balance Sheet Adjustments

SAP ERP posts the offsetting adjustment entry to the GL account configured under transaction key GA0. None of these transaction keys have any account modifiers associated with them, so for one reconciliation account, you can associate only one adjustment GL account to which all adjustment postings are made.

Now let's discuss what options are available for you to automate month-end accrual processing.

2.3   Accrual Transactions

You use accrued expense or accrued revenue to record expenditure or revenue for activities that have already occurred but for which you haven't received or generated invoices or official documents. This functionality can be useful for any periodic postings that are based on a specific amount or specific value. Examples of such postings are contract transactions such as insurance contracts or leasing contracts, periodic subscriptions, and so on.

The approach used for processing accruals in SAP ERP depends on the nature, volume, frequency, and complexity of accrual postings. For simple scenarios in which an accrual posting is to be reversed on a specific future date, you can use Transactions FBS1 and F.81.

On the other hand, for complex or large-volume accrual entries, SAP ERP provides a useful functionality called the Accrual Engine, which lets you set up accruals based on highly complex, user-defined criteria. Then SAP ERP handles calculations, recalculations, and all postings on a periodic basis.

> **Note**
>
> The discussion in this section focuses only on what SAP ERP calls manual accruals that use the Accrual Engine. However, the functionality of the Accrual Engine is also used for several other processes in SAP ERP, such as for accruals for rights management, provisioning for rewards, and so on. Because conceptually these processes use similar GL account determination techniques, you will be able to extrapolate concepts discussed in this section to other processes as well.

2.3.1   Accrual Engine

Figure 2.12 shows the different objects involved in the configuration of the Accrual Engine. The Accrual Engine posts accrual amounts for an accrual object, which can be any contract, order, or agreement that is to be accrued over a period of time.

The company code and accrual method are assigned to the accrual object as its attributes. An accrual method is just a technical function module that determines how the accrual is calculated. SAP ERP provides function modules for standard accrual methods, such as linear accruals, period-specific linear distribution, day-specific linear distribution, and so on. You can use these function modules as the base to customize accrual calculations for your company.

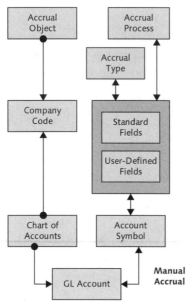

Figure 2.12 Accrual Engine

The accrual type is a user-defined type of accrual, such as cost, revenue, discount, and so on. An accrual object is assigned one of the accrual types as its attribute. There can be multiple accrual types assigned to an accrual object only if the accrual object has multiple components. This can be the case, for example, if a contract has a revenue component as well as a cost component, which both must be accrued over the life of the contract.

The accrual process in the Accrual Engine determines what types of postings are implemented for the accrual. There are three different types of accrual processes:

▶ **Opening posting (I)**
Creates the accrual by posting the total value that is to be accrued.

▶ **Periodic posting (P)**
Posts a periodic amount (usually) from the accrual account to the income statement account.

▶ **Final posting (F)**
This posting is made only if the accrual is terminated before the end of the accrual period. Depending on the configuration setting, either no further accrual posting occurs, or the remaining portion of the accrual amount is posted immediately in the period in which termination occurs.

For the purpose of GL account determination in the Accrual Engine, you can use standard fields that are available in a standard SAP ERP system as well as user fields for which you must do additional configuration. Standard fields include accounting principle, accrual process, accrual type, and others.

The following subsection describes how GL accounts are determined based on account determination objects associated with the Accrual Engine.

2.3.2 Simple Account Determination

The two types of GL account determination for the Accrual Engine process are simple account determination and extended account determination. In a simple account determination setup for accruals, for a combination of standard fields and user fields, the following two GL accounts are assigned:

▶ **Start account:** Account to be posted from (credit).

▶ **Target account:** Account to be posted to (debit).

Obviously, the start account and the target account are different depending on the accrual process (opening, periodic, or final) and accrual type (cost, revenue, or discount). For example, the target account is an accrual account for the opening posting, whereas it functions as an income statement account for the periodic posting. Configuration for simple account determination is carried out under Financial Accounting IMG • General Ledger Accounting • Business Transactions • Manual Accruals • Accrual/Deferral Posting • Account Determination • Simple Account Determination.

Figure 2.13 shows an example of simple account determination for the Accrual Engine setup. In this simple but adequate setup, you associate a start account and a target account for different processing activities of the accrual object such as start of accrual (I), periodic accrual recognition (P), change of the accrual start (U), transfer of periodic accrual recognition (C), and completion of the accrual (F). The figure also shows how the same GL account can be a start account for one accrual activity but is the target account for a different accrual activity.

Accrual Engine - Account Determination: Change Rule Values									

Derivation rule   G/L Account determination

No value filter active

Chart of	Chart of Accounts Name	Transact	Transaction in Accrual Engine	As	Start Account	S	Target account	T
INT	Sample chart of accounts	I	Inception	=	18999000		25900000	
INT	Sample chart of accounts	U	Change of the Inception	=	25900000		18999000	
INT	Sample chart of accounts	P	Periodic Recognition	=	25900000		18999000	
INT	Sample chart of accounts	C	Transfer of Periodic Recognition	=	25900000		18999000	
INT	Sample chart of accounts	F	Completion	=	18999000		18999000	

Figure 2.13 Simple Account Determination for the Accrual Engine

For business scenarios that require more complex functionality of accrual processing, you can use extended account determination for the Accrual Engine.

2.3.3 Extended Account Determination

Simple account determination described previously becomes inefficient to maintain if the business requirements involve a large number of field combinations that point to relatively few GL accounts. For such scenarios, SAP ERP offers extended account determination.

Configuration activities for extended account determination for the Accrual Engine start out the same as the activities for simple account determination. However, in the account derivation rule, instead of specifying actual GL accounts, you specify symbolic GL accounts. This is a scenario in which SAP ERP uses a simplified condition technique combined with a symbolic account technique to carry out GL account determination.

Figure 2.14 shows two configuration screens of extended account determination for the Accrual Engine. The first screen looks very similar to the configuration screen for simple account determination (see Figure 2.13). However, as described earlier, instead of actual GL accounts, these rules are assigned symbolic GL accounts ACCSYMB_O, ACCSYMB_P, and ACCSYMB_E. The bottom part of the figure shows the configuration activity in which actual GL accounts are assigned to relatively simple combinations of chart of accounts and account symbols. These characteristic combinations used in GL account assignment give you considerable flexibility in implementing complex GL account determinations for complex accrual processes. Configuration for extended account determination is carried out under FINANCIAL ACCOUNTING IMG • GENERAL LEDGER ACCOUNTING • BUSINESS TRANSACTIONS • MANUAL ACCRUALS • ACCRUAL/DEFERRAL POSTING • ACCOUNT DETERMINATION • EXTENDED ACCOUNT DETERMINATION.

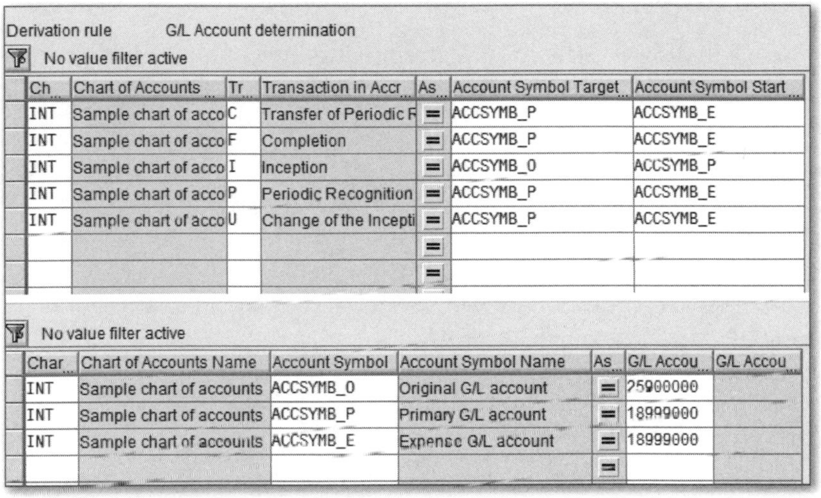

Figure 2.14 Extended Account Determination

You will find SAP ERP transactions to process manual accruals under the SAP ERP menu ACCOUNTING MENU • FINANCIAL ACCOUNTING • GENERAL LEDGER • PERIODIC PROCESSING • MANUAL ACCRUALS.

2.4 Summary

We have discussed several GL account determination functionalities in SAP ERP's GL accounting component. These functionalities primarily assist in period-end closing activities.

The currency revaluation process discussed in this chapter focused on GL account determination. However, when implementing the currency valuation functionality, you should also take into account all applicable statutory guidelines to determine which GL accounts to process, which exchange rates to use, and how to treat exchange rate differences. SAP ERP provides very comprehensive functionality for foreign currency revaluation.

The Accrual Engine is a powerful tool that provides a virtual accrual subledger with the ability to create self-correcting, mass processing of accruals that are tied together via business documents such as contracts or orders. The symbolic account technique that is available for extended account determination for the Accrual Engine provides you with a relatively simple framework to configure SAP ERP to carry out complex accrual postings to accurate GL accounts.

In Chapter 3, we will discuss GL account determination techniques for two other most commonly used SAP ERP Financials subcomponents: Accounts Receivable and Accounts Payable.

2.5   Reference

This section provides technical details relevant to GL account determination for GL transactions.

2.5.1   Configuration Transactions

Table 2.1 provides a list of the configuration transactions for the account determination objects discussed in this chapter.

Transaction Code	Description
OBA1	GL account determination for foreign currency valuation
OBYA	Maintain intercompany clearing GL accounts
OB53	Maintain retained earnings accounts
OBBV	Assign AR/AP adjustment accounts
OBXD	Maintain bad debt reserve accounts
ACACAD	Accrual account determination (simple or extended)
ACACADMETASGL	Accrual account determination strategy
ACACTREE01	Create accrual objects

Table 2.1 Configuration Transactions

2.5.2   Tables and Structures

Table 2.2 contains a list of the tables and structures used to store data relevant for the GL account determination discussed in this chapter.

Table/Structure	Description
T030S	For ending balance GL accounts
T030D	For open item GL accounts
FAGL_T030TR	For currency translation
T030	For retained earnings accounts, bad debt accounts
T030U	For AR/AP adjustment accounts
R030	For intercompany clearing accounts
ACEDSASSGMT	Standard account assignment for accrual objects
ACEDSOI_ACCOUNTS	For accrual postings per accrual item
ACEOBJ	For accrual objects

Table 2.2   Tables and Structures

2.5.3   Enhancements

Table 2.3 provides a list of the enhancements that can be used to influence GL account determination in transactions discussed in this chapter.

Enhancement	Description
F1040001	Reserve for bad debt—calculate percentages

Table 2.3   Enhancements

3   Accounts Receivable/Accounts Payable Transactions

In the SAP ERP system, Accounts Receivable/Accounts Payable (AR/AP) transactions refer to business transactions with customers or vendors. There are some basic business transactions such as sending an invoice to a customer, receiving payments from a customer, receiving an invoice from a vendor, and sending a payment to a vendor. However, there are many other business transactions that can occur with customers and vendors, such as receiving or making advance payments, offering discounts, making use of discounts for early payments, and so on.

This chapter covers GL account determination for customers, vendors, and commonly used AR/AP transactions. You should note that this chapter views GL account determination strictly from the entries posted directly in the Financial Accounting (FI) component of SAP ERP. Obviously, in an integrated system, customer and vendor transactions also originate in other components. For example, a customer invoice in AR is typically generated from a billing document in the Sales and Distribution (SD) functionality, which in turn is generated based on a sales order entered in the SD functionality. Similarly, a purchase order in the Materials Management (MM) functionality serves as a base for posting inventory accounts at the time of goods receipt, and a vendor invoice in AP is posted based on a logistics invoice posted in the MM functionality. In Chapter 8 and Chapter 9, we will discuss GL account determination for customer and vendor transactions that originate in SD and MM.

For the transactions posted directly in the AR and AP subcomponents, SAP ERP uses two techniques for GL account determination: direct assignment and the transaction key technique. For example, reconciliation accounts are directly assigned to the customer and vendor account master, whereas for AR/AP transactions, different transaction keys are used for GL account determination. We will start with the discussion of reconciliation accounts, continue with different GL account determinations required in basic AR/AP transactions, and then toward the end of this chapter, we will discuss the GL account determination for other special business requirements.

3.1   Reconciliation Accounts

A reconciliation account is a balance sheet GL account in which transactions from subledgers are automatically updated. For the purposes of discussion in this chapter, we will focus on only customer and vendor subledgers. Chapter 6 discusses reconciliation accounts for fixed assets. It is fairly common to have several reconciliation accounts for the same type of subledger. For example, you would use different reconciliation accounts to separate receivables from external customers and internal, affiliated companies. Even for external customers, you may want to separate receivables from domestic customers and receivables from foreign customers. You must assign a reconciliation account to a customer or a vendor account before you can post any accounting transactions in AR/AP involving that account.

3.1.1   Primary Reconciliation Accounts

As shown in Figure 3.1, you can mark a GL account as a reconciliation account by specifying the subledger type (CUSTOMERS, VENDORS) in the GL account master. You maintain this field value using CHANGE GL ACCOUNT (TRX. FS00), and accessing the RECON. ACCOUNT FOR ACCT TYPE field on the CONTROL DATA tab.

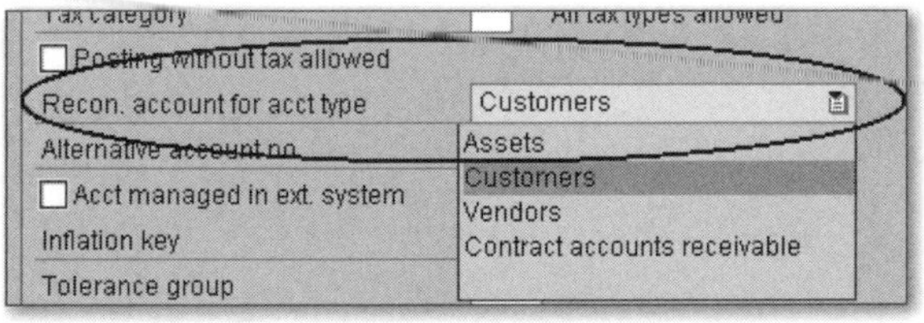

Figure 3.1   Define the Reconciliation Account

After you've defined the required reconciliation accounts, the next step is to assign them to customer accounts and vendor accounts. You maintain this field value using CHANGE CUSTOMER ACCOUNT (TRX. FD02) OR CHANGE VENDOR ACCOUNT (TRX. FK02) • COMPANY CODE DATA, and then selecting the RECON. ACCOUNT FOR ACCT TYPE field in the CONTROL DATA tab. Figure 3.2 shows this assignment. This assignment ensures that any monetary value posted to any customer accounts or vendor accounts are also posted automatically and simultaneously to the corresponding reconciliation account in GL. We will refer to these reconciliation accounts as primary reconciliation accounts in this chapter to avoid confusion with other reconciliation accounts.

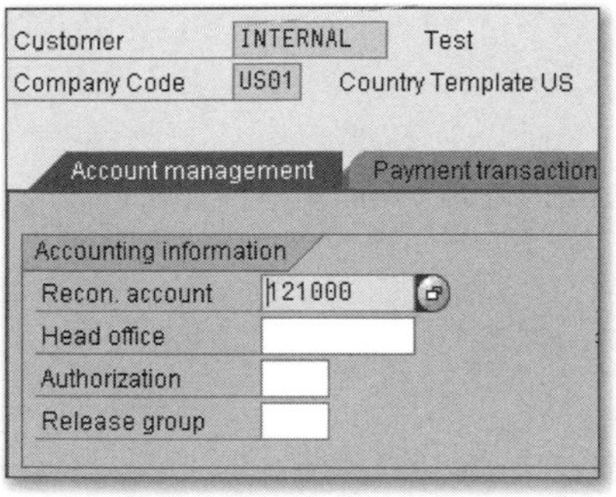

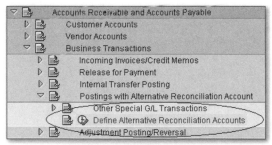

Figure 3.2 Assign Reconciliation Account

There are two possible scenarios in which SAP ERP will post to a different reconciliation account than the one defined in the customer or vendor master. Either configuration settings allow the manual change of reconciliation accounts while posting, or you are posting a special transaction. Both of these scenarios are described next.

3.1.2 Alternative Reconciliation Accounts

Figure 3.3 shows the configuration menu path where you can define alternative reconciliation accounts for each reconciliation account.

Figure 3.3 Menu Path for Alternative Reconciliation

This is one of the required configuration steps to enable users to enter a different reconciliation account at the time of posting than the one from the customer/vendor master. Figure 3.4 shows this assignment of alternative reconciliation account.

In Figure 3.4, "(01)" represents a reconciliation account from the customer/vendor master, and "(02)" represents an alternative reconciliation account that can be entered in AR/AP transactions. The key for this configuration assignment is the GL account (G/L Acc) and alternative GL account (Alt. G/L), so you can define multiple alternative reconciliation accounts for one reconciliation account. The ID field simply enables you to enter a short mnemonic for alternative GL account assignment, so that you can quickly enter the alternative account in transactional entries.

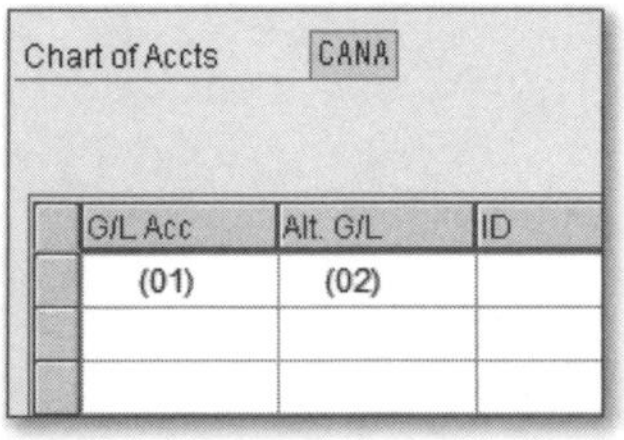

Figure 3.4 Assign Alternative Reconciliation Accounts

However, in addition to configuring alternative GL accounts as described previously, you also have to set a flag in the GL account master of the reconciliation account that allows entry of alternate reconciliation accounts at the time of transaction entry. You carry out this setting in the GL account master using CHANGE GL ACCOUNT (TRX. FS00) transaction and then selecting RECON. ACCT READY FOR INPUT field on the CREATE/BANK/INTEREST tab.

The functionality for alternative reconciliation accounts can come in handy if you want to treat some customer/vendor transactions differently from the regular customer/vendor transactions for the purposes of specific functionalities. Let's see what that means.

Excluding Reconciliation Accounts

Figure 3.5 shows a configuration of the reconciliation accounts so that you can choose to exclude them from credit management, automatic payment, or dunning.

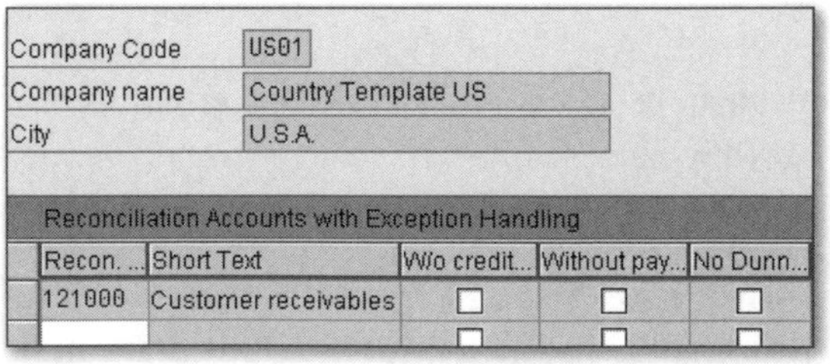

Figure 3.5 Reconciliation Account Exception Handling

Using these settings, you can configure the following for all transactions posted to the reconciliation accounts:

- W/O CREDIT...
  Transactions do not update credit management, and thus do not count against the credit limit.

- WITHOUT PAY...
  The reconciliation account is not included in automatic payments, thereby giving you full control of when and how the payments are processed.

- NO DUNN...
  Transactions are not considered for dunning.

One of the menu paths for this configuration activity is IMG • FINANCIAL ACCOUNTING • ACCOUNTS RECEIVABLE AND ACCOUNTS PAYABLE • BUSINESS TRANSACTIONS • OUTGOING PAYMENTS • AUTOMATIC OUTGOING PAYMENTS • PAYMENT METHOD/BANK SELECTION FOR PAYMENT PROGRAM • DEFINE RECONCILIATION ACCOUNTS WITHOUT AUTOMATIC PAYMENTS.

This transaction is accessible through different menu paths under configuration activities for credit management, automatic payments, and dunning. However, you can make all three settings from any of the menu paths. The next section discusses GL reconciliation accounts for special GL transactions.

3.1.3 Special Reconciliation Accounts

There is another scenario in which SAP ERP uses a different reconciliation account in AR/AP transactions than the one specified in the corresponding customer/vendor master. This is the scenario when you post special GL transactions for a customer or a vendor account. We briefly discussed special GL transactions in Chapter 2 while discussing bad debt reserve accounts. In this section, we will discuss special GL transactions in more detail.

Figure 3.6 shows a list of special GL transactions that are available in SAP ERP for posting to accounts receivables and accounts payables.

There are a few special GL transactions such as down payments and bill of exchange, for which you have to carry out additional configuration for enabling and using that functionality. You will find those configuration activities under respective configuration menus in IMG under AR and AP business transactions.

S	Description
A	Down Payment
B	Nonrediscountable Bills of Ex.
C	RE Rent deposit
E	Individual Value Adjustment
F	Down Payment Request
G	Guarantees Given
H	Security Deposit
I	BR: Vendor Operation
J	RE Advance Payment Request
K	RE AP Operating Costs
P	Payment Request
Q	B/e residual risk
R	Bill of Exchange Payt Request
S	Check/Bill of Exchange
T	Down Payment
U	RE AP sales-based rent
W	Rediscountable Bills of Exch.
Z	Interest Receivable

Figure 3.6 Special GL Transactions

For all other special GL transactions, you simply have to assign a different reconciliation account—let's call it special reconciliation account—to each primary reconciliation account. You carry out this assignment for each special GL transaction that you intend to use in SAP ERP. For example, if you use down payments in your AR and AP transactions, and if you use bank guarantees in your AP transactions; you only have to configure special reconciliation accounts for those three special GL transactions.

You assign special reconciliation accounts via menu path IMG • FINANCIAL ACCOUNTING • ACCOUNTS RECEIVABLE AND ACCOUNTS PAYABLE • BUSINESS TRANSACTIONS • POSTINGS WITH ALTERNATIVE RECON ACCOUNT • OTHER SPECIAL G/L TRANSACTIONS • DEFINE ALTERNATIVE RECON ACCOUNTS FOR CUSTOMERS/VENDORS.

As shown in Figure 3.7, you have to configure alternative reconciliation accounts for all relevant combinations of ACCOUNT TYPE and SPECIAL G/L IND. Per the definitions that are valid across the SAP ERP system, account type D is used for customers, and account type K is used for vendors. SPECIAL G/L IND. is used to identify special GL transactions (refer to Figure 3.6) such as a bank guarantee, letter of credit, and so on.

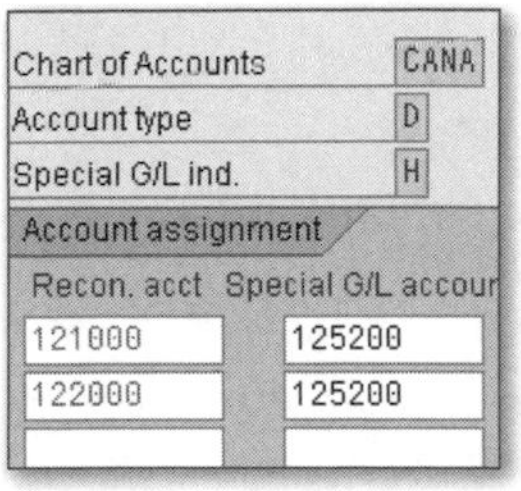

Figure 3.7 Alternative Reconciliation Account

Offsetting GL Accounts

Of course, entries made to any of the special GL transactions require another place-holder to post offsetting entries. You specify these accounts via the menu path IMG • FINANCIAL ACCOUNTING • ACCOUNTS RECEIVABLE AND ACCOUNTS PAYABLE • BUSINESS TRANSACTIONS • POSTINGS WITH ALTERNATIVE RECON ACCOUNT • OTHER SPECIAL G/L TRANSACTIONS • DEFINE ACCOUNTS FOR AUTOMATIC OFFSETTING ENTRY.

These offsetting accounts are specified using transaction key SGA (automatic statistical posting entry). The following rule modifiers are available:

▸ Debit/credit (not changeable)

▸ Account type/special GL indicator

Before we move on to the next topic, there is one more possible scenario you should keep in mind. As we will discuss in Chapter 8, it is also possible to determine a customer reconciliation account dynamically while processing sales documents. This requires the configuration of reconciliation account determination (Chapter 8, Section 8.1.7).

Let's now discuss GL account determination in basic AR and AP transactions.

3.2 Basic Accounts Receivable/Accounts Payable Transactions

Most of the AR/AP transactions use the transaction type technique to determine GL accounts. One thing to keep in mind is that because AR and AP share some common functionalities, you may be able to access the same configuration activities through multiple menu paths under AR/AP business transactions configuration.

You may have already noticed this when we discussed alternative reconciliation accounts in Section 3.1.2.

Figure 3.8 shows a configuration menu path that contains most of the configuration activities discussed in this section.

> **Note**
>
> A few business processes can be considered AR/AP business transactions but are not discussed in this chapter. GL account determination for withholding taxes is discussed in Chapter 4. GL account determination for the bill of exchange process is discussed in Chapter 5. And, we already discussed GL account determination for foreign exchange gain/loss in Chapter 2.

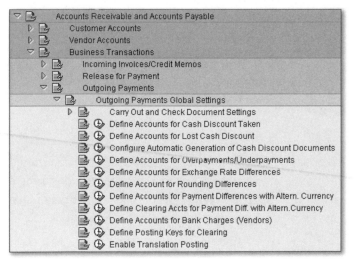

Figure 3.8 Accounts Receivable/Accounts Payable Transactions

3.2.1 Vendor Discounts

Most vendors offer discount terms for early or even timely payment of their invoices. For incoming invoices containing discount terms, you can choose to post them using one of two methods: net method or gross method.

You set this method in the document type configuration using IMG • FINANCIAL ACCOUNTING • FINANCIAL ACCOUNTING GLOBAL SETTINGS • DOCUMENT • DOCUMENT HEADER • DEFINE DOCUMENT TYPE. On the configuration screen, you set the flag NET

DOCUMENT TYPE to indicate that the document is posted using the net method. If this flag is not selected, then the document is posted using the gross method. SAP ERP provides document type KN to post vendor invoices using the net method. The more commonly used document type KR is used to post vendor invoices with the gross method.

> **Note**
>
> The net method is available only for vendor invoices. You cannot post customer invoices using the net method.

Cash Discounts Taken

This GL account determination is relevant for the gross method of posting vendor invoices. Under this method, any discount is calculated and posted only at the time when actual payment is made against the invoice. Any discount taken on outgoing payments is posted to the GL accounts determined using this configuration. Following are the details relevant for configuring GL accounts for the cash discounts taken:

▸ **Configuration menu path**
  IMG • FINANCIAL ACCOUNTING • ACCOUNTS RECEIVABLE AND ACCOUNTS PAYABLE • BUSINESS TRANSACTIONS • OUTGOING PAYMENTS • OUTGOING PAYMENTS GLOBAL SETTINGS • DEFINE ACCOUNTS FOR CASH DISCOUNTS TAKEN.

▸ **Transaction key**
  SKE (cash discount received).

▸ **Rule modifiers**
  Debit/credit (not changeable), tax code.

For an automatic payment program, the system calculates the cash discount based on the actual date of payment and the discount dates and net payment date per the payment terms.

In the net method of posting vendor invoices, the system automatically deducts cash discount from vendor invoices when they are posted. This is with the assumption that you will make payment to get the maximum discount. Another effect of posting incoming invoices with the net method is that if the invoice is for inventory materials that are valuated using moving average price (MAP), then the discount amount has no effect on the new MAP. Otherwise, you may absorb the full vendor invoice amount in your MAP, but you may get the discount that can't be allocated to inventory. In some countries, statutory requirements dictate that posting of all vendor invoices be done using the net method. This method requires configuring two GL accounts.

Cash Discount Clearing

Under the net method, any cash discount on an incoming invoice is posted to the cash discount clearing account at the time of posting the vendor invoice. The GL accounts are determined using the following:

▶ **Configuration menu path**
   IMG • FINANCIAL ACCOUNTING • ACCOUNTS RECEIVABLE AND ACCOUNTS PAYABLE • BUSINESS TRANSACTIONS • INCOMING INVOICES/CREDIT MEMOS • DEFINE ACCOUNT FOR NET PROCEDURE.

▶ **Transaction key**
   SKV (cash discount clearing – net method).

▶ **Available rule modifiers**
   Debit/credit (not changeable), tax code.

Lost Cash Discount

When these invoices are paid, any difference between the discount calculated when the invoice is posted and the discount calculated at the time of payment is posted to the lost cash discount account. This GL account is determined using the following:

▶ **Configuration menu path**
   IMG • FINANCIAL ACCOUNTING • ACCOUNTS RECEIVABLE AND ACCOUNTS PAYABLE • BUSINESS TRANSACTIONS • OUTGOING PAYMENTS • OUTGOING PAYMENTS GLOBAL SETTINGS • DEFINE ACCOUNTS FOR LOST CASH DISCOUNT.

▶ **Transaction key**
   VSK (lost cash discount – net method).

▶ **Rule modifiers**
   Debit/credit (not changeable), tax code.

You maintain payment terms using the configuration path IMG • FINANCIAL ACCOUNTING • ACCOUNTS RECEIVABLE AND ACCOUNTS PAYABLE • BUSINESS TRANSACTIONS • INCOMING INVOICES/CREDIT MEMOS • DEFINE TERMS OF PAYMENT.

In the next section, we will discuss posting customer discounts.

3.2.2 Customer Discounts

Similar to the vendor discounts available in the AP process, your company may offer discounts to customers for early or timely payment of your invoices. As mentioned previously, there is no net method of posting customer invoices and customer discounts. The customer discounts are posted only when the actual customer payment is received.

Cash Discounts Granted

The GL accounts for cash discounts granted (customer discounts) are determined using the following:

▶ **Configuration menu path**
  IMG • FINANCIAL ACCOUNTING • ACCOUNTS RECEIVABLE AND ACCOUNTS PAYABLE • BUSINESS TRANSACTIONS • INCOMING PAYMENTS • INCOMING PAYMENTS GLOBAL SETTINGS • DEFINE ACCOUNTS FOR CASH DISCOUNTS GRANTED.

▶ **Transaction key**
  SKT (cash discount expenses).

▶ **Rule modifiers**
  Debit/credit, tax code.

You maintain payment terms using the configuration path IMG • FINANCIAL ACCOUNTING • ACCOUNTS RECEIVABLE AND ACCOUNTS PAYABLE • BUSINESS TRANSACTIONS • OUTGOING INVOICES/CREDIT MEMOS • DEFINE TERMS OF PAYMENT.

In the next section, we will discuss posting overpayments and underpayments.

3.2.3 Overpayments and Underpayments

Whenever there is difference between the payment amount and the corresponding invoice amount, the system uses the following methodology to post this difference amount. First the system tries to adjust this difference against the discount amount, if applicable and available. If there is still any payment difference after adjusting for the discount amount, or if there is no available discount amount, the system tries to post this difference as an underpayment or overpayment.

The system automatically determines the GL accounts for underpayment or for overpayment based on whether the payment amount is less than or more than the corresponding invoice amount. These GL accounts are determined using the following:

▶ **Configuration menu path**
   IMG • FINANCIAL ACCOUNTING • ACCOUNTS RECEIVABLE AND ACCOUNTS PAYABLE • BUSINESS TRANSACTIONS • OUTGOING PAYMENTS • OUTGOING PAYMENTS GLOBAL SETTINGS • DEFINE ACCOUNTS FOR OVERPAYMENTS/UNDERPAYMENTS.

▶ **Transaction key**
   ZDI (payment differences by reason).

▶ **Rule modifiers**
   Debit/credit, tax code, reason code.

Incidentally, the same transaction key is used for GL account determination whether the overpayment or underpayment occurs in customer payments or in vendor payments. While analyzing postings for overpayments and underpayments, it is important to be familiar with the concept of tolerance limits in SAP ERP.

Tolerance Limits

The tolerance limits provide control over how much payment difference is acceptable for overpayment and for underpayment in vendor and customer transactions. To implement tolerance limits, you first configure tolerance groups and then assign these tolerance groups to every customer and vendor accounts. Of course, you can also create a high-level tolerance group for a company code that is relevant in case the customer account or vendor account does not contain a tolerance group.

The tolerance group specifies several parameters. Figure 3.9 shows the parameters that are mainly relevant for our discussion in this section.

Permitted Payment Differences			
	Amount	Percent	Adjust Discount By
Gain	999.00	10.0 %	1.00
Loss	5.00	2.5 %	1.00

Figure 3.9 Configuration of Tolerance Limit

A tolerance limit specifies the maximum permitted difference as an absolute amount and as a percentage. It also specifies the amount that can be automatically adjusted against the discount amount. This specification is made for both scenarios, that is, when there is gain (i.e., the difference is favorable to your company) and when there is loss (i.e., the difference is not favorable to your company).

Note

The overpayment or underpayment difference is validated against the tolerance limits assigned to the customer or vendor and the employee (user ID). The lowest of the determined tolerance is considered applicable.

The payment difference that cannot be adjusted against discount amounts and underpayment/overpayment tolerance amounts is posted back to the customer account or vendor account. Let's now discuss GL account determination for rounding differences.

3.2.4 Rounding Differences

These GL accounts are posted with the amount differences that arise due to inaccuracies in the calculation of automatic postings. This can be especially the case in foreign currency transactions that involve different number of decimal places and use exchange rates that are defined with up to four or five decimal points. See the following transaction key and rule modifiers:

▶ **Configuration menu path**
  IMG • FINANCIAL ACCOUNTING • ACCOUNTS RECEIVABLE AND ACCOUNTS PAYABLE • BUSINESS TRANSACTIONS • INCOMING PAYMENTS • INCOMING PAYMENTS GLOBAL SETTINGS • DEFINE ACCOUNT FOR ROUNDING DIFFERENCES.

▶ **Transaction key**
  RDF (internal currencies rounding difference).

▶ **Rule modifiers**
  Debit/credit.

If the transactions are in a foreign currency and different exchange rates are applicable for different line items, then the total difference is split into two parts. One part corresponds to the difference due to the exchange rate variance, which is posted to GL accounts that are determined as discussed in Chapter 2. The other part of the difference corresponds to calculation/rounding differences. That is the only difference posted to the GL accounts discussed in this section.

3.2.5   Alternative Payment Currency

These accounts are applicable if the payment transaction currency is different from the currency of the invoice. We discussed configuration of this transaction key in Chapter 2, Section 2.1.3), so only the high-level information about configuring these accounts is given here.

Alternative Currency—Payment Difference

SAP ERP posts any payment differences that arise due to the use of an alternative payment currency to GL accounts determined using the following:

▶ **Configuration menu path**
IMG • FINANCIAL ACCOUNTING • ACCOUNTS RECEIVABLE AND ACCOUNTS PAYABLE • BUSINESS TRANSACTIONS • OUTGOING PAYMENTS • OUTGOING PAYMENTS GLOBAL SETTINGS • DEFINE ACCOUNTS FOR PAYMENT DIFFERENCES WITH ALTERN CURRENCY.

▶ **Transaction key**
KDW (payment difference for alternative currency).

▶ **Rule modifiers**
Debit/credit, tax code.

Alternative Currency—Offsetting Payment Difference

The offsetting entry to the preceding posting is posted to GL accounts determined using the following:

▶ **Configuration menu path**
IMG • FINANCIAL ACCOUNTING • ACCOUNTS RECEIVABLE AND ACCOUNTS PAYABLE • BUSINESS TRANSACTIONS • OUTGOING PAYMENTS • OUTGOING PAYMENTS GLOBAL SETTINGS • DEFINE CLEARING ACCOUNTS FOR PAYMENT DIFF WITH ALTERN CURRENCY.

▶ **Transaction key**
KDZ (payment difference for alternative currency offset).

▶ **Rule modifiers**
Debit/credit (not changeable), tax code.

3.2.6 Bank Charges

When you use payment methods such as a wire transfer, bill of exchange, and so on, banks may collect an additional processing charge. Any such bank charges that are separately identified while posting payments are posted to a different GL account. This GL account determination is carried out using the following details:

▶ **Configuration menu path**
IMG • FINANCIAL ACCOUNTING • ACCOUNTS RECEIVABLE AND ACCOUNTS PAYABLE • BUSINESS TRANSACTIONS • INCOMING PAYMENTS • INCOMING PAYMENTS GLOBAL SETTINGS • DEFINE ACCOUNTS FOR BANK CHARGES.

▶ **Transaction group**
BAN (bank transactions).

▶ **Transaction key**
BSP (bank charges).

▶ **Rule modifiers**
No rule modifiers for this transaction key.

Now let's discuss GL account determination for down payments.

3.2.7 Down Payments

In many industries, applying a down payment on an order is a common practice. This process could mean your company is making down payments to a vendor, or your company is processing down payments received from a customer. In either scenario, you can process down payments in SAP ERP using either the net method or the gross method.

If you process down payments using the net method, posting to the business partner (customer or vendor) account is not inclusive of the tax amount. However, for down payments processed using the gross method, posting to the business partner includes tax amount.

This means that under the gross method of posting down payments, where tax is included in the down payment posting to a business partner, the system also requires an offsetting or clearing account where it can post the tax entries. In SAP ERP, you configure tax clearing accounts for this purpose. Following are the details for configuring these GL accounts.

Down Payments—Output Tax Clearing

For output tax clearing (down payments received from customers), a GL account is determined using the following setup:

- ▶ **Configuration menu path**
  IMG • Financial Accounting • Accounts Receivable and Accounts Payable • Business Transactions • Down Payment Received • Define Account for Tax Clearing • Output Tax Clearing on Down Payments.

- ▶ **Transaction key**
  MVA (output tax clearing on down payments).

- ▶ **Rule modifiers**
  Debit/credit, output tax code.

Down Payments—Input Tax Clearing

For input tax clearing (down payments made to vendors), a GL account is determined using the following setup:

- ▶ **Configuration menu path**
  IMG • Financial Accounting • Accounts Receivable and Accounts Payable • Business Transactions • Down Payment Made • Define Account for Tax Clearing • Input Tax Clearing on Down Payments.

- ▶ **Transaction key**
  VVA (input tax clearing on down payments).

- ▶ **Rule modifiers**
  Debit/credit, input tax code.

So far, we have discussed GL account determination for common AR and AP transactions. In the next section, we will discuss GL account determination for processing payment cards in SAP ERP.

3.3   Payment Card Accounts

SAP ERP provides robust functionality that enables you to receive payments from your customers via credit cards. In SAP ERP, credit cards, corporate cards, affinity cards, and all other similar cards are collectively referred to as *payment cards*.

Therefore, credit card and payment card are used interchangeably for the purposes of our discussion.

Let's first briefly understand the process of payments using payment cards. To accept customer payments by credit card, your company has to first open an account at a clearing house. The clearing house acts as a go-between between your company and the financial institutions issuing the payment cards. When your company accepts customer payment by credit card, the first step in the process is to get the amount authorization from the financial institution that issued that credit card. At this point, you can also carry out additional security checks such as address check, ZIP code check, or CVV (card verification value) check. Also at this point, you "reserve" the corresponding amount on the payment card.

Subsequently, after goods are shipped and services are performed, your company will send an invoice to the customer and, at the same time, will also charge the amount on the customer's credit card. This charge on the customer's credit card is placed via the clearing house. During the settlement process, instead of posting a receivable from your customer, you post a receivable from your clearing house. Typically after a few days of carrying out the settlement process, you receive the corresponding payment from the clearing house.

One point to keep in mind is that depending on the type and size of your business, and the types of payment cards that your company accepts, you may process your payment cards through more than one clearing house. There is no impact on accounting during the credit card authorization process. However, at the time of the settlement process, there are two touch points that require GL account determination. These are discussed in the next section.

3.3.1   Clearing House Account

This GL account is posted at the time of processing customer invoices. Because the customer has already paid by credit card, at the time of processing invoices, the system automatically clears the receivables in the customer account. To make this clearing entry, the process in SAP ERP credits the customer account to clear the receivables and debits the clearing house account.

The determination of the clearing house account is done using the condition technique we discussed in Chapter 1. You can make configuration settings for the GL account determination for the clearing house account via menu path IMG • Sales and Distribution • Billing • Payment Cards • Authorization and Settlement • Maintain Clearing House • Account Determination.

The standard system provides by default the Sales Organization and Payment Card Type in the field catalog. These fields are available for clearing house account determination (see Figure 3.10). However, you can choose to use any other field or fields from structures KOMCV or KOMKCV for this GL account determination.

SlsOrg/Card cat.						
App	CndTy.	ChAc	SOrg.	Type	G/L account ...	G/L account ...
VD	A001	CANA	0001	VISA		
VD	A001	CANA	0001	MC		
VD	A001	CANA	0001	AMEX		

Figure 3.10 Payment Card General Ledger Account Determination

The other GL account required at the time of payment card processing is a cash clearing account.

3.3.2 Cash Clearing Account

When you carry out the settlement process in SAP ERP, credit card transaction details are sent to the clearing house. The cash clearing account is used to record this receivable from the clearing house. At this point, the cash clearing account is debited with the total receivable amount from the clearing house. After the clearing house processes the credit card transactions in a settlement request, it sends payment to you after deducting the relevant charges and fees. At this point, the cash clearing account gets credited, and the bank account is debited. For this reason, you should assign a separate GL account for every credit card receivable account.

The cash clearing account is set up via the menu path IMG • Financial Accounting • Accounts Receivable and Accounts Payable • Business Transactions • Payments with Payment Cards • Assign G/L Account to Cash Clearing Account.

It is important to note that this account should be set with the Open Item Management flag selected (see Chapter 1, Section 1.2.6). Figure 3.11 shows an example of assigning the cash clearing account.

ChAc	Receivable	Short Text	Clearing	Short Text
CANA	125300	A/R - Payment Cards	113030	Paymnt Card Acct

Figure 3.11 Cash Clearing Account

> **Note**
>
> Even though it isn't specifically mentioned at the beginning of this section, you obviously also require a bank account to receive the credit card payments.

3.3.3 Bank Account

This account can be considered part of the credit card transaction process—although it is just like any other bank account. It is posted when payment from the clearing house is received toward one or more settlement runs.

This posting can be automatic if you are using the automatic bank statement functionality. Otherwise, you can also post this entry manually.

The GL account for the bank account is assigned in configuration by navigating to the menu path IMG • Financial Accounting • Bank Accounting • Bank Accounts • Define House Bank Accounts.

This brings us to an end of the discussion about GL account determination in the payment card process. In the next section, we will discuss GL account determination for the interest calculation process.

3.4 Interest Calculation

The interest calculation process in SAP ERP provides comprehensive functionality to calculate interest on arrears (past due items) and based on account balances. Even though this discussion is included here in the chapter on AR and AP, you can use the interest calculation functionality on GL accounts as well.

Figure 3.12 shows seemingly complicated links between different account determination objects involved in the interest calculation process.

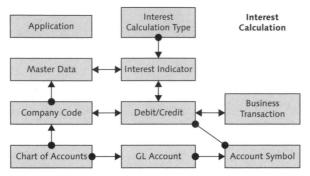

Figure 3.12 Interest Calculation Account Determination Objects

3.4.1 Account Determination Objects

In addition to the obvious objects, such as a company code and a chart of accounts, the interest calculation process uses several other account determination objects.

Application

An *application* in this context refers to a task area corresponding to a specific business process. You carry out all GL account determination configuration for interest calculation within a task area, that is, specific for an application.

Table 3.1 lists the relevant values for the purposes of the current discussion. These values are predefined and not changeable. Depending on the configuration task, the value for this characteristic is automatically selected.

Application	Description
0002	Interest calculation on AR arrears
0009	Interest calculation on AP arrears
0005	Interest calculation on AR balances
0006	Interest calculation on AR balances

Table 3.1 Application Values for Interest Calculation

Interest Calculation Type

An *interest indicator type* specifies whether interest calculation is for the interest calculation on arrears (per item) or on account balance. For the purposes of the current discussion, the following values of interest calculation type are relevant:

- ▶ P (item interest calculation)
- ▶ S (balance interest calculation)

These values are also predefined and cannot be changed. However, as you will see, you use these values while configuring one or more interest indicators.

Interest Indicator

An *interest indicator* is a two-character code that you can freely define and use in the interest calculation process. An interest indicator is configured with detailed specifics such as what reference interest rate should be used, what type of items should be included in interest calculation (if applicable), what is the frequency of interest calculation, and so on.

You define interest indicators using the configuration IMG • Financial Accounting • Accounts Receivable and Accounts Payable • Business Transactions • Interest Calculation • Interest Calculation Global Settings • Define Interest Calculation Types.

Under the same menu area, you will find configuration transactions that you can use to configure detailed specifics of interest rate indicators, for arrears calculation as well as for balance interest calculation. You can define as many interest indicators as necessary. For example, you may create separate interest indicators for different reference interest rates, for different interest calculation frequency, and so on.

An interest indicator can be only of one interest calculation type—either based on items or based on account balance. You assign interest indicators to master data records.

Master Data

You must assign the appropriate interest indicators to all account master records that you want to include in automatic interest calculation processes. The master data in this context refers to GL account master, customer account master, or vendor account master. The following list describes where you can assign the interest indicator for each type of master record:

- ▶ **GL account master**
  Change GL Account Master (TRX. FS00) transaction and then select Interest Indicator field in the Interest Calculation Information In Company Code section on the Create/Bank/Interest tab.

► **Customer account master**

CHANGE CUSTOMER MASTER (TRX. FD02) transaction and then select INTEREST INDICATOR field in the INTEREST CALCULATION section on the ACCOUNT MANAGEMENT tab.

► **Vendor account master**

CHANGE VENDOR MASTER (TRX. FK02) transaction and then select INTEREST INDICATOR field in the INTEREST CALCULATION section on the ACCOUNT MANAGEMENT tab.

You can only assign one interest indicator to a master data account. However, this assignment is company code specific, so you can potentially assign different interest indicators for the same master account in different company codes. Let's now discuss the business transaction.

Business Transaction

A *business transaction* in this context is a predefined four-character value that uniquely identifies a type of business transaction for interest posting. While configuring the GL account determination for interest calculation, you have to consider all possible business transactions that are relevant for your company.

Table 3.2 lists sample values of business transactions that are relevant for the interest calculation posting configuration. We will discuss the remaining account determination objects in the next section.

Value	Name
1000	Interest received posting
1020	Debit interest—value date in the past
2000	Interest paid posting
2020	Credit interest—value date in the past

Table 3.2 Business Transaction Values for Interest Calculation

3.4.2 General Ledger Account Determination

You will find configuration transactions for interest calculation under the menu area IMG • FINANCIAL ACCOUNTING • ACCOUNTS RECEIVABLE AND ACCOUNTS PAYABLE • BUSINESS TRANSACTIONS • INTEREST CALCULATION • INTEREST POSTING.

You will find here different configuration transactions for the GL account determination configuration depending on whether you are configuring interest calculation for AR or AP, and whether interest calculation is based on arrears or on account balances. SAP ERP uses the symbolic account technique for GL account determination for the interest calculation process.

We discussed the account determination objects application, business transaction, and interest indicator in the previous section. For configuring any GL account determination, you follow these steps:

1. Define account symbols to correspond to different GL accounts.

2. Assign two account symbols to every combination of business transaction, interest indicator, company code, and business area characteristics—one account symbol for debit posting and another one for credit posting.

3. Assign GL accounts to corresponding account symbols.

Figure 3.13 shows an example of GL account determination configuration. As you can see in this example, you can access the commands for branching to the account symbol definition and the GL account assignment from the same transaction.

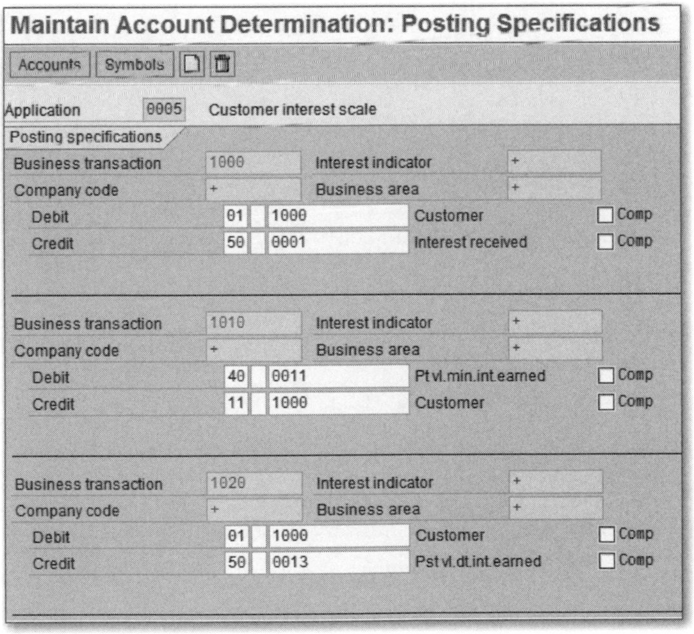

Figure 3.13 General Ledger Account Determination: Interest Calculation

3.5 Summary

GL account determination for standard AR/AP transactions is relatively easy. All the necessary configuration transactions are grouped neatly, in the configuration guide, under different business transactions.

The assignment of alternative reconciliation accounts, which is explained in this chapter, is relevant only for documents posted in FI. For the customer billing documents posted from SD, reconciliation account determination can be done using the condition technique. This is covered in Chapter 8.

Because SAP ERP is a highly integrated system, AR/AP GL account determination is closely tied to Purchasing and SD. Therefore, the GL account determination described in this chapter is applicable in most cases for transactions originating in Purchasing or SD also.

Another subject matter closely integrated with AR and AP is tax calculation. Chapter 4 discusses GL account determination for posting sales and purchase tax.

3.6 Reference

This section provides you with a technical reference for the AR and AP transactions discussed in this chapter.

3.6.1 Configuration Transactions

Table 3.3 provides a list of the configuration transactions for the account determination objects discussed in this chapter.

Transaction Code	Description
AKOF	Reconciliation accounts with exception handling
OBXR	Reconciliation accounts for down payments received from customers
OBXY	Reconciliation accounts for other special GL transactions for customers

Table 3.3 Configuration Transactions

Transaction Code	Description
OBYR	Reconciliation accounts for down payments made to vendors
OBXT	Reconciliation accounts for other special GL transactions for vendors
OBXS	Offsetting accounts for special GL transactions
OB00	For rounding differences
OBXU	For cash discount taken
	For cash discount clearing
OBXV	For cash discount lost
OBXK	For bank charges
OBXL	For overpayments/underpayments
	For input tax clearing
	For output tax clearing
OBXO	For alternative payment currency
OBXQ	For alternative payment currency—offset
OV81	Payment cards—condition tables
OV83	Payment cards—field catalog
OV85	Payment cards—condition types
OV86	Payment cards—determination procedure
OV87	Payment cards—GL account determination
	Payment cards—cash clearing account
FI12	Maintain bank account

Table 3.3 Configuration Transactions (Cont.)

3.6.2 Tables and Structures

Table 3.4 contains a list of tables or structures used to store data relevant for the GL account determination discussed in this chapter.

Table/Structure	Description
TAKOF	Reconciliation accounts with exception handling
T074	Special GL reconciliation accounts
T030	Offsetting GL accounts for special transactions
T030	For AR/AP transactions
MV12A	Payment card—condition generator
T681F	Payment card—field catalog
T685	Payment card—condition types
T683	Payment card—determination procedures
C???	Payment card—GL account determination (see Note following this table)
TCCAA	Payment card—clearing account
T012K	House bank accounts

Table 3.4 Tables and Structures

> **Note**
>
> GL account determination is stored in condition tables corresponding to the tables specified in the condition generator.

3.6.3 Enhancements

Table 3.5 shows a list of the enhancements that can be used to influence GL account determination in transactions discussed in this chapter.

Enhancement	Description
SDVFC001	Account determination from payment card plan item

Table 3.5 Enhancements

4 Tax Transactions

This chapter covers GL account determination for tax calculation and postings. The SAP ERP system supports the calculation of several types of taxes such as sales tax, purchase tax, withholding tax, and payroll taxes. This chapter primarily focuses on GL account determination for sales tax, purchase tax, and withholding taxes. The chapter on payroll transactions (Chapter 10) provides more detail on GL account determination for payroll taxes.

Tax calculations are highly specific to individual countries. Even within a country, different industries may be subject to different types of taxes, so it is difficult to provide a single source for all types of tax calculations that are applicable to all scenarios. However, because the focus of this guide is on GL account determination and not on tax calculations, it will suffice to use one of the tax procedures as an example and describe GL account determination for it. SAP ERP provides tax calculation procedure templates for several countries.

In this chapter, we will use the tax calculations procedure template provided for the U.S. as the example procedure to describe GL account determination. From here, you can extrapolate or extend your understanding of GL account determination to other tax procedures. The remarkable flexibility and functionality of the condition technique enables you to implement GL account determination for almost any type of sales or purchase taxes. The standard U.S. tax procedure provides calculation of the following types of taxes:

▶ **Calculation of purchase tax on inbound goods and services**
The tax amount is posted as a separate line item in an invoice.

▶ **Calculation of purchase tax on inbound goods and services**
The tax amount is distributed to other line items in an invoice.

▶ **Calculation of purchase tax on inbound goods and services**
The tax amount calculation and posting where the vendor should have but did not charge tax.

▶ **Calculation of sales tax on outbound goods and services**
Sales tax and purchase tax calculations in SAP ERP are implemented using

different approaches depending on whether the Sales or Purchasing functionalities of SAP ERP are implemented in addition to SAP ERP Financials.

In each case, the GL account determination method is slightly different. We will first discuss tax GL account determination in SAP ERP Financials, and then gradually expand the discussion to address other variations. First let's begin with a quick overview of account determination objects that are part of GL account determination for tax calculations.

4.1 Account Determination Objects

Figure 4.1 shows account determination objects involved in tax GL account determination in SAP ERP Financials. Here SAP ERP uses a simplified condition technique for tax calculation and GL account determination.

The *tax procedure* in the tax configuration corresponds to the calculation procedure in the condition technique. The tax procedure contains the necessary specifications and postings for different types of tax calculations that are relevant for a country.

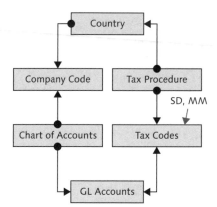

Figure 4.1 Tax Account Determination for Finance

As mentioned before, the standard SAP ERP system provides many country-specific calculation procedures that can be used as is or modified as required. Figure 4.2 shows some of the tax procedures that are available in SAP ERP. These procedures are maintained via the menu path FINANCIAL ACCOUNTING IMG • FINANCIAL ACCOUNTING GLOBAL SETTINGS • TAX ON SALES/PURCHASES • BASIC SETTINGS • CHECK CALCULATION PROCEDURE.

Proce...	Descript.
TAXCA	Sales Tax - Canada
TAXCAJ	Sales Tax - Canada
TAXCL	Sales Tax - Chile
TAXCN	Sales Tax - China
TAXCO	Sales Tax - Colombia
TAXD	Sales Tax - Germany
TAXF	Sales Tax - France
TAXHK	Sales Tax - Hongkong
TAXHU	Sales Tax - Hungary
TAXINJ	Sales Tax India
TAXIT	Sales Tax - Italy
TAXJP	Sales Tax - Japan
TAXPE	Sales Tax - Peru
TAXPH	Sales Tax - Philippines
TAXUS	Sales Tax - USA
TAXUSJ	Sales Tax USA w. Jurisdictions
TAXUSX	Tax USA m Jurisdictions (ext.)

Figure 4.2 Standard Tax Procedures

One tax procedure is assigned to a country. Considering that sales and purchase tax calculations are highly country-specific, you will often find a separate tax procedure for each country. However, it is technically possible to assign the same tax procedure to multiple countries. So, for example, you can develop a tax procedure for one European region as it applies to your business and assign that same tax procedure to all European countries. The actual configuration of the tax procedure isn't relevant for the topic of this Essentials guide. However, for reference, Figure 4.3 shows an example of a tax procedure for the United States.

Step	CTyp	Description	ActKy	Accrls
100	BASB	Base Amount		
200		A/P Distributed		
210	AP1I	A/P Sales Tax 1 Inv.	NVV	
220	AP2I	A/P Sales Tax 2 Inv.	NVV	
230	AP3I	A/P Sales Tax 3 Inv.	NVV	
240	AP4I	A/P Sales Tax 4 Inv.	NVV	
300		A/P Undistributed		
310	AP1E	A/P Sales Tax 1 Exp.	VS1	
320	AP2E	A/P Sales Tax 2 Exp.	VS2	
330	AP3E	A/P Sales Tax 3 Exp.	VS3	
340	AP4E	A/P Sales Tax 4 Exp.	VS4	
400		A/P Use Tax Distributed		
410	AP1U	A/P Sales Tax 1 Use	MW1	
420	AP2U	A/P Sales Tax 2 Use	MW2	
430	AP3U	A/P Sales Tax 3 Use	MW3	

Figure 4.3 Sample U.S. Tax Procedure

Figure 4.4 shows the assignment of the tax procedure to a country. This assignment is carried out via the menu path FINANCIAL ACCOUNTING IMG • FINANCIAL ACCOUNTING GLOBAL SETTINGS • TAX ON SALES/PURCHASES • BASIC SETTINGS • ASSIGN COUNTRY TO CALCULATION PROCEDURE.

After you have configured the tax procedure, you configure multiple tax codes for that tax procedure. These tax codes typically correspond to tax rates specified by the country-specific regulatory authority. Some countries such as the United States and Canada use multiple tax jurisdiction levels at which tax is calculated. For a tax code configured in such implementations, you can specify a separate tax rate corresponding to each jurisdiction level.

TP	East Timor	
TR	Turkey	TAXTR
TT	Trinidad,Tobago	
TV	Tuvalu	
TW	Taiwan	TAXTW
TZ	Tanzania	
UA	Ukraine	TAXUA
UG	Uganda	
UM	Minor Outl.Isl.	
US	USA	TAXUSJ
UY	Uruguay	

Figure 4.4 Country—Tax Process Assignment

Tax codes are configured for a tax procedure. Out of all the conditions available in the tax procedure, tax rates or percentages for a tax code are assigned only to a few relevant conditions. Other conditions in the procedure may not be tax-relevant. This concept will become clear when we discuss tax calculations in Sales and Purchasing later in this chapter. You carry out tax code configuration via the menu path FINANCIAL ACCOUNTING IMG • FINANCIAL ACCOUNTING GLOBAL SETTINGS • TAX ON SALES/PURCHASES • CALCULATION • DEFINE TAX CODES FOR SALES AND PURCHASES.

For example, in Figure 4.5, TAX CODE "O1" is configured for tax PROCEDURE "TAXUS". The specification of tax percentage 6.250 with A/R sales tax (and the corresponding account key, which is not shown in the figure) indicates to the system that this percentage is for sales tax (outbound) and not purchase tax (inbound).

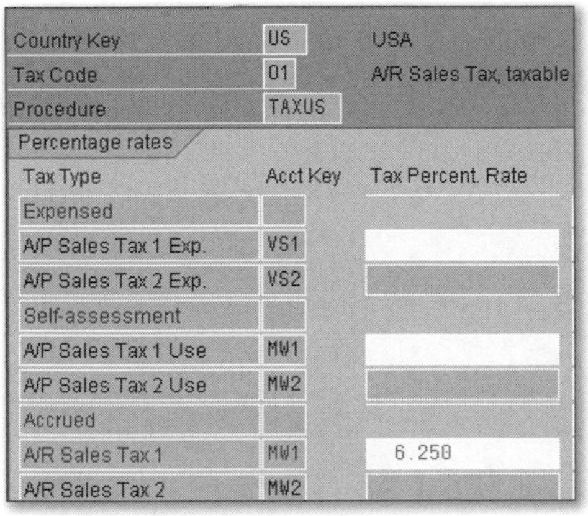

Figure 4.5 Tax Code Definition

The next section shows you how these objects are used to determine GL accounts for tax posting.

4.2 General Ledger Account Determination

Let's continue with the example of tax procedure discussed in the previous section. As discussed, for a tax code configured for a tax procedure, you assign tax rates to all relevant tax procedure conditions. For every condition in a tax procedure to which a tax rate is assigned, you must enter a GL account to which the corresponding tax accounting entry will be posted. Keep in mind that tax rates are assigned separately for each tax code. However, you have to assign GL accounts only once for each condition to which a tax rate may be assigned.

For example, as shown in Figure 4.6 for the TAX CODE "O1" configuration, tax rates are defined only for account keys MW1, MW2, and MW3. Therefore, when you select the TAX ACCOUNTS command button in the Tax Code Maintenance (Transaction FTXP), the pop-up window expects you to assign GL accounts only for those three account keys. Subsequently if you were to set up another tax code O2 for the same tax procedure, that tax code would use the same GL accounts for account keys MW1, MW2, and MW3. However, if tax code O2 had a tax rate for account key MW4, then you will need to configure a corresponding GL account, which in turn will be shared by any other tax codes.

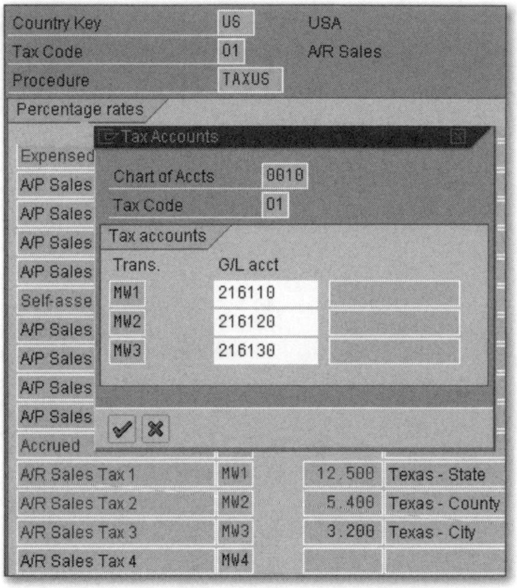

Figure 4.6 Tax General Ledger Account Determination

This also highlights another aspect of the tax condition procedure configuration. If you want the same type of tax to post to different GL accounts, you need to set up separate conditions and separate account keys in the tax procedure.

So far we have only discussed a simple form of tax GL account determination. The remainder of this section is devoted to other variables and combination of parameters that influence tax GL account determination. Let's look at some of these variations.

4.2.1 Tax Jurisdiction Code

In many countries, tax is levied at multiple levels of government. For example, in the United States, tax is levied at the state, county, and city levels. A business transaction may be taxable at all, some, or none of these levels.

Because tax codes are created for different tax percentages, if you are required to create a separate tax code for each combination of tax levels, there could literally be thousands of tax codes—one for each unique combination of state, county, and city. Use of tax jurisdiction code functionality eliminates the need to create so many tax codes. A tax jurisdiction code helps in uniquely identifying a geographical area from a tax calculation standpoint. You define a jurisdiction code structure so that different values of jurisdiction code can uniquely identify a geographical area. Subsequently, you use the same tax code with different values of jurisdiction codes to maintain tax rate combinations. You define the jurisdiction code structure for a tax procedure using FINANCIAL ACCOUNTING IMG • FINANCIAL ACCOUNTING GLOBAL SETTINGS • TAX ON SALES/PURCHASES • BASIC SETTINGS • SPECIFY STRUCTURE FOR TAX JURISDICTION CODE.

Even though the definition of the tax jurisdiction code has an impact on the tax rate determination, it does not have any impact on the GL account determination. GL accounts specified for an accounting key in a tax procedure are shared across all tax codes and all tax jurisdiction codes.

Therefore, irrespective of whether the tax jurisdiction functionality for a country is active or not, you can determine GL accounts after the tax procedure and account keys are known.

4.2.2 External Tax Systems

Depending on the number of tax authorities and the frequency of changes in tax rates and tax regulations, it may not be practical to maintain the complete tax calculation configuration within SAP ERP.

SAP ERP provides the ability to interface with external tax software programs that are highly specialized in providing tax calculations and keeping all tax rates and tax rules up to date. The existence of such an interface necessitates additional configuration in the system—particularly in the areas of derivation of a tax jurisdiction code based on an address, and tax calculations based on a business transaction. You carry out settings for external tax calculations under the configuration area FINANCIAL ACCOUNTING IMG • FINANCIAL ACCOUNTING GLOBAL SETTINGS • TAX ON SALES/PURCHASES • BASIC SETTINGS • EXTERNAL TAX CALCULATION.

If your implementation uses external tax software, then, in SAP ERP, instead of assigning actual tax rates to tax conditions, you assign 100% value to the appropriate conditions. The tax interface passes these values to the external software, which in turn determines accurate applicable tax rates and calculates appropriate tax amounts. However, there is no impact on the GL account determination process. Tax codes are still defined in SAP ERP, and GL accounts are still assigned to the tax codes as described earlier.

4.2.3 Non-Taxable Transactions

As discussed in the introduction to this chapter, GL account attributes determine whether an account is taxable and, if so, what types of business transactions can be posted to it.

When a non-taxable business transaction is posted to a taxable GL account, SAP ERP refers to the configuration in the menu path FINANCIAL ACCOUNTING IMG • FINANCIAL ACCOUNTING BASIC SETTINGS • TAX ON SALES/PURCHASES • POSTING • ASSIGN TAX CODES FOR NON-TAXABLE TRANSACTIONS.

As shown in Figure 4.7, you specify tax codes for input tax and output tax to be used for non-taxable transactions. These tax codes have zero percent assigned to them, so that calculation procedure doesn't calculate tax for the corresponding tax conditions. Even for these scenarios, GL account determination takes place as described earlier. However, because the effective tax amount is zero, the process doesn't generate any accounting entry to the tax accounts.

Co...	Company name	City	Input...	Output
0001	SAP A.G.	Walldorf	V0	A0
0MB1	IS-B Musterbank Deut...	Walldorf		
AR01	Country Template AR	Argentinien	C0	D0
ARG1	Country Template AR	Argentinien		
AT01	Country Template AT	Austria	V0	A0
AU01	Country Template AU	Australia	P0	S0
BE01	Country Template BE	Belgium	V0	A0
BR01	Country Template BR	Brazil	I0	A0
CA01	Country Template CA	Canada	V0	A0

Figure 4.7 Non-Taxable Transactions

4.2.4 Tax Calculation in Sales

A typical implementation scenario consists of the SAP Sales and Distribution (SD) functionality and SAP ERP Financials. In such a scenario, tax code determination occurs in the SD functionality, and relevant information is passed to the SAP ERP Financials component, where determination of tax rates and tax GL accounts takes place.

You must first configure applicable tax determination rules in the source country. These rules are merely the conditions used in the Sales pricing procedure. This configuration is carried out via the menu path SALES & DISTRIBUTION IMG • BASIC FUNCTIONS • TAXES • DEFINE TAX DETERMINATION RULES.

Figure 4.8 shows an example of a tax rule determination for the United States. In this configuration activity, TAX CATEGORY refers to the tax conditions maintained in the pricing procedure. In the example shown, three conditions correspond to three levels of tax calculations. The SEQUENCE NUMBER determines which tax condition is evaluated first. Each tax condition is configured with condition type TAXES; and it is assigned to an appropriate access sequence.

Tax...	Name	S..	Tax ca...	Name
SG	Singapore	1	MWST	Output Tax
SK	Slovakia	1	MWST	Output Tax
TR	Turkey	1	MWST	Output Tax
US	USA	1	UTXJ	Tax Jurisdict.Code
US	USA	2	UTX2	County Sales Tax
US	USA	3	UTX3	City Sales Tax
VE	Venezuela	1	MWST	Output Tax

Figure 4.8 Sales Tax Rule Determination

The maintenance of tax conditions and access sequences for a pricing procedure is carried out in the menu path SALES & DISTRIBUTION IMG • BASIC FUNCTIONS • PRICING • PRICING CONTROL.

Typically, the access sequence assigned to these condition types provides, at a minimum, the ability to differentiate between domestic transactions and foreign transactions.

Figure 4.9 shows the tax code determination for foreign transactions, for condition UTXJ, (condition table 78), and access sequence UTX1. Per this configuration, for sales transactions originating in the United States, tax code O1 is assigned if the customer ship-to location (destination) is in BRAZIL or in CANADA. On the other hand, if the customer ship-to location is in CHINA or in INDIA, SAP ERP assigns TAX CODE O0 to such sales transactions.

After the tax code is determined, the tax calculation and tax GL account determination occurs in SAP ERP Financials. This process is the same as the process described at the beginning of this section.

Country US USA

Valid On 01/01/2006

Departure Country / Destination Country

R...	Name	Valid From	Valid to	Tax..
BR	Brazil	01/01/2006	12/31/9999	01
CA	Canada	01/01/2006	12/31/9999	01
CN	China	01/01/2006	12/31/9999	00
IN	India	01/01/2006	12/31/9999	00
JP	Japan	01/01/2006	12/31/9999	02

Figure 4.9 Tax Code Determination in Sales

For sales transactions, two additional objects influence tax code determination: the tax classification indicator for customers and the tax classification indicator for materials. These indicators are defined and assigned in the Sales component via the menu path SALES & DISTRIBUTION IMG • BASIC FUNCTIONS • TAXES • DEFINE TAX RELEVANCY OF MASTER RECORDS. These indicators differentiate and classify customers and products for the purpose of taxation (as taxable, partially taxable, non-taxable, etc.). For example, government and non-profit customers may be non-taxable, whereas special products may be non-taxable due to a tax holiday or any similar business conditions. Or the same product may be taxable for some customers and non-taxable for others.

In the customer master, these indicators are maintained on the BILLING DOCUMENT tab in the SALES AREA data. In the material master, these indicators are maintained on the SALES ORG 1 tab for sales organization-specific data. These indicators are available in the access sequence, so they can be used for tax code determination.

If you are using only the SD functionality of SAP ERP without SAP ERP Financials, then you can facilitate tax calculation by creating conditions for the different types of tax calculations. You maintain values for these conditions directly in the SAP SD functionality. In such a scenario, GL account determination is done using the account keys associated with conditions. This process is discussed in detail in Chapter 8.

4.2.5 Tax Calculation in Purchasing

Similar to the business scenario described previously for the order-to-cash cycle, for the procure-to-pay cycle, you implement both Purchasing and SAP ERP Financials. In this case, the applicable tax code is determined in Purchasing, and the maintenance of tax codes, tax rates, and tax GL accounts is determined in SAP

ERP Financials. You should read this section (Section 4.2) from the beginning, if you haven't already done so. In the order-to-cash cycle, you have to calculate and collect taxes for most, if not all, of your customers. In the procure-to-pay cycle, however, most commonly your suppliers include tax in their invoices so that you pay it along with the invoice amount. So the tax configuration in Purchasing is relatively simple compared to the tax configuration in Sales.

Typically, your supplier invoice already includes the tax amount in most cases, so your primary responsibility is to verify the tax already charged on the vendor invoice. However, if the purchasing transaction is taxable, and the vendor invoice does *not* include tax, then your local tax regulations may require you to self-assess that tax (*use tax* in the United States).

For the procure-to-pay cycle, it is important to maintain accurate tax classification for materials, plants, and account assignments. We discussed these tax indicators in the previous section. For Purchasing, you maintain and assign product tax indicators via the menu path MATERIALS MANAGEMENT IMG • PURCHASING • TAXES • SET TAX INDICATOR FOR MATERIAL/PLANT/ACCOUNT ASSIGNMENTS.

> **Note**
>
> In the material master, material tax indicators for Purchasing are maintained separately and independently from the material tax indicators for Sales. This reflects the reality of any business environment where the same material may be taxed differently depending on whether it is being purchased or sold. The material tax indicators for Sales transactions are maintained in the material master on the SALES ORG 1 tab, and you have to specify a separate material tax indicator for every possible destination country. On the other hand, material tax indicators for Purchasing transactions are maintained in the material master on the PURCHASING tab, and you can assign only one tax indicator per receiving plant.

In Purchasing, tax code determination is carried out based on the conditions assigned to the calculation schema. The standard SAP ERP system provides condition MWST for this purpose. This condition is assigned an access sequence, which can make use of any or all of the tax indicators described earlier to determine a tax code. At the very minimum, the access sequence should be able to provide a separate tax code determination for domestic purchases and foreign purchases.

Maintenance of the conditions and access sequences for the calculation schema is carried out via the menu path MATERIALS MANAGEMENT IMG • PURCHASING •

Conditions • Define Price Determination Process • Define Access Sequences/ Condition Types/Calculation Schema.

Figure 4.10 shows the tax code determination for foreign transactions, for condition MWST, and for one of the access alternatives (condition table 11) of access sequence MWST. Per this configuration, for transactions originating in the United States and with the destination in Japan, the tax code is determined as V9 regardless of the tax classification. On the other hand, if the destination is in Brazil, and if both tax classifications are 1 (taxable), then the tax code is I1. In all other cases, it is determined as I0.

R...	T.	T.	Name		Valid From	Valid to	Tax..
BR	0	0	Tax Exempt	No tax	01/01/2006	12/31/9999	I0
BR	0	1	Tax Exempt	Full tax	01/01/2006	12/31/9999	I0
BR	1	0	Liable for Taxe	No tax	01/01/2006	12/31/9999	I0
BR	1	1	Liable for Taxe	Full tax	01/01/2006	12/31/9999	I1
JP	0	0	Tax Exempt	No tax	01/01/2006	12/31/9999	V9
JP	0	1	Tax Exempt	Full tax	01/01/2006	12/31/9999	V9
JP	1	0	Liable for Taxe	No tax	01/01/2006	12/31/9999	V9
JP	1	1	Liable for Taxe	Full tax	01/01/2006	12/31/9999	V9

Figure 4.10 Purchase Tax Determination

However, if your requirements are not very complicated, you can maintain the tax code in the Purchasing info record for the combination of vendor and material. This tax code gets transferred along with other details from the info record to the purchase order. You maintain vendor info records using the transactions under menu path SAP Menu • Logistics • Materials Management • Purchasing • Master Data • Info Record. On the Info Record maintenance screen, you maintain the tax code on the Purch organization data 1 tab. After the tax code has been determined, the tax calculation and GL account determination for the tax code happens on the SAP ERP Financials side as described earlier.

In the next section, we will look at other relevant information such as tax account maintenance and GL account attributes.

4.3 Other Relevant Information

This section covers additional relevant information that did not belong in the previous section.

4.3.1 Tax Account Maintenance

We have already discussed how GL account assignment can be done from the Tax Code maintenance screen. However, you can also maintain all sales/purchase tax-relevant accounts using the configuration menu path FINANCIAL ACCOUNTING IMG • FINANCIAL ACCOUNTING GLOBAL SETTINGS • TAX ON SALES/PURCHASES • POSTING • DEFINE TAX ACCOUNTS.

Figure 4.11 shows the maintenance of GL accounts for different transaction keys (account keys) that use Transaction %TX. This configuration activity displays all the tax account keys from all the tax procedures in the current client of SAP ERP. However, an interesting aspect of this configuration activity is that if the same account key is used in several tax procedures and assigned to different tax codes, you will be able to configure GL accounts for all tax codes in one place.

Description	Transaction
India Basic Excise	JI1
India Addl Excise	JI2
India Special Excise	JI3
Additional tax	LUX
Sales tax 1	MW1
Sales tax 2	MW2
Output tax GST	MW5
Output tax	MWS
Non-deduct.input tax	NAV
Entertainment tax	NZ1
Reduction	NZ2
Sales tax 1	VS1
Sales tax 2	VS2
Input Tax PST Gross	VS5
Input Tax HST s/a	VS6
Input tax GST s/a	VS7

Figure 4.11 Tax Account Maintenance

Figure 4.12 shows an example of GL accounts assigned to different tax codes associated with transaction or account key MW1. These tax codes may be associated with different tax procedures.

| Chart of Accounts | 0010 |
| Transaction | MW1 |

Account assignment	
Tax code	Account
00	216100
01	216130
02	216130
S0	216410
S1	216410
S2	216410
SP	216410
U1	216200

Figure 4.12 General Ledger Accounts—Transaction Key View

4.3.2   General Ledger Account Attributes

We have already discussed GL account attributes that can have an impact on GL account determination. For the purposes of the discussion in this chapter, the value in the field TAX CATEGORY is very important.

The tax category value in the GL account master controls the type of tax transactions that can be posted to that GL account. You can even control the transactions being posted to an account at the individual tax code level. Figure 4.13 shows some of the values available for the field tax category.

St	Name
-	Only input tax allowed
+	Only output tax allowed
*	All tax types allowed
<	Input Tax Account
>	Output Tax Account
-B	Input tax - down payments managed
+B	Output tax - down payments managed
E0	A/P Sales Tax, exempt
E1	A/P Sales Tax, taxable, posted to
I0	A/P Sales Tax, exempt
I1	A/P Sales Tax, taxable, distribute
O0	A/R Sales Tax, exempt

Figure 4.13 Tax Category in General Ledger Accounts

Table 4.1 provides brief explanations of what types of transactions can be posted to a GL account for different tax category values.

Tax Category	Transactions Allowed for the GL Account
*	You can post transactions containing input tax or output tax.
-	You can only post transactions that contain input tax.
+	You can only post transactions that contain output tax.
Individual tax codes	You can only post transactions that contain the specific tax code.
<	The GL account is an input tax account.
>	The GL account is an output tax account.

Table 4.1 Tax Category Values

It is also important to note that if you have selected the POSTING WITHOUT TAX ALLOWED setting on the CONTROL DATA tab of the GL account master, you can post a transaction to that GL account regardless of whether it contains a tax code.

The next section discusses GL account determination for the withholding tax functionality in SAP ERP.

4.4 Withholding Tax

Most commonly, payment recipients are required to accurately report all of their income and pay appropriate taxes on it. However, for any statutory or tax reasons, tax authorities may request the payer to withhold tax from the payments made to a payee, and remit the tax directly to the tax authorities. SAP ERP provides two types of withholding tax functionalities: simple withholding tax and extended withholding tax.

4.4.1 Simple Withholding Tax

Simple withholding tax calculation provides limited but mostly adequate functionality for withholding tax calculation. You can use the simple withholding tax functionality if taxes are to be withheld only from accounts payable, and if a payee only has one type of payment that is subject to withholding tax. For simple withholding tax, you assign GL accounts directly to withholding tax codes (see Figure 4.14) that are associated with the payee account. You carry out this assignment in the configuration activity accessed via the menu path FINANCIAL ACCOUNTING IMG • FINANCIAL ACCOUNTING GLOBAL SETTINGS • WITHHOLDING TAX • WITHHOLDING TAX • POSTING • DEFINE ACCOUNTS FOR WITHHOLDING TAX.

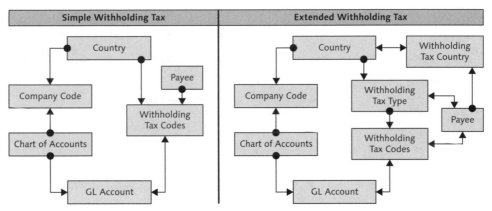

Figure 4.14 Simple and Extended Withholding Tax

SAP ERP uses transaction key QST for GL account determination for simple withholding tax. You can also use account modifiers debit/credit indicator and withholding tax code for carrying out GL account determination at a more granular level.

GL accounts specified for this transaction key are posted when open items in customer or vendor accounts are cleared—that is, when a payment transaction is posted.

Let's now look at the extended withholding tax process in SAP ERP.

4.4.2 Extended Withholding Tax

Figure 4.14, shown previously, also includes a schematic diagram for extended withholding tax for easier comparison purposes. The extended withholding tax process provides considerably more complex functionality for withholding tax calculations. For example, you can use it to process multiple withholdings for the same payee, self-withhold for the scenarios where your business is subject to a withholding process, calculate withholding tax at the time of invoicing instead of at the time of payment, and so on.

Additionally, the extended withholding tax process makes available the concepts of the withholding tax country and the withholding tax type. The WITHHOLDING TAX COUNTRY field lets you specify a different country for withholding tax calculation and reporting purposes. For example, in the United States, taxes withheld on certain income of foreign individuals or corporations are reported on IRS Form 1042. This withholding tax depends on the payee's country. The WITHHOLDING TAX TYPE field, on the other hand, enables you to separate different types of withholdings such as federal withholding, state withholding, and so on. You maintain withholding tax country, withholding tax types, and withholding tax codes in the payee's master records. You assign GL accounts for extended withholding tax using configuration activities under the menu path FINANCIAL ACCOUNTING IMG • FINANCIAL ACCOUNTING GLOBAL SETTINGS • WITHHOLDING TAX • EXTENDED WITHHOLDING TAX • POSTING • ACCOUNTS FOR WITHHOLDING TAX.

You configure GL account determination for the following types of transactions:

▸ **Transaction key WIT (extended withholding tax)**
GL accounts configured under this transaction key are used to post withholding tax deducted from outgoing payments.

▸ **Transaction key GRU (offsetting entry without deduction)**
SAP ERP uses GL accounts configured under this transaction key to post an offsetting entry for the grossing-up option. This function is only relevant in Argentina for foreign vendors.

▸ **Transaction key OPO (self-withholding)**
SAP ERP uses GL accounts configured under this transaction key to post withholding tax calculated and deducted from incoming payments.

▸ **Transaction key OFF (offsetting entry with deduction)**
SAP ERP uses GL accounts configured under this transaction key to post the offsetting entry. This option is relevant if the withholding tax code configuration requires SAP ERP to generate two withholding tax line items with opposing debit/credit signs.

Each of these transactions provides account modifiers for the debit/credit indicator, withholding tax type, and withholding tax code. By enabling all of the rule modifiers, you can carry out GL account determination at the lowest level. On the other hand, you also should consider the complexity involved in maintaining this type of account determination on an ongoing basis and the efforts required at the time of month-end reconciliation.

4.5 Summary

As discussed in this chapter, in a typical implementation, tax calculations and tax GL account determination is done in SAP ERP Financials, whereas functionalities in Sales and Purchasing provide necessary functionality for tax code determination.

Transaction OB40 provides an overview of all of the tax accounts assigned to all tax procedures. The complexity of sales and purchase taxes mainly lies in the tax calculations rather than the GL account determination.

Using withholding tax functions, you can withhold taxes on incoming or outgoing payments and invoices. Depending on the industry and customer base of your company, you can choose to implement simple withholding tax or extended withholding tax.

If payments to and from customers and vendors are posted in SAP ERP manually, there is no additional GL account determination involved. However, if these payment transactions are automated, you must configure GL account determination for payment transactions, which is the subject of Chapter 5.

4.6 Reference

Now let's look at the technical and configuration issues for tax transactions.

4.6.1 Configuration Transactions

Table 4.2 provides a list of the configuration transactions for the account determination objects discussed in this chapter.

Transaction Code	Description
FTXP	Maintain tax codes
M/06	Maintain condition types (Purchasing)
M/07	Maintain access sequences (Purchasing)
OB40	Maintain tax accounts
OBCL	Tax codes for non-taxable transactions
OBCO	Maintain tax jurisdiction code structure
OVK1	Tax determination rules (Sales)
OVK3	Maintain tax relevancy of customers (Sales)
OVK4	Maintain tax relevancy of materials (Sales)
V/09	Maintain condition types (Sales)
V/10	Maintain access sequences (Sales)

Table 4.2 Configuration Transactions

4.6.2 Tables and Structures

Table 4.3 contains a list of the tables and structures used to store the relevant data for the GL account determination discussed in this chapter.

Table/Structure	Description
T005	Country tax procedure assignment
T681A	Applications
T681F	Allowable fields per usage and application
T683	Calculation procedure
T683S	Calculation procedure data
T685	Condition types per usage and application
T687	Account keys per application

Table 4.3 Tables and Structures

5   Bank Transactions

This chapter discusses GL account determination in SAP ERP's bank transactions. This content is applicable if you are already using or are planning to use banking transactions such as automatic cash application of customer payments to open invoices, automatic reconciliation of bank statements electronically received from your bank, or automatic interest calculation and posting. Toward the end of this chapter, we will briefly cover GL account determination for the bill of exchange payment method as well.

5.1   House Bank and Other Subaccounts

Even if your company doesn't use any electronic banking functionalities of SAP ERP, you will most certainly use the Accounts Payable (AP) functionality. To carry out payment runs in AP, you have to define house banks and house bank accounts. In this section, we will discuss GL account determination for house bank accounts and subaccounts.

5.1.1   House Bank Account

A house bank is the bank where your company maintains its bank accounts. In SAP ERP, you define house bank IDs and associate them with a company code. Subsequently, you define bank account IDs for individual bank accounts and assign them to the house bank IDs. You can assign multiple house banks and multiple bank accounts for a company code. As shown in Figure 5.1, the G/L account field contains the assignment of a GL account to your bank ACCOUNT ID. This setup is carried out via the menu path IMG • FINANCIAL ACCOUNTING • BANK ACCOUNTING • BANK ACCOUNTS • DEFINE HOUSE BANKS • HOUSE BANKS • BANK ACCOUNTS.

You'll notice another DISCOUNT ACCT field in Figure 5.1. This is not the GL account for cash discounts. That field is for discounted bill of exchanges. We will discuss bill of exchanges later in this chapter.

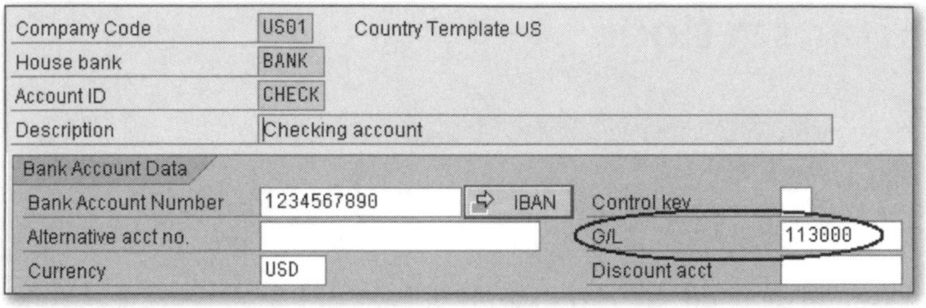

Figure 5.1 Assignment of the General Ledger Account to the Bank Account

Another aspect relevant for bank transactions, in particular for outgoing payments, is setting up bank subaccounts. Let's discuss subaccounts in the next section.

5.1.2 Bank Subaccounts by Payment Method

A typical outgoing payment debits a vendor account and clears corresponding vendor documents, while crediting the house bank account. However, depending on the payment mode (check, wire transfer, etc.), the actual payment may not credit the house bank for several days. To accurately capture this "float" amount, you can set up bank subaccounts for all relevant payment methods (Figure 5.2). For all outgoing payments, this subaccount gets credited instead of the main house bank account. Subsequently, at the time of processing bank reconciliation statements, the credit amount gets transferred from the bank subaccount to the main house bank account. This setup is carried out via the menu path IMG • FINANCIAL ACCOUNTING • ACCOUNTS RECEIVABLE AND ACCOUNTS PAYABLE • BUSINESS TRANSACTIONS • OUTGOING PAYMENTS • AUTOMATIC OUTGOING PAYMENTS • PAYMENT METHOD/BANK SELECTION FOR PAYMENT PROGRAM • SET UP BANK DETERMINATION FOR PAYMENT TRANSACTIONS • BANK SELECTION • BANK ACCOUNTS.

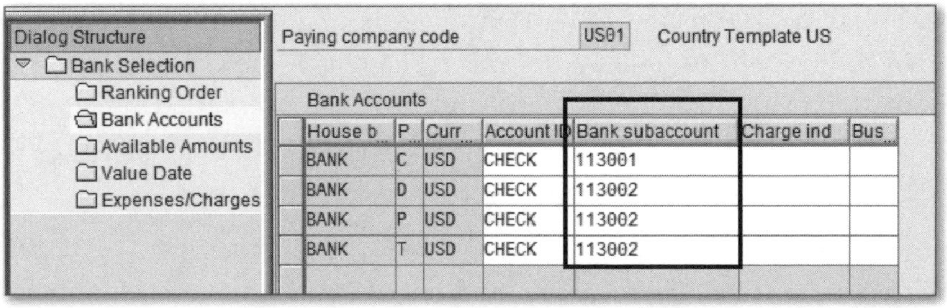

Figure 5.2 Define Bank Subaccounts

In the example shown in Figure 5.2, for payment methods C, D, P, and T, the outgoing payments process will post credits to the corresponding bank subaccounts instead of the main house bank account. If you are implementing electronic or manual bank statement reconciliation processes in the SAP ERP system, then this configuration is a required step. Otherwise, whether you want to set up these bank subaccounts depends on your business process.

In the next section, we will discuss the account determination objects involved in the electronic bank statement process.

5.2 Account Determination Objects

Figure 5.3 shows the account determination objects relevant in the electronic bank statement configuration. This configuration is relevant if you are implementing automatic bank statement upload and reconciliation in SAP ERP.

We will start with the relatively complex GL account determination for electronic bank statement configuration. The reason for starting with a complex process instead of a simpler one is that the electronic bank statement configuration uses all of the account determination objects relevant in banking transactions (see Figure 5.3).

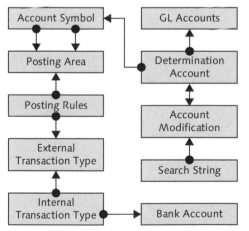

Figure 5.3 Account Determination Objects for Electronic Bank Transactions

On the other hand, other banking transactions, such as manual bank statements, processing of incoming checks, and others, use only some of these account determination objects. So after you understand the relationship between all account determination objects involved in electronic bank configuration, it will be easier to understand account determination for the simpler processes.

You will notice that most of the settings related to electronic bank statement configuration can be carried out in a single transaction (see Figure 5.4), which you can access via the menu path BANK ACCOUNTING IMG • BUSINESS TRANSACTIONS • PAYMENT TRANSACTIONS • ELECTRONIC BANK STATEMENT • MAKE GLOBAL SETTINGS FOR ELECTRONIC BANK STATEMENT.

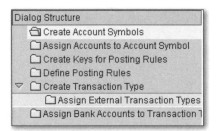

Figure 5.4 Bank Transaction Configuration

Usually it is your bank that determines the electronic format(s) in which bank transaction data is made available to its customers. Additionally, banks in different countries use different data formats for providing bank transaction data to their corporate customers. Some examples of these formats are SWIFT, BAI, MultiCash, and MT940. As you would expect, each format provides precise specifications in which different pieces of bank transaction data are made available. In SAP ERP, you create an internal transaction type to correspond to a data format provided by your house bank.

5.2.1 Internal Transaction Type

You identify a data format provided by your house bank in SAP ERP via the account determination object called the internal transaction type (TRANS. TYPE). As shown in Figure 5.5, SAP ERP provides transaction types for many such formats, and you can create additional internal transaction types as necessary. You can assign only one internal transaction type to one bank account. However, notice that the internal transaction type is simply a mnemonic code. For example, if you have two bank accounts for which you receive bank transaction data in MultiCash format, but the details or transactions for each bank account are slightly different, you can create two internal transaction types—MC01 and MC02—that both refer to the MultiCash format, and assign it to each bank account.

Trans. type	Name
BAI	Bank Administration Institue (USA)
BE	Belgium : CODA
FIN	Finland: Merita
ITAU	Brazil: Banco Itau
MC	MultiCash
NO	Norway - Multicash
SE	Sweden - Multicash

Figure 5.5 Internal Transaction Types

5.2.2 External Transaction Type

For each internal transaction type, you maintain several external transaction types. External transaction types identify different types of bank transactions specific to that internal transaction type and thus specific to the data format in which you receive bank transaction data. You will need to create an external transaction type for each type of transaction that is valid for that bank account. For example, incoming payment by check, incoming payment by wire transfer, bank charges, outgoing payment by check, interest income, foreign exchange fees, returned check, and interbank transfer are all different external transaction types. Typically, a bank has a list of few hundred transaction codes that can uniquely identify every possible transaction that the bank will process. However, you can choose to create only those external transaction types in SAP ERP that are relevant for your bank account.

Figure 5.6 shows the configuration of an external transaction type for the BAI2 format. In this example, each row represents a different transaction such as 115 (lockbox deposit), 165 (preauthorized ACH credit), 195 (incoming money transfer), and 214 (foreign exchange credit).

Assign External Transaction Types to Posting Rules			
Ext...	+/-...	Posting...	Interpretation Algorithm
115	+	Y06	001: Standard algorithm
165	+	Y04	001: Standard algorithm
195	+	Y02	001: Standard algorithm
214	+	Y09	001: Standard algorithm

Figure 5.6 External Transaction Type

Now you may be able to appreciate the advantage of using an internal transaction type as an intermediate link between bank accounts and bank transaction codes (external transaction types). By assigning the same internal transaction type to multiple bank accounts, you can share the same set of external transaction codes across multiple bank accounts. Otherwise, you would have to define external transaction codes multiple times—one for each bank account.

In the configuration, each external transaction type is assigned an interpretation algorithm and a posting rule.

5.2.3 Interpretation Algorithm

The interpretation algorithm determines how SAP ERP "interprets" the reference document number available in the transaction data. SAP ERP provides a large number of interpretation algorithms that help interpret the reference document number as the check number (011, 012, and 013), accounting document number (020), reference document number in an accounting document (021), document from an invoice list (025), payment order number (029), and so on. Additionally, you can create up to nine more custom interpretation algorithms to interpret bank transaction data.

Unlike the posting rule discussed next, the interpretation algorithm only has an indirect influence on GL account determination.

5.2.4 Posting Rule

The posting rule assigned to an external transaction type controls the determination of the debit and the credit GL accounts that are posted automatically for that external transaction type. This will become clearer after you understand the configuration of a posting rule. Let's consider the example shown in Figure 5.6, shown previously, in which external transaction type 165 is assigned a posting rule Y04.

You can assign up to two posting areas to a posting rule. Posting area 1 is used to post entries to GL accounts, such as interest income, bank charges, transfers between bank accounts, clearing cash-in-transit accounts, and so on. Specifications made for posting area 2, on the other hand, correspond to subledger postings, such as the clearing of a vendor invoice for an outgoing payment or the clearing of a customer invoice for an incoming payment.

Figure 5.7 shows the configuration of a POSTING RULE ("Y04"). It specifies posting keys and the account symbol for the debit and credit posting. You may want to refer to the discussion of the symbolic account technique in Chapter 1, Section 1.3.2, where we discussed the benefits of using account symbols in GL account determination.

The COMPRESSION indicator in the rule definition does not have any direct influence on GL account determination. However, it can be used to post a summarized entry instead of individual detailed entries on the debit side, the credit side, or both.

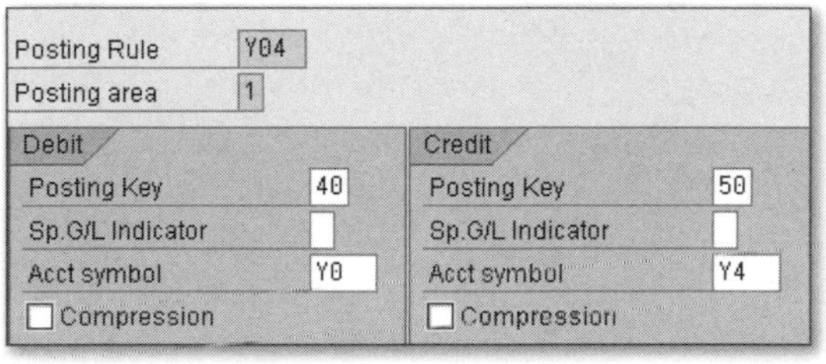

Figure 5.7 Posting Rule Configuration

In the next section, we will discuss how these account symbols are used for GL account determination.

5.3 General Ledger Account Determination in Banking Processes

In this section, we will discuss GL account determination for different banking processes between your company and your house bank.

5.3.1 Electronic Bank Statement

This subsection is relevant if you are setting up an interface with your bank to electronically receive bank transaction data and post those transactions automatically in SAP ERP. In this subsection, we will discuss electronic bank statements. In subsequent subsections, we will discuss other transactions such as manual bank statement, lockbox, and others. In the previous section, we discussed how you assign the following elements:

- ▶ External transaction types to an internal transaction type
- ▶ Posting rules to external transaction types
- ▶ Account symbol to the posting rules

The final step of GL account determination is determining the GL accounts from account symbols. This configuration is carried out via the menu path BANK ACCOUNT-ING IMG • BUSINESS TRANSACTIONS • PAYMENT TRANSACTIONS • ELECTRONIC BANK STATEMENT • MAKE GLOBAL SETTINGS FOR ELECTRONIC BANK STATEMENT • ASSIGN ACCOUNTS TO ACCOUNT SYMBOLS.

There are two ways you can assign GL accounts to account symbols. You can either assign a GL account directly to an account symbol, or you can add one more level of abstraction by using generic accounts. In Figure 5.8, a single GL account (G/L ACCT) is assigned to an account symbol irrespective of currency. There is no account modifier.

Assign Accounts to Account Symbol				
Act Symbol	Acct Moc	Currency	G/L acct	Acct Symb. Desc
Y0	+	+	113000	Master Account

Figure 5.8 Single GL Account Assignment

> **Note**
>
> In Figure 5.8, the G/L ACCT field refers to an account symbol (ACT SYMBOL) and not the GL account. So in this case, you still have to carry out a separate configuration activity to assign GL account 113000 to account symbol 113000.

However, such simple account assignment may not be practical or advisable in all business scenarios. To meet the business requirements of additional flexibility in GL account determination, you can use the functionality of generic accounts provided in SAP ERP.

Using generic accounts, you can reduce your configuration maintenance efforts by replacing common digits of account numbers with plus signs (+). At the time of posting, SAP ERP picks up these common digits from the GL account number maintained in the house bank master. For example, you can post to different accounts, depending on the transaction currency, using generic accounts. Consider a scenario with multiple house bank accounts where each bank account has transactions in multiple currencies. In this scenario, you can design the chart of accounts so that the last three digits of a bank subaccount number represent the currency—001 for INR, 002 for USD, and so on—while the main bank account number has 000 as its last three digits.

Figure 5.9 shows the usage of a generic bank account in a configuration. If two house banks are assigned GL accounts 1300000 and 1400000, then the configuration shown in Figure 5.9 will post all INR transactions to subaccounts ending in 001 (e.g., 1300001 and 1400001), all USD transactions to subaccounts ending in 002, and all other transactions to main bank accounts.

Act Symbol	Acct Mod.	Currency	G/L acct	Acct Symb. Desc.
Y0	+	+	+++++++000	Master Account
Y0	+	INR	+++++++001	Master Account
Y0	+	USD	+++++++002	Master Account

Figure 5.9 Generic Account Assignment

This type of automatic account determination approach is successful only if the chart of accounts is designed with appropriate numbering logic for main bank accounts and bank subaccounts. If you are trying to implement this process in an already productive SAP ERP system, you may not be able to use generic account logic. In that case, you will have to create separate posting rules for each of the postings.

The following is a list of actions that summarizes this entire discussion:

1. A bank account is assigned an internal transaction type.

2. An internal transaction type is assigned multiple external transaction types.

3. A transaction in the incoming data from the bank contains an external transaction type.

4. An external transaction type is assigned a posting rule.

5. A posting rule is assigned debit and/or credit GL account symbols.

6. A GL account symbol determines one or more GL accounts.

After you know how GL account determination in electronic bank statements works, the GL account determination in manual bank statement processing is relatively simple.

5.3.2 Manual Bank Statement

You can choose to use the manual bank statement functionality instead of developing an electronic interface to your house bank. Manual bank statement functionality enables you to manually enter a bank statement in SAP ERP instead of electronically uploading the transactions.

The configuration for a manual bank statement is only slightly different from that required for an electronic bank statement. Because there is no electronic upload of data from external house bank accounts, there is no requirement to maintain external transaction types or map external transaction types to an internal transaction type.

Instead, you maintain your own business transaction codes and assign them to posting rules. Mapping between a business transaction code and a posting rule is carried out via the menu path BANK ACCOUNTING IMG • BUSINESS TRANSACTIONS • PAYMENT TRANSACTIONS • MANUAL BANK STATEMENT • CREATE AND ASSIGN BUSINESS TRANSACTIONS. Figure 5.10 shows this configuration activity.

Attributes that are assigned to an external transaction type in electronic bank statements are assigned to a business transaction in a manual bank statement. For example, while configuring manual bank statement transactions, the account modifier and interpretation algorithms are assigned to a business transaction. The remaining configuration activities, such as configuring a posting rule and assigning GL accounts to an account symbol, are exactly the same as the ones carried out for electronic bank statement configuration.

Trans. type	1			
Tran	+-	Post. rule	Acct mod	Int algthm
0001	+	0001		1
0001	-	0001		
0002	+	0002		
0002	-	0002		
0003	+	0003		

Figure 5.10 Manual Bank Statement Transactions

While entering bank statement items manually (Transaction FF67), you enter every transaction in a bank statement with the corresponding business transaction code. At the time the bank statement is posted, SAP ERP carries out GL account determination and posts each transaction to appropriate GL accounts. In the previous example, each transaction code represents different business transactions, such as credit memo (0001), check credit memo (0002), bearer check (0003) and so on.

The TRANS. TYPE field in Figure 5.10 shows the value "1", indicating that these business transactions are relevant and configured for a manual bank statement. If this value is "2", it means that the business transactions are relevant and configured for deposited check transactions.

5.3.3 Deposited Check Transactions

You use deposited check transactions to enter the details of the checks that have been received. Similar to the processing of bank statements, you can enter deposited check details manually or upload the details electronically in SAP ERP. Either the house bank or a service provider certified by the house bank usually provides the details for checks deposited into a bank account.

This functionality uses a configuration that is very similar to the configuration of manual bank statements (see Figure 5.11), with two main differences. The first difference is that you create business transactions to process deposited checks under TRANS. TYPE 2 instead of TRANS. TYPE 1. The second difference is that you are not able to assign an interpretation algorithm to a business transaction that is relevant for the deposited checks process.

Trans. type		2		
Tran	+-	Post. ru...	Acct mod	Text
0001	+	0003		Check deposting via interim
0002	+	0004		Direct check deposit

Figure 5.11 Deposited Check Configuration

From the posting rule onward, the GL account determination is similar to that already described for electronic bank statements in Section 5.3.1.

5.3.4 Lockbox Process

In the previous section, we discussed the processing of deposited checks. The banks in the United States provide a value-added service known as lockbox processing. In this process, your customers send their payments to a specific bank location, instead of sending payments to your company and then having someone in your company deposit them to your bank. The lockbox process provides benefits in terms of time and accuracy of processing incoming payments. Lockbox is a fairly common banking process used by many large and small U.S. companies.

Configuration for lockbox-specific parameters is done in the configuration activity under BANK ACCOUNTING IMG • BUSINESS TRANSACTIONS • PAYMENT TRANSACTIONS • LOCKBOX.

However, as far as the GL account determination process is concerned, the entire configuration is carried out exactly as described in the section on electronic bank statements (Section 5.3.1), using the same configuration transactions.

5.3.5 Payment Request Process

One of the most commonly used SAP ERP transactions for processing outgoing payments is Transaction F110. This transaction is used to process outbound payments based on open items posted on customer or vendor accounts. Payment requests provide another option for processing outgoing payments. In some SAP ERP system components (e.g., Treasury), a payment request is automatically generated when an accounting document with payment due is posted. Subsequently, you run an automatic payment Transaction F111 that generates outbound payments based on payment requests instead of accounting documents.

In most cases, these payments can be processed automatically. The credit side of the outbound posting is made to a GL account that is associated with the paying house bank (Section 5.1.1), or is a bank subaccount for the house bank (Section 5.1.2). However, if a payment request corresponds to a bank transfer, then you have to consider several additional aspects.

1. First you have to configure an activity that determines the clearing account for the receiving bank. To configure this clearing account, use configuration activity BANK ACCOUNTING IMG • BUSINESS TRANSACTIONS • PAYMENT TRANSACTIONS • PAYMENT REQUEST • DEFINE CLEARING ACCOUNTS FOR RECEIVING BANK FOR ACCOUNT TRANSFER.

   Figure 5.12 shows a sample configuration of this clearing account configuration. In this configuration activity, the COUNTRY and the payment method (PMT METHOD) refer to the paying company code. All of the other fields such as company code (CoCo...), HOUSE BK, CURRENCY, and ACCOUNT ID refer to the receiving company code. Thus, in this example, all payment requests that correspond to transfer *into* the house bank BANKB of company code 1000 or 1010 with payment method 1 are posted to clearing account 113008. All similar payment requests that use payment method 3 are posted to clearing account 113027.

CoCo	House Bk	Country	Pmt Method	Currency	Account ID	Clrg acct
1000	BANKB	US	1			113008
1000	BANKB	US	3			113027
1010	BANKB	US	1			113008
1010	BANKB	US	3			113027

Figure 5.12 Payment Request Clearing Account

2. There is one more level of complexity you need to consider if such bank transfers occur between bank accounts in different countries. For such scenarios, you have to specify another clearing account under configuration activity BANK ACCOUNTING IMG • BUSINESS TRANSACTIONS • PAYMENT TRANSACTIONS • PAYMENT REQUEST • DEFINE CLEARING ACCOUNTS FOR CROSS-COUNTRY BANK ACCOUNT TRANSFERS.

   You need to configure this GL account for each company code that may receive cross-country bank transfers. For the purpose of this transaction, SAP ERP considers cross-country bank transfer as the transfer between bank accounts that are either located in different countries, or that belong to company codes that use different local currencies.

3. Last, you have to configure bank subaccount configuration for the paying bank. Carry out this configuration under BANK ACCOUNTING IMG • BUSINESS TRANSACTIONS • PAYMENT TRANSACTIONS • PAYMENT HANDLING • BANK CLEARING ACCOUNT DETERMINATION • DEFINE ACCOUNT DETERMINATION.

   This subaccount determination configuration is similar to the subaccount determination we discussed in Section 5.1.2, with two important differences: This subaccount determination is only used for payment requests for bank transfers and only if the originating application hasn't already included a bank subaccount in the payment request.

In the next section, we will discuss GL account determination for cash journals.

5.3.6 Cash Journal

You can use the cash journal functionality in SAP ERP to record cash transactions. Every company has a petty cash account from which payment or receipt of small value transactions are carried out in cash. What is considered a petty cash transaction depends on the individual company, but some examples of such expenses are office supplies in small quantities and dinner orders for hardworking SAP consultants. Companies that carry out transactions with retail consumers may have a substantial part of their business done in cash.

To use the cash journal functionality, you first have to set up the cash journal GL account in the company code via the menu path BANK ACCOUNTING IMG • BUSINESS TRANSACTIONS • CASH JOURNAL • SET UP CASH JOURNAL. Figure 5.13 illustrates this setup. In this example, GL account 100000 corresponds to cash journal 0001 in company code 0001. The currency field indicates that all transactions in this cash journal are recorded in EUR.

Manitain View for Cash Journals				
Co...	CJ ...	G/L accoun...	Curr...	CJ Closed
0001	0001	100000	EUR	☐

Figure 5.13 Cash Journal Setup

In the next step, you have to define transactions that you will be posting to the cash journal and the corresponding GL account that should receive an offsetting entry from the cash journal. At some level, these transactions are similar to the business transactions you would define for a manual bank statement (Section 5.3.2). Examples of such transactions are dinner expenses and postage expenses. Figure 5.14 shows the setup of these cash journal transactions. Remember that the GL accounts configured in this activity are the offsetting accounts. The credit entries for any payments and debit entries for any receipts are posted to the GL account associated with the cash journal setup.

Maintain View for Cash Journal Transaction Names					
Co...	Tra...	B	G/L accoun...	T...	Cash journal business trans.
0001	2	E	476100		DINNER - OVERTIME HRS
0001	3	E	476500		POSTAGE STAMPS
0001	01	E	476000		OFFICE SUPPLIES

Figure 5.14 Cash Journal Transactions

The BUSINESS TRANSACTION TYPE field (column B, in the figure) determines the type of cash journal transaction. The value in this field indicates whether a cash journal transaction is a revenue (R), expense (E), receipt from bank (C), payment to bank (B), customer posting (D), or vendor posting (K). Your company's business requirements may necessitate the setup of multiple cash journals. However, the cash journal transaction configuration is not specific to one cash journal. So you can use these transactions across all cash journals that are configured for a company code.

In Section 5.4, we will examine the details of the bill of exchange special payment method.

5.4   Bill of Exchange Transactions

Bill of exchange (BoE) is a popular payment method in European countries. If BoE is used as the method of payment, the payer has until the terms specified in the BoE to make payments to the payee. The following business transactions are possible for the BoE payment method:

▶ The payee can sell the BoE to the bank in advance of its due date (discounting).

▶ The payee can present the BoE to the payer for payment on the due date (presentment).

▶ The payee can present the BoE to the bank to collect money from the payer (collection).

▶ The payee can deem the BoE expired after the term and protest period of the BoE has elapsed.

In SAP ERP, you have to configure BoE transactions as special GL transactions. You have the capability to configure the BoE as both an incoming (receivable) as well as an outgoing (payable) payment method. Refer to Chapter 3 for more details on special GL transactions.

5.4.1   Bill of Exchange Receivable Transactions

Because SAP ERP treats BoE transactions as special GL transactions, BoE receivables are maintained in alternative reconciliation accounts. These accounts have to be set up for each type of BoE transaction (e.g., BoE payment request or re-discountable

BoE). This configuration is done via the menu path BANK ACCOUNTING IMG • BUSINESS TRANSACTIONS • BoE TRANSACTIONS • BoE RECEIVABLE • POST BoE RECEIVABLE • DEFINE ALTERNATIVE RECON ACCTS FOR BoE RECEIVABLE.

You also have to assign GL accounts for different fees and charges associated with BoE transactions. This setup is done via the menu path BoE TRANSACTIONS IMG • BoE RECEIVABLE • POST BoE RECEIVABLE • DEFINE ACCOUNTS FOR BoE TRANSACTIONS.

SAP ERP uses the transaction key technique to determine GL accounts for BoE transactions. Figure 5.15 shows the transaction keys relevant for BoE transactions grouped under transaction GROUP "WEC" (bills of exchange).

Group	WEC	Bills of exchange	
Procedures			
Description			Transaction
Bank discount charges	(01)		BDS
Bank collection charges	(02)		BIK
Bank bill of exchange tax	(03)		BWS
Revenue from discount charges	(04)		DSK
Revenue from collection charges	(05)		INK
Bill of exchange payment request	(06)		WAN
Bill of exchange from request	(07)		WBW
Bill of exchange charges - debit	(08)		WSB
Revenue from bill of exchange tax	(09)		WST
Bill of Exchange Usage	(10)		WVW

Figure 5.15   Bill of Exchange General Ledger Account Determination

Figure 5.15 also shows the transaction keys WAN (06), WBW (07), WSB (08), and WVW (10). These transaction keys are used only for the determination of the posting key. They are not relevant for GL account determination. The six remaining transaction keys are explained here:

▸ **BoE charge posting**
   The bank charges you fees for BoE discounting and BoE collection. You (the payee) can pass on approximate charges for these fees to the customer (the payer).

When these customer receivable entries are posted, offsetting entries are made to GL accounts determined from transaction keys DSK (04), which is revenue from discount charges, and INK (05), which is revenue from collection charges.

Depending on whether the BoE is presented to the bank for discounting or collection, the actual charges for these services are posted using transaction keys BDS (01), which are bank discount charges, or BIK (02), which are bank collection charges.

▶ **BoE tax posting**
Similar to bank charges, any specific BoE tax can also be passed on to the customer. SAP ERP uses the GL account determined from transaction key WST (09), which is revenue from BoE tax, to post the offsetting entry for the customer receivable.

The actual BoE tax is posted to the GL account determined using transaction key BWS (03), or BoE tax.

For the actual charges and tax, no rule modifiers are available; that is, only one GL account can be posted. For revenue transaction keys, the tax code rule modifier is available, so you can post to different GL accounts based on the tax code.

In addition to the GL accounts just defined, two additional configuration activities are relevant for GL account determination for the receivable BoE transactions.

Bill of Exchange Liability Posting

When you (the payee) present the BoE to the bank for discounting, you also need to record the liability on your books. This ensures that if the payer fails to honor the BoE, the bank has recourse and can collect from you.

This liability is reflected in separate bank subaccounts. These accounts are maintained under the menu path BOE TRANSACTIONS IMG • BOE RECEIVABLE • PRESENT BOE RECEIVABLE AT BANK • DEFINE BANK SUBACCOUNTS.

Bank subaccounts must at least be defined for each BANK ACCT used for BoE transactions (see Figure 5.16). However, you can determine different bank subaccounts based on combinations of the BoE usage, special GL indicator, and customer AR reconciliation account.

ChAc	Bank acct	Usage		SGL	Cust recon	Bank subacct
INT	113100	Discounting	B			113107
INT	113100	Discounting	W			113107
INT	113100	Forfeiting	B			113107
INT	113100	Forfeiting	W			113107
INT	113100	Collection	B			113112
INT	113100	Collection	W			113112

Figure 5.16 Define Bank Subaccounts

Bill of Exchange Usage Posting

When the payee presents the BoE to the bank for usage (presentment), the charges levied by the bank are posted to different GL accounts. These accounts are configured under the menu path BoE Transactions IMG • BoE Receivable • Present BoE Receivable at Bank • Maintain Account Determination.

Bank charge accounts can be specified for a combination of the house bank, bank account, and BoE usage.

Now let's look at the GL account determination for BoE payable transactions.

5.4.2 Bill of Exchange Payable Transactions

This subsection describes the configuration requirements from the payer's standpoint, or when you submit the BoE as a method of payment to your vendors (payee). You can review this in Section 5.3 before continuing on.

Compared to BoE receivables, the roles are reversed in BoE payables. Therefore, your vendor will calculate and invoice you for BoE charges in the BoE payable. However, you will still have to specify alternative bank reconciliation accounts and bank subaccounts to process these BoE transactions.

In addition, you also need to maintain GL accounts for processing a BoE presented to your house bank by your vendor or by your vendor's bank. These accounts are maintained under the menu path BoE Transactions IMG • BoE Payable • Returned BoE Payable • Define Account for Returned BoE.

As shown in Figure 5.17, this account configuration is maintained for a combination of house bank, bank account, and BoE payment methods.

House bk	Acct ID	PM	Acct for ret. BoE
BQE01	CPT1	E	511401
BQE02	CPT2	E	511402

Figure 5.17 General Ledger Accounts for Returned Bill of Exchange

5.5 Summary

The content of bank transactions, especially in electronic format, can vary considerably from country to country, and possibly within a country from bank to bank. However, for the purposes of GL account determination, SAP ERP uses a standard framework to arrive at the appropriate GL account.

Bank transactions or manual transactions are mapped to a posting rule, and the posting rule, with the help of account symbols, determines the GL accounts to be posted. It is important to consider possible bank interface requirements when designing a chart of accounts. This is especially true for designing bank accounts and bank subaccounts. This is one of the reasons why the template charts of accounts provided in SAP ERP have a gap of 10 account numbers between each bank GL account.

SAP ERP supports the end-to-end BoE cycle, whether BoEs are received from customers or used to pay vendors.

5.6 Reference

Now let's look at the configuration transactions and table references pertaining to bank transactions.

5.6.1 Configuration Transactions

Table 5.1 provides a list of the configuration transactions for the account determination objects discussed in this chapter.

Transaction Code	Description
OBYN	Set alternative reconciliation accounts for BoE
OBYH	Define other accounts for BoE transactions
OBYK	Define bank subaccounts for BoE presentment

Table 5.1 Configuration Transactions

5.6.2 Tables and Structures

Table 5.2 contains a list of tables and structures used to store data relevant for the GL account determination discussed in this chapter.

Table/Structure	Description
T012K	House bank accounts
T033I	Account symbols
T033G	GL account to account symbol assignment
T028D	Posting rule key
T033F	Posting rule posting area definition
T028V	Internal transaction types
T028G	External transaction types to internal transaction type assignment
T028B	Sending bank transaction type
T074	Alternative BoE reconciliation accounts
T030	Standard BoE accounts
T045B	Charge account determination for BoE
T046A	Return BoE accounts

Table 5.2 Tables and Structures

6   Asset Transactions

This chapter gives you an overview of the GL account determination process in Asset Accounting (AA).

Asset accounting, in general, is usually associated with fixed assets (such as plant equipment, computer equipment, and office equipment); relevant capital cost tracking; and depreciation calculation. However, the Asset Accounting (AA) component in SAP ERP provides much more functionality than just fixed assets.

You can use this component to maintain intangible assets, such as patents or goodwill; to calculate the replacement value of assets for insurance purposes; to revaluate assets that are in inflation-prone countries; or to calculate the details of capital lease payments.

All of these functionalities share two common traits: the ability to track multiple values independent of each other on a single object, and the ability to post periodic decreases or increases in these values.

As you will see, in SAP ERP, you can define any type of assets you choose to track, and you can track multiple values for the same asset independent of each other. You can also post a decrease or an increase in these values using highly customizable calculation formulas.

6.1   Account Determination Objects

Figure 6.1 shows the different account determination objects that are involved in GL account determination in the AA component. These objects enable you to determine GL accounts based on different viewpoints. For example, asset class lets you group assets based on their type, whereas depreciation areas let you group assets based on their depreciation calculation methods. These account determination objects, combined with the chart of accounts, provide a structured framework for GL account determination in asset accounting. Let's discuss each account determination object.

6.1.1 Asset Class

An asset class represents a group of similar assets that is defined by the user. For example, you can choose to have an asset class called "Computer Hardware" that groups all types of computer hardware in your company, or you can create multiple asset classes such as "Networking Equipment," "User Desktops and Accessories," and "Data Servers" for different types of computer hardware. A very important consideration while designing asset classes is that in SAP ERP, asset class definitions are valid across all company codes and across all charts of depreciation. This design makes it easier to generate enterprise-wide asset catalog.

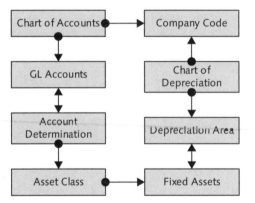

Figure 6.1 Account Determination Objects for Asset Transactions

Another way to look at the design of asset classes is to review the fixed asset section of a balance sheet and create one or more asset classes for each GL account in that section. As shown in Figure 6.2, the standard SAP ERP system provides many commonly used asset classes. If required, you can create additional asset classes to meet your business requirements.

Asset class creation and maintenance is done via the menu path IMG • ASSET ACCOUNTING • ORGANIZATION STRUCTURES • ASSET CLASSES • DEFINE ASSET CLASSES.

Class	Short text
1000	Real estate
1100	Buildings
1200	Land Improvements
1500	Leasehold Improvmnts
2000	Machinery
3000	Fixtures & fittings
3100	Vehicles
3200	Hardware
3210	Computer Software
4000	Assets under constr.
4001	Investment measure
5000	LVA
6000	Leasing (oper.)
6100	Leasing (capital)
7000	Formation expenses
8000	Objects of art

Figure 6.2 List of Available Asset Classes

6.1.2 Depreciation Area

A depreciation area corresponds to a depreciation book. You can carry out asset valuation in a depreciation area independent of any other depreciation areas on the same asset by independently assigning depreciation calculation parameters for each depreciation area of an asset. This allows you to have one depreciation area for calculating book depreciation per GAAP requirements and another depreciation area for calculating asset depreciation per tax requirements.

You can set and view parameters for a depreciation area in the menu path IMG • ASSET ACCOUNTING • ORGANIZATION STRUCTURES • COPY REFERENCE CHART OF DEPRECIATION TO COMPANY CODE • COPY/DELETE DEPRECIATION AREAS.

As you can see in Figure 6.3, a depreciation area has several value maintenance attributes that control the type of asset transactions that you can post to that depreciation area. Even though it is unlikely that you will get a GL account determination error due to an incorrect setting in any of these attributes, it can certainly result in errors in asset posting transactions.

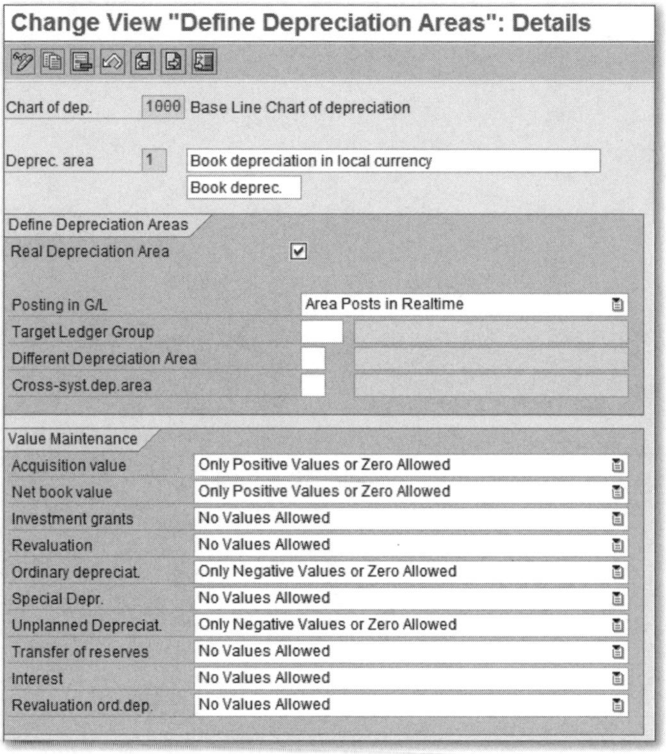

Figure 6.3 Define Depreciation Area Details

One of the important attributes of a depreciation area is how SAP ERP posts its values to GL accounting. For each depreciation area, you can specify this attribute using one of the following values:

▶ (0) Area does not post

▶ (1) Area posts in real time

▶ (2) Area posts APC and depreciation on periodic basis

▶ (3) Area posts depreciation only

▶ (5) Area posts APC only

You should note that you can select only one depreciation area to post to the GL in real time (option 1). Usually, this is the book depreciation area that posts to GL accounts used to prepare financial statements. When you carry out the month-end depreciation run (Transaction AFAB), depreciation values in only that depreciation area are posted to GL.

> **Note**
>
> For other depreciation areas that post to the GL on a periodic basis, an account determination setup similar to the one described in this chapter should be maintained. Values from these depreciation areas are transferred to the GL when the periodic posting program is run.

We already discussed that you can associate multiple depreciation areas to an asset. That brings us to our next topic of discussion: a chart of depreciation.

6.1.3 Chart of Depreciation

In AA, multiple depreciation areas are grouped into a chart of depreciation. Apart from the book depreciation area, a chart of depreciation can include other depreciation areas such as those for group consolidation, tax purposes, insurance purposes, and property tax. Most commonly, GAAP and tax requirements for asset depreciation calculations remain the same for all companies within a country. So you will find that the same chart of depreciation is frequently assigned to all company codes that operate in the same country.

SAP ERP provides a template chart of depreciation for many countries in the world. Each template chart of depreciation also suggests depreciation areas and associated depreciation calculation parameters. Figure 6.4 shows some of the suggested depreciation areas provided in the template chart of depreciation for the United States. When implementing AA, you can choose to retain or remove any of these depreciation areas, except the book depreciation area.

Define Depreciation Areas	
Ar.	Name of depreciation area
1	Book depreciation in local currency
10	Federal Tax ACRS/MACRS
11	Alternative Minimum Tax
12	Adjusted Current Earnings
13	Corporate Earnings & Profits
30	Consolidated balance sheet in local curre
31	Consolidated balance sheet in group curr
32	Book depreciation in group currency
40	State modified ACRS
80	Insurance values

Figure 6.4 U.S. Chart of Depreciation

You can set and view parameters for a chart of depreciation via the menu path IMG • ASSET ACCOUNTING • ORGANIZATION STRUCTURES • COPY REFERENCE CHART OF DEPRECIATION • COPY REFERENCE CHART OF DEPRECIATION.

> **Note**
>
> You should use a separate chart of depreciation for each country. For group consolidation, you can always use a separate depreciation area in a group currency that depreciates assets per the group depreciation rules.

The chart of depreciation is assigned to a company code. Each company code can have only one chart of depreciation, but many company codes can share one chart of depreciation. This assignment is carried out in menu path IMG • ASSET ACCOUNTING • ORGANIZATION STRUCTURES • ASSIGN CHART OF DEPRECIATION TO COMPANY CODE.

6.1.4   Account Determination

An account determination object in AA corresponds to a group of GL accounts. You create account determination objects using the menu path IMG • ASSET ACCOUNTING • ORGANIZATION STRUCTURES • ASSET CLASSES • SPECIFY ACCOUNT DETERMINATION.

An account determination object serves as an intermediary between an asset class and a group of GL accounts. As you will see later in this chapter, different AA transactions require posting to different GL accounts. If several asset classes shared the same group of GL accounts, you would have to complete that task separately for each asset class. Instead, you can assign a group of GL accounts to an account determination object and then assign that account determination object to as many asset classes as necessary without having to carry out repetitive configurations.

You assign GL accounts to an account determination object using Transaction AO90 or the menu path IMG • ASSET ACCOUNTING • INTEGRATION WITH THE GENERAL LEDGER • ASSIGN G/L ACCOUNTS.

The relationships between other account determination objects (review Figure 6.1), such as the chart of accounts, company code, and GL account, were discussed in Chapter 1.

6.1.5   Other Asset Accounting Objects

Before we proceed to the discussion of GL account determination for AA transactions, let's begin with a brief overview of other AA objects. These objects do not directly influence GL account determination. However, they play an extremely important role in AA functionalities, and thus any discussion of AA would be incomplete without at least some discussion of these objects.

▸ **Depreciation key**

A depreciation key in the AA component is a key that controls depreciation calculation. Additionally, as you will see, a depreciation key is used to calculate imputed interest and to process investment support or subsidies received for an asset.

You configure default depreciation keys for each depreciation area in a chart of depreciation. Subsequently, you can change the depreciation key assigned to it while creating or processing an asset. A depreciation key definition is unique within a chart of depreciation. A depreciation key, in turn, contains several other calculation methods and parameters that control depreciation calculation.

You configure depreciation keys using the menu path IMG • ASSET ACCOUNTING • DEPRECIATION • VALUATION METHODS • DEPRECIATION KEY • MAINTAIN DEPRECIATION KEY.

▸ **Calculation methods**

As the name implies, a calculation method controls calculation parameters for a specific type of calculation. AA configuration provides the following calculation methods:

  ▸ **Base method:** Among other things, a base method specifies one of several depreciation methods for depreciation calculation. Examples of depreciation methods include sum of the year's digits, percentage from a useful life, stated percentage, and immediate depreciation.

  ▸ **Declining-balance method:** A declining-balance method specifies a multiplication factor for determining the depreciation percentage rate (e.g., 150% or 200%) and the upper and lower limits for the depreciation percentage rate.

  ▸ **Maximum amount method:** A maximum amount method specifies a maximum depreciation amount that cannot be exceeded before a certain calendar date. As applicable and as necessary, the depreciation process reduces the calculated depreciation so that it doesn't exceed the maximum amount specified for this method.

▶ **Multi-level method:** A multi-level method allows different depreciation calculations during different phases—or levels—of asset depreciation. For example, you can use a multi-level method to use one depreciation calculation for the first two years of asset depreciation and then use different depreciation calculation until the net book value (NBV) of an asset becomes zero.

▶ **Period control method:** A period control method determines how depreciation calculation is carried out for different asset transactions with reference to a period beginning or period end. Examples of period control are pro-rata at period start date, pro-rata at mid-period, next month, next quarter, at mid-quarter, at mid-year, and so on.

Each depreciation key is assigned one value for each of these five calculation methods, though by using appropriate calculation method parameters, you can make a calculation method irrelevant. Configure calculation methods using the configuration menu path IMG • ASSET ACCOUNTING • DEPRECIATION • VALUATION METHODS • DEPRECIATION KEY • CALCULATION METHODS.

▶ **Transaction type**
A transaction type in AA specifies a unique business transaction. It controls several important factors such as whether the transaction debits an asset or credits an asset, what document type is used for posting to the GL, whether the transaction type can be used manually, and others.

For the consolidation purpose, a transaction type also includes parameters that indicate whether the transaction type posts to an affiliated company and that identify the corresponding consolidation transaction type. SAP ERP provides several hundred transaction types that cover almost all possible asset transactions. However, if necessary, you can also create custom transaction types for posting to fixed assets.

Carry out configuration for asset transaction types with the appropriate configuration menus under the configuration area IMG • ASSET ACCOUNTING • TRANSACTIONS • << BUSINESS TRANSACTION >>. In this menu path, << BUSINESS TRANSACTION >> corresponds to different asset transactions such as acquisitions, retirements, transfers, and intercompany transfers.

Now let's move on to discuss the GL account determination process in AA.

6.2 General Ledger Account Determination

There are two ways you can approach the configuration of GL account determination for AA. One option is to use a single configuration transaction that lets you carry out GL account determination for almost all business transactions in AA, such as depreciation accounts, acquisition and production cost accounts, and imputed interest accounts. Alternately, you can choose to use several configuration transactions where you can carry out GL account determination for specific business transactions in AA, such as for special depreciation and ordinary depreciation. To access the single configuration transaction, use the menu path IMG • FINANCIAL ACCOUNTING • ASSET ACCOUNTING • INTEGRATION WITH THE GENERAL LEDGER • ASSIGN G/L ACCOUNTS.

As shown in Figure 6.5, GL accounts in this configuration are conveniently grouped into balance sheet accounts, depreciation accounts, and special reserves accounts. To configure GL accounts, you must first select the chart of accounts, then the account determination rule, and then one of the three groups in the window on the left side in Figure 6.5.

Of course, the depreciation area you select in this configuration transaction should be set to allow posting to GL accounting whether completely or partially, in real time or as a periodic posting.

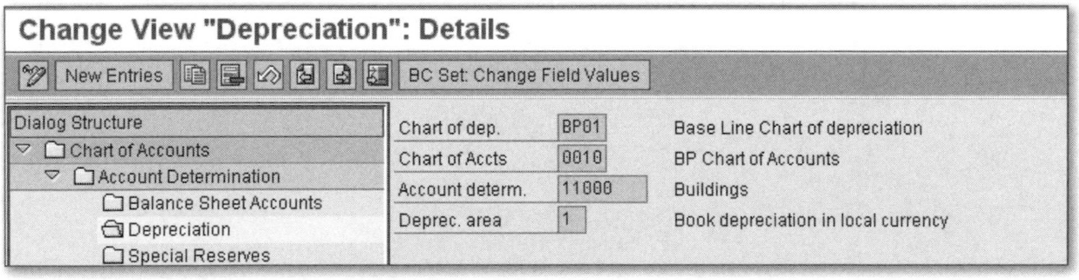

Figure 6.5 General Ledger Account Configuration

Because almost all GL accounts for AA can be set in this transaction, a slightly different approach is used in this chapter to talk about GL account determination.

Figure 6.6 and Figure 6.7 show the groups of GL accounts that you can set under the balance sheet accounts group and under the depreciation accounts group. GL accounts in these figures are marked with sequential numbers. Throughout this section, while discussing GL accounts configuration, you'll see references to the associated numbers. You can refer back to these figures to find the exact section in which to configure these accounts.

We will start with the most commonly used basic asset transactions.

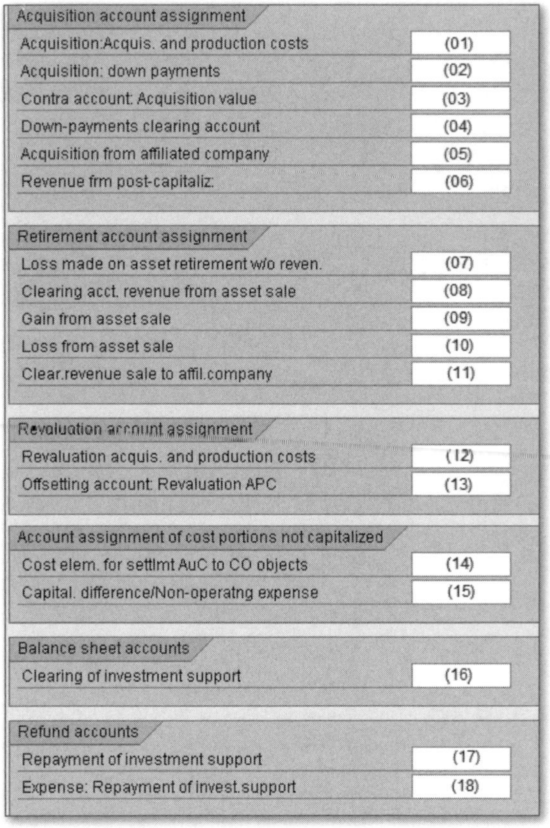

Figure 6.6 Balance Sheet Accounts for Assets

Ordinary depreciation account assignment	
Acc.dep. accnt.for ordinary depreciation	(19)
Expense account for ordinary depreciat.	(20)
Expense account for ord. dep. below zero	(21)
Revenue from write-up on ord.deprec.	(22)

Special depreciation account assignment	
Accumulated dep. account special dep.	(23)
Expense account for special depreciation	(24)
Expense account for spec.dep.below zero	(25)
Revenue from write-up on special deprec.	(26)

Unplanned depreciation account assignment	
Accumulated dep. account unpl. deprec.	(27)
Expense account for unplanned deprec.	(28)
P&Lact.unpl.dep.below 0	(29)
Revenue from write-up on unplnd. deprec.	(30)

Account assignment for transfer of reserves	
Val. adj. acct. for transfer of reserves	(31)
Contra account for transferring reserves	(32)
Revenue from w-up transfer of reserves	(33)

Account assignment for revaluation on depreciation	
Reval. accumulated ord. depreciation	(34)
Offsetting accnt: Reval. ordinary deprc.	(35)

Interest account assignment	
Expense account for interest	(36)
Clearing interest posting	(37)
Intrst expense when book val.below zero	(38)

Figure 6.7 Depreciation Accounts for Assets

6.2.1 Basic Transactions

This subsection describes the "must have" GL account assignments to use the most commonly used functionality of the AA component.

▶ **Asset capitalization**
These GL accounts carry the acquisition and production cost of an asset, that is, the capitalized amount of an asset that is reported in the GL. When an asset is acquired, either from external procurement or from in-house production, you post the capitalization cost to a balance sheet account. This cost (APC) is posted to the asset capitalization account (01).

Any subsequent adjustments or additions to an asset value are also posted to this GL account. You may come across the functionality of subassets and group assets in the AA component. Capitalization costs for all subassets and group assets are also posted on the same capitalization account as the one for the main asset.

▶ **Asset depreciation**
With the exception of a few asset types such as land and goodwill, all assets depreciate over a predetermined useful life. For all other types of assets, you carry out a monthly depreciation run to make depreciation postings that reduce the book value of an asset and post the depreciation expense.

The depreciation run posts reduction in asset value as a credit to the accumulated depreciation account (19) and a debit to the depreciation expense account (20). This is standard depreciation, also called *ordinary depreciation* in SAP ERP. In Section 6.2.3, we will discuss other types of depreciation postings.

▶ **Asset sale or retirement**
You may choose to sell or retire an asset while it still has some book value. Depending on whether the sale proceeds of an asset are more or less than its book value, you post accounting entries to the asset gain or asset loss account. If an asset is sold for more than its NBV, SAP ERP posts the difference as a gain on the asset sale (09) account. If an asset is sold for less than its NBV, the difference is posted as a loss from the asset sale (10) account. The asset NBV is calculated as the difference between the capitalized value of an asset (01) and the accumulated depreciation on the asset (19).

▶ **Asset scrap or disposal**
Sometimes an asset cannot or should not be sold due to performance, usability, or even statutory reasons. In such cases, you can retire the asset by posting an asset scrap transaction. An asset scrap transaction is similar to an asset retirement transaction, except that there are no sales proceeds. If an asset is scrapped, its entire NBV is posted to loss due to the asset scrap (07) account. Asset NBV is calculated in the same manner as described for the asset sale or retirement.

▶ **Asset transactions with affiliated companies**
There are times when you need to carry out an asset acquisition or asset sale. If an acquisition or the sale of an asset occurs with an affiliated company (within the same corporate group), SAP ERP uses accounts acquisition from the affiliated company (05) and revenue sale to the affiliated company (11).

> **Note**
>
> It is important that you record and report asset acquisitions or sales with affiliated companies separately to allow these transactions to be treated as asset transfers while consolidating all of the company codes. This allows the appropriate reporting of gain or loss to be posted in the selling company

▶ **Using offsetting entry accounts**

If you acquire assets from a vendor that is already set up in your SAP ERP system, when you post the asset acquisition, the payable is directly posted to that vendor account. Similarly, during the asset sale, if an existing customer in is specified in the transaction, the receivable is directly posted to the customer account.

If a customer account or a vendor account is not set up in the SAP ERP system, you can use a clearing account to which you post the offsetting entry at the time of asset acquisition, asset sale, or retirement. These accounts can be set up under the offsetting entry for asset acquisition (03) and the offsetting entry for asset sale (08).

Even if the customer account or the vendor account involved in the asset transaction is already set up, you may still want to use a clearing account and post entries from Accounts Payable (AP) or Accounts Receivable (AR) to the clearing account. Subsequently, you can clear entries from asset acquisitions or asset sales with the entries posted from the AR or AP functionality.

▶ **Offsetting entry for post-capitalization**

As we discussed just now, when you post an asset acquisition directly in AA using acquisition transaction types, SAP ERP offers the offsetting entry for asset acquisition (03). However, the GL account determination is different if you are posting asset acquisition that is post-capitalization. Asset post-capitalization is when you post an asset acquisition that should have been posted in one of the previous fiscal years but was not posted at that time due to some reason. Now you have to post the asset acquisition in the current fiscal year, even though the asset should be depreciated from its original capitalization date in one of the previous fiscal years.

When you enter a post-capitalization transaction in AA, SAP ERP offers the GL account specified as the revenue from post-capitalization (06) in configuration as the account for posting the offsetting entry. Note that this is just a default proposal for a GL account. You can choose to change it at the time of posting the asset transaction.

Now let's look at a special type of asset class, assets under construction.

6.2.2 Assets Under Construction Transactions

An outright asset acquisition is usually possible for relatively small assets or for assets that are available in single units, such as a computer, equipment for a plant, a copier machine, or even a car. However, large projects such as the construction of a plant or an SAP ERP implementation contract that go on for several decades require a different approach to capitalize them.

The assets under construction (AuC) class provides that functionality in the AA component. AuC is a special type of asset class that lets you track and report all costs that are posted to a cost collector in SAP ERP. In most implementations, this cost collector is an internal order, a production order, a project defined in project systems, or any combination thereof. However, in the absence of any such cost collectors, you can even create a special type of asset under the AuC class that acts as a bucket to track and report all costs that are posted to it.

AuC assets are not depreciated. However, as appropriate, costs collected on an AuC are settled to one or more fixed assets. This settlement can be a complete settlement for all costs or only a partial settlement. You can carry out this process periodically, at the end of each phase of a project, or based on any other business-dependent criteria. You can settle any costs collected on an AuC that shouldn't be capitalized to a cost center or a GL account, for example.

► **AuC settlement**
In Asset Accounting GL account determination configuration, you have to configure two cost elements for this process. The first one is the cost element (14) that is used when settling line items from an AuC to a cost center, an order, or a work breakdown structure (WBS) element of a project system. This cost element is relevant during line-item settlement in AA.

The second cost element is used to post any capitalization differences and non-operating expenses. This cost element (15) is used to post non-operating expenses or any difference in capitalization costs that may arise because an asset is capitalized differently for the local books than for the consolidated books.

▶ **Capitalization of down payments**

As you may imagine, an AuC that represents a long-term project that is being capitalized may also involve making down payments before the asset is actually completed or delivered. Without any down payments, you capitalize costs on an AuC when the full or partial portion of an asset is completed and delivered. However, if you have made a down payment to the vendor prior to capitalizing any assets, you can choose to capitalize that down payment, too. Of course, whether or not you capitalize this down payment depends on your business requirements.

If you choose to capitalize the down payment, SAP ERP uses two accounts. The first one is the acquisition down payments (02) account that is used for posting capitalization of down payments. The second one is the down payments clearing account (04) that is used for posting offsetting entries. When posting a vendor invoice, this entry is reversed, and it is cleared against the corresponding down payment.

We discussed ordinary depreciation posting in Section 6.2.1. Let's now look at GL account determination for other depreciation postings.

6.2.3 Other Depreciation Postings

In this section, we will look at a special scenario related to ordinary depreciation and other types of depreciation that SAP ERP supports in the AA component.

▶ **Depreciation below zero**

Typically, after the NBV of an asset is reduced to zero, you stop depreciating the asset for local reporting purposes. However, for business or statutory reasons, you may continue depreciating the asset even if the NBV of the asset is below zero. SAP ERP uses EXPENSE ACCOUNT FOR ORD. DEP. BELOW ZERO (21) to post any ordinary depreciation after the NBV of an asset is zero.

If the depreciation posted to an asset must be reversed, reversal of the ordinary depreciation is posted to the GL account revenue from the write-up on the ordinary depreciation (22). Write-up to depreciation can occur for any reason—the depreciation calculated in the past might have been too high, a credit memo might have been posted to an asset that reduced the capitalized cost, or another reason.

So far, we have only discussed ordinary depreciation, that is, depreciation calculated per the statutory requirements for planned wear and tear of an asset. However, SAP ERP also provides the following additional types of depreciation:

▶ **Unplanned depreciation**

For unplanned or unforeseen wear and tear of an asset (e.g., damage due to natural disaster), you can post unplanned depreciation to reduce the NBV of an asset. SAP ERP provides the following GL accounts to post unplanned depreciation. Usage of these accounts is similar to that described for corresponding accounts with reference to ordinary depreciation.

- ▶ Accumulated depreciation (27)
- ▶ Depreciation expense (28)
- ▶ Depreciation if the NBV is below zero (29)
- ▶ Revenue from depreciation write-up (30)

▶ **Special depreciation**

From time to time, statutory laws may allow special depreciation in the form of a tax break, special incentives to promote growth, or for another reason. For example, in the United States, there have been several economic stimulus acts in the past decade that allowed businesses to claim additional depreciation for assets acquired during a specific calendar period. Though you do require additional configuration in terms of new depreciation keys that calculate special depreciation, for the purposes of GL account determination, you can track those depreciation postings in different GL accounts than the ordinary depreciation.

SAP ERP uses the GL accounts in the following list to post special depreciation. Usage of these accounts is similar to that described for corresponding accounts with reference to ordinary depreciation or unplanned depreciation.

- ▶ Accumulated depreciation (23)
- ▶ Depreciation expense (24)
- ▶ Depreciation if the NBV is below zero (25)
- ▶ Revenue from depreciation write-up (26)

Amounts calculated for unplanned and special depreciation are not posted during the regular depreciation run. To post these amounts, you must carry out a periodic asset posting run.

6.2.4 Asset Revaluation Postings

Asset revaluation is a fairly complex topic. Your company may have to revalue its fixed assets for one of several reasons using one of several approaches. For example, if your company has assets in a country that is prone to inflation, you may want to periodically revalue your assets using the revaluation program for inflation adjustments. For insurance purposes, you may use the index replacement series to revalue your assets each year.

Each method has its pros and cons, and each method meets a specific set of requirements. For example, the index replacement series is useful if a majority of the assets are located in a high-inflation country for which a reliable and generally accepted inflation index is available. The asset revaluation measure is more appropriate if only one-off, one-time revaluation of assets is required.

The detailed discussion of revaluation reasons and revaluation methods falls outside of the scope of this book, so let's just focus on GL account determination for asset revaluation processes. In all such cases, SAP ERP uses the following accounts to post revaluation adjustments and offsetting entries to the APC and to accumulated depreciation:

▸ Revaluation of APC cost adjustments (12)

▸ Revaluation of APC cost offsetting (13)

▸ Revaluation of accumulated depreciation (34)

▸ Revaluation of accumulated depreciation offsetting (35)

6.2.5 Imputed Interest Calculation

SAP ERP provides the functionality to calculate imputed interest on the capital that is tied up in fixed assets. This information can be useful in cost accounting, for example, to analyze what-if scenarios. Using this information, you can evaluate whether buying fixed assets represents an optimal choice to deploy your capital.

In AA, the process to carry out imputed interest calculation is the same as the process to carry out depreciation calculation. You have to first configure a depreciation key that specifies the interest rate for this calculation and then assign this depreciation key to a separate depreciation area that is used for interest calculation. You must also decide whether to analyze this interest calculation in the AA component of SAP ERP, or whether to post the interest calculation to GL accounts.

If you choose to post the interest calculations to GL accounts, SAP ERP uses the following GL accounts to post the results of interest calculation:

► **Expense interest posting** (36)
This GL account serves a similar purpose as the depreciation expense account. Any imputed interest calculated on an asset is posted to this account.

► **Offsetting interest posting** (37)
This GL account is used to post an offsetting entry for the imputed interest calculation, that is, the offsetting entry for the interest posted to the expense interest posting account (36).

► **Expense interest posting when the NBV is below zero** (38)
This GL account serves a similar purpose as the expense interest posting account (36), but it is posted if the NBV of an asset is zero.

As you will notice, these accounts are similar to the accounts you configure for posting ordinary, unplanned, or special depreciation. On the other hand, GL account determination for imputed interest calculation doesn't contain any configuration for accumulated depreciation or write-up of imputed interest back to GL accounts.

6.2.6 Investment Support Transactions

Investment support in this context refers to the subsidies or the loan you may receive toward your capital expenditure or investment to procure or produce an asset. Whether and how much investment subsidy you receive depends on the type of an asset, the industry in which your company operates, and the purpose for which the asset will be put to use.

You can choose to take one of the two approaches to maintain this investment support in the AA component of SAP ERP: You can maintain this investment support on the asset side as a reduction in the asset acquisition and procurement cost (APC), or you can maintain this investment support on the liability side as a special reserve.

▶ **Investment support on the asset side**
If you maintain this investment support on the asset side as a reduction in the asset APC, the asset acquisition cost is reduced by the amount that corresponds to the investment support or subsidy. For the purpose of depreciation calculation, you use the reduced asset cost after taking into account the investment subsidy. Even though, in this case, depreciation calculation of an asset is processed similarly to other fixed assets, SAP ERP doesn't provide much automation for processing the investment support—such as making monthly payments, processing early termination, and so on. So under this scenario, you have to manually post investment support transactions to the GL.

▶ **Investment support on the liability side**
You can also maintain this investment support on the liability side as a special reserve. Under this method, you depreciate the original asset acquisition cost on the asset side, similarly to any other fixed asset. At the same time, you also "depreciate" investment support on the liability side. Obviously, you require additional configuration for this method of maintaining investment support in SAP ERP. However, the advantage of this method is that most entries for processing the investment support are automated.

> **Note**
>
> Some of the GL accounts mentioned in this section become visible in the configuration transaction only after you have configured at least one investment measure. You carry out investment support configuration via the menu path IMG • FINANCIAL ACCOUNTING • ASSET ACCOUNTING • SPECIAL VALUATION • INVESTMENT SUPPORT.

Figure 6.8 shows the GL accounts involved in the GL account determination for investment support in AA.

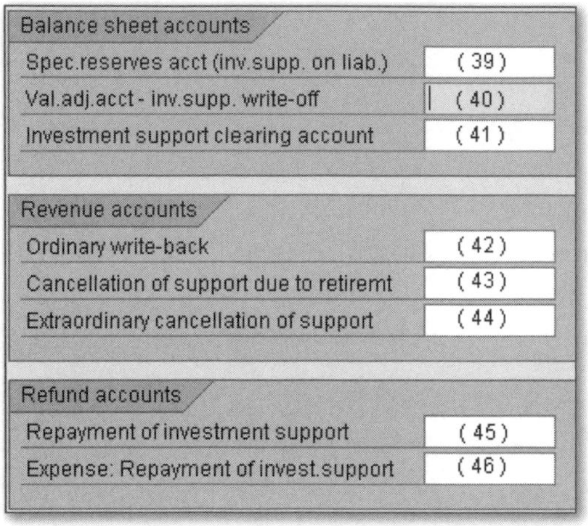

Figure 6.8 Investment Support on the Liability Side

Now let's look at the GL account determination relevant for the scenarios in which the investment support measure is maintained on the liability side:

▶ For a new investment support, SAP ERP uses the GL account maintained as SPEC. RESERVES ACCT (INV.SUPP. ON LIAB.) (39) to post the investment support entry. The corresponding offsetting entry is posted to the INVESTMENT SUPPORT CLEAR-ING ACCOUNT (41)/(16), as shown in Figure 6.8. Remember that these entries are made only if an investment support is maintained on a liability side as a special reserve.

▶ You have to carry out periodic asset posting runs to post periodic entries to the investment support. During these periodic posting runs, the planned write-off amount is posted from the special reserves account to the ORDINARY WRITE-BACK ACCOUNT (42).

You may terminate the procurement or production of an asset before the retention period of the investment support. The retention period is the time frame for which the investment subsidy is valid. The following two constellations arise depending on whether the asset is terminated before the retention period, and whether the investment support has to be paid back:

▶ If investment support has to be repaid, and if the asset is terminated before the retention period, the repayment entries are created by posting the original sup-port amount to the repayment of investment support (45)/(17) account, and by posting the planned write-off amount to the expense: repayment of the invest-ment support (46)/(18) account.

▶ If investment support doesn't have to be paid back, and if the asset is terminated before the retention period, the remaining amount of investment support is simply written off to the value adjust account—investment support write-off (40).

As you will notice, the process of GL account determination in the AA component is somewhat simplified because a single configuration transaction provides you with access to all relevant GL account determination scenarios.

6.3 Summary

AA is one of the components in SAP ERP in which design and decisions about account determination objects are as important as, if not more important than, the actual GL account determination.

Proper design and decisions about the chart of depreciation, the account determination rules, and the asset class make it fairly easy to expand the future scope of an AA implementation.

Because account determination rules are linked to the chart of accounts instead of the individual company codes, the effort to implement AA for other company codes is greatly reduced. If company codes share the same chart of accounts, the effort is reduced to merely maintaining some basic settings specific to the company code and transferring asset data from legacy systems.

Chapter 7 discusses GL account determination as it relates to travel expense transactions. We will then proceed to discussing components outside of SAP ERP Financials.

6.4 Reference

As usual, this section provides you with a technical reference that corresponds with the discussion in this chapter.

6.4.1 Configuration Transactions

Table 6.1 provides a list of the configuration transactions for the account determination objects discussed in this chapter.

Transaction Code	Description
ACSET	Maintain additional account assignment
AM05	Deactivate asset class in chart of depreciation
AO88	GL account assignment for investment support
AO90	GL account assignment
EC08	Copy reference chart of depreciation
OADX	Define how depreciation areas post to the GL
OAOA	Define asset classes
OAOA	Assign account determination to asset classes
OAOB	Assign chart of depreciation to company codes
OAYZ	Depreciation areas in asset class

Table 6.1 Configuration Transactions

Transaction AO90, shown in Table 6.1, provides GL account configuration for almost all of the functionality of AA. However, if required, other transactions starting with AO can be used to implement specific business functionalities.

6.4.2 Tables and Structures

Table 6.2 contains a list of the tables and structures that are used to store data relevant for the GL account determination discussed in this chapter.

Table/Structure	Description
ANKA	Asset classes
T093	Depreciation areas in chart of depreciation
T095	Balance sheet accounts for account determination
T095A	Account determination rules
T095B	Depreciation accounts for account determination
T096	Chart of depreciation

Table 6.2 Tables and Structures

6.4.3 Enhancements

Table 6.3 provides a list of the enhancements that can possibly be used to influence GL account determination in transactions discussed in this chapter.

Enhancement	Description
AINT0002	Substitution of offsetting accounts for asset transactions

Table 6.3 Enhancements

7 Travel Expense Transactions

This chapter describes GL account determination for travel expense transactions. The Travel Expenses subcomponent is part of the SAP Travel Management (TV) module. FI-TV also includes the Travel Request (handles the functionality of travel request and approvals) and Travel Planning (provides the functionality of travel planning and booking) subcomponents. The Travel Expenses subcomponent oversees the travel expense processing. While you can implement these three subcomponents in different combinations, only the Travel Expenses subcomponent is relevant for the discussion on GL account determination, so this chapter will focus on its transactions.

Travel expense accounting is also an easy introduction to GL account determination because it relates to the HR and Payroll applications with SAP. This is because the concepts and the account determination techniques used in GL account determination for travel expense transactions are "simpler" versions of the techniques we will discuss in Chapter 10 on payroll transactions. This is important because GL account determination in SAP HR and SAP Payroll applications make use of a few unique concepts and techniques such as infotypes and features.

In the next section, we will first discuss these new concepts and then the account determination objects relevant to travel expense transactions.

7.1 Account Determination Objects

Let's first discuss the concepts of an infotype and a feature. As mentioned at the beginning of this chapter, these concepts are also relevant for the GL account determination of payroll transactions discussed in Chapter 10.

7.1.1 Infotypes

An *infotype* groups together data relevant to a specific purpose or a subject matter. Infotypes help HR applications manage and store employee data efficiently. An infotype is identified by its four-digit alphanumeric keys, and all infotype data is delimited by time periods, so that you can easily maintain data that changes over time. The following are some examples of employee infotypes:

▶ **Organizational Assignment (0001)**
This infotype contains enterprise structure (company code, cost center), personnel structure (employee group, employee subgroup, payroll area), and organizational plan (position, job key).

▶ **Travel Privileges (0017)**
This infotype contains various groupings for the employee that can be used during configuration to determine other parameters such as expense reimbursement limits, travel costs, and any restrictions on travel privileges.

▶ **Bank Details (0009)**
This infotype is used to maintain employee bank account details. This information can be used, for example, to directly deposit expense reimbursements.

▶ **Personal Data (0002)**
This infotype contains personal data of an employee and other data that is relevant to HR.

The standard SAP ERP system provides hundreds of infotypes, each catering to a unique information data set of employees. Throughout this chapter, we will discuss or reference different infotypes as they relate to the expense accounting discussion.

7.1.2 Features

A *feature* is a decision tree technique used in SAP HR and SAP Payroll applications and in the Travel Expenses subcomponent to determine default values for a parameter based on a certain set of characteristic values. It is also used to control and determine the transactional flow of a business process. In the latter case, the parameter value corresponds to the next step in a process flow. The beauty of this decision tree technique is that it consists of a multi-level decision tree, where at each decision point, you can configure multiple decision branches for subsequent actions depending on the value of a parameter. Not only that, but at any level, one branch of a decision tree can be as deep and as complex as necessary without impacting the depth of other decision branches.

For instance, let's say you want to determine an employee group using this decision tree technique. Your sales companies in the North American region have a large number of employees with multiple organizational levels, whereas your sales companies in the European region has only one company per country, with just a few employees.

Using the feature decision tree technique, you can determine the employee group under the North American region using all of the organizational levels (e.g., department, product line, strategic business unit, company code, etc.), while for the European region, you can determine the employee group using just the company code.

Another interesting aspect of features is that they can be used to determine the value for any type of parameter. For example, the features discussed in this chapter are not used to determine GL accounts but instead values for the GL account determination objects.

Figure 7.1 shows the different account determination objects involved in travel expense transactions.

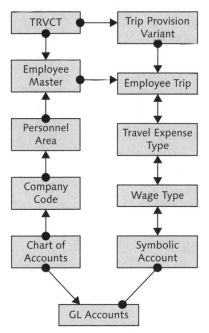

Figure 7.1 General Ledger Account Determination Objects for Travel Expense Transactions

Let's now discuss individual account determination objects depicted in that figure, beginning with a trip provision variant.

7.1.3 Trip Provision Variant

A *trip provision variant* is a group of control parameters that classify trip provisions according to different criteria such as reimbursement of travel receipts in foreign currency, tax treatment of expense reimbursement, per-diem amounts, minimum and maximum amounts, and others.

Usually, every country has a specific set of rules that control employee expense reimbursement and trip cost accounting, and their treatment for tax purposes. So a trip provision variant is always assigned to one country. However, it is possible to have more than one trip provision variant assigned to a country. This may the case, for example, if a country has separate guidelines for different industries or if a country has multiple trip cost accounting methods. SAP ERP provides sample trip provision variants for many countries such as U.S. Accounting (10), U.S. Accounting (High-Low) (80), French Accounting (06), Mexican Accounting (32), and others.

A trip provision variant is associated in all control and valuation data tables of a trip costing. A trip provision variant is defined using the menu path IMG • FINANCIAL ACCOUNTING • TRAVEL MANAGEMENT • TRAVEL EXPENSES • MASTER DATA • CONTROL PARAMETERS FOR TRAVEL EXPENSES • DEFINE/DELETE/RESTORE TRIP PROVISION VARIANTS.

Each trip provision variant has several global parameters associated with it. The following are some of the global parameters that you can set for a trip provision variant:

▶ The currency for travel trips associated with this trip provision variant

▶ The currency in which settlement of foreign currency travel receipts is done

▶ Domestic and international tax specifications for the travel receipts

▶ The unit of measure for entering distance on travel receipts (kilometers or miles)

▶ The exchange rate type used for converting

These global parameters have significant influence over how you process and settle travel expenses in the Travel Expenses subcomponent. These parameters are configured under the same menu path as shown earlier, but they use DEFINE GLOBAL SETTINGS as the final menu node.

In the next subsection, we will discuss the travel feature that is used to derive a trip provision variant TRVCT.

7.1.4 TRVCT Feature

The Travel Expenses subcomponent uses the feature TRVCT to derive the trip provision variant for an employee trip. Figure 7.2 shows a sample decision tree of a trip provision variant using different characteristics. For example:

▶ At the highest level is the characteristic MOLGA that represents a country grouping, which in most cases is interpreted as an employee's country. For most country groupings, there is a one-to-one assignment of a trip provision variant. For example, Great Britain is the only country for country grouping 08.

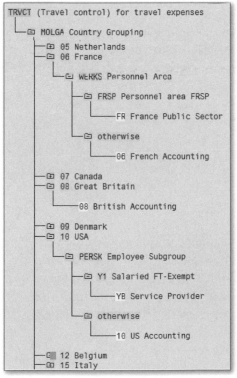

```
TRVCT (Travel control) for travel expenses
    └─ MOLGA Country Grouping
        ─ 05 Netherlands
        ─ 06 France
            └─ WERKS Personnel Area
                ─ FRSP Personnel area FRSP
                    └─ FR France Public Sector
                ─ otherwise
                    └─ 06 French Accounting
        ─ 07 Canada
        ─ 08 Great Britain
            └─ 08 British Accounting
        ─ 09 Denmark
        ─ 10 USA
            └─ PERSK Employee Subgroup
                ─ Y1 Salaried FT-Exempt
                    └─ YB Service Provider
                ─ otherwise
                    └─ 10 US Accounting
        ─ 12 Belgium
        ─ 15 Italy
```

Figure 7.2 Travel Control Feature TRVCT

▶ For the country grouping France (06), a trip provision variant is determined based on the characteristic WERKS, which represents an employee's personnel area. So if an employee belongs to a public sector, then the Travel Expense subcomponent uses a different trip provision variant.

▶ On the other hand, for the country grouping U.S. (10), it is the employee's subgroup that determines a trip provision variant for its travel trips. For full-time or exempt employees, the Travel Expenses subcomponent uses one trip provision variant; for all other employees, it uses a different trip provision variant.

You maintain this feature in configuration via the menu path IMG • FINANCIAL ACCOUNTING • TRAVEL MANAGEMENT • TRAVEL EXPENSES • MASTER DATA • CONTROL PARAMETERS FOR TRAVEL EXPENSES • ASSIGN ORGANIZATIONAL AREAS AND TRVCT FEATURE.

Now let's discuss another account determination object: a personnel area.

7.1.5 Personnel Area

In Section 7.1.1 we discussed infotypes and examples of infotypes, such as the one for employee organizational assignment data (Infotype 0001). This infotype includes, among other assignments, employee assignment to a personnel area (see Figure 7.3).

Figure 7.3 Personnel Area Assignment

A personnel area is part of an enterprise structure definition in SAP ERP. You define personnel areas using the menu path IMG • ENTERPRISE STRUCTURE • DEFINITION • HUMAN RESOURCES MANAGEMENT • PERSONNEL AREAS. You assign personnel areas to company codes using the menu path IMG • ENTERPRISE STRUCTURE • ASSIGNMENT • HUMAN RESOURCES MANAGEMENT • ASSIGNMENT OF PERSONNEL AREA TO COMPANY CODE.

A personnel area represents an organizational unit in SAP ERP from the viewpoint of SAP HR, SAP Payroll, and Time Management functionalities. A personnel area has a many-to-one relationship with a company code definition. This means that a personnel area can be assigned to only one company code, but a company code may consist of multiple personnel areas. For example, a company with headquarters in the United States but branch offices (not separate legal entities) in Canada and the United Kingdom will have three personnel areas created for a company code.

So far, we have discussed most of the organizational objects involved in GL account determination such as features, trip provision variants, and personnel areas. Now let's get to the transactional objects that are involved in GL account determination.

7.1.6 Employee Trip

The employee trip object, which represents an employee trip, plays an important role in SAP ERP's travel management module. You use an employee trip for planning, travel requests, trip bookings, account assignments, travel expense maintenance, and expense settlements.

Depending on your access authorization and your preferences, you enter an employee trip using one of the following scenarios:

▸ **Planning manager (Transaction TP01)**
This transaction contains all steps of a trip for managing travel requests, travel plans, and travel expenses.

▸ **Travel expense manager (Transaction PR05)**
This transaction provides an overview of all of the employees' trips. You can edit one travel expense report at a time.

▸ **Travel calendar (Transaction PR02)**
This transaction provides an overview in a calendar form for processing all employees' trips. The calendar form is intended to be used only for managing domestic trips.

▸ **Weekly report (Transaction PR04)**
The weekly report provides an overview of all of the employee's weekly travel reports. This is another form in which you can process trip data.

An employee trip object provides a container to maintain almost all data associated with a trip. The following are some examples of trip data that you can maintain for an employee trip object:

▶ **Trip rules data**

Trip rules data consists of company-specific rules and guidelines for items such as routes and trip destinations, trip categories, service classes, trip duration, time scaling, and priorities. If applicable, your trip rules data also includes travel request and travel approval information. You assign company-specific travel rules to an employee using Infotype 0470 (travel profile).

> **Note**
>
> You can also maintain employee-specific travel preferences using Infotypes 0471 (flight preferences), 0472 (hotel preferences), 0473 (rental car preferences), 0474 (train preferences), and 0475 (customer program). You may want to consider this aspect while trying to analyze seemingly non-standard expense postings to a travel expenses GL account. It may be due to inappropriate assignment of parameters in the travel profile of travel preference infotypes.

▶ **Trip data**

Examples of this type of data include destination, freely enterable trip reason, one of the preapproved trip activities, and booking data for travel services such as flight, hotel, and rental car reservations. Of course, you can enter multiple legs of a travel plan under the same trip ID, and maintain all of this data for each travel leg, whether it includes multiple destinations within a country or across multiple countries.

▶ **Trip status data**

This data consists of several trip statuses such as trip request status, trip approval status, trip settlement status, trip transfer status to payroll, trip transfer status to accounting, and trip transfer status to DME (Data Medium Exchange).

▶ **Expense details**

These details include trip advances, expense receipts, both reimbursable and non-reimbursable parts of expenses, supporting details (such as number of attendees, or explanation for unusual charges), and assignment to different cost center or a company code for reimbursement.

In the next section, we will discuss the use of expense types to enter expense details for an employee trip.

7.1.7   Expense Type

Employee trip expenses are recorded via *expense types*. An expense type in the Travel Expenses subcomponent controls several parameters that not only help in categorizing travel expenses but also enforce (to some degree) travel expense policies. All expense types are defined within a trip provision variant. There are two types of expense types that you can configure for travel expenses.

▶ **Expense types for per diems/flat rate**
These types of expenses are reimbursed at a flat rate or per diem. For these types of expenses, you have to enter the unit of the corresponding activity, and the Travel Expenses subcomponent automatically calculates the corresponding expense amount.

For example, for lunch and dinner, you simply enter the number of days, and the Travel Expenses subcomponent multiplies it by the predefined per diem rate and calculates the reimbursement amount. Similarly, after you enter the number of miles/kilometers you drove, the Travel Expenses subcomponent multiplies it by a flat rate and calculates the reimbursement amount. You configure these expense types using the menu path IMG • Financial Accounting • Travel Management • Travel Expenses • Master Data • Travel Expense Types • Create Travel Expense Types for Per Diems/Flat Rates.

▶ **Expense type per individual travel receipts**
Except the few examples mentioned in the previous paragraph, almost all other expenses such as flight airfare, meals, business entertainment, hotel, and others are created using per receipt expense types. For these types of expenses, you have to enter the actual expense amount corresponding to receipts.

For example, for lunch, dinner, and rental car reimbursements, you have to enter expense amounts that correspond to the receipt amounts. You configure these expense types using the menu path IMG • Financial Accounting • Travel Management • Travel Expenses • Master Data • Travel Expense Types • Create Travel Expense Types for Individual Receipts.

There are limited attributes for per diem/flat rate expense types. You can only assign an expense type category to these types of expense types. However, the expense types based on receipts provide you with several configurable parameters that let you enforce your corporate travel policy up to a certain extent.

Figure 7.4 shows an example of an expense type for individual receipts. As you can see, here you can assign it one of the predefined codes for the travel expense category, travel provider category, permissible trip expense type, use of expense types, expense reimbursement amounts, and so on.

Travel Exp.Type	AIR	Flight
Travel Expense Types for Receipt : US Accounting		
Travel Expense Cat.		Other
Provider Category		Airline
ExpTy.Permissibility		123456789
Amounts are		To be reimbursed to the employee
Usage		In business trip and in weekly report

Figure 7.4 Expense Type—Individual Receipt

The value specified in the AMOUNTS ARE reimbursement field influences GL account postings, so it is important to be familiar with how each expense type is set up. The following are possible values for this field:

- Expense amounts are reimbursed to employee
- Expense amounts are paid by company
- Expense amounts are taxable by employee, not paid to employee
- Expense amounts are taxable by employee, paid to employee
- Expense amounts are estimated costs only, no reimbursement to employees
- Expense amounts are already paid by the company, taxable by employee

Now let's move on to the next account determination object: a wage type.

7.1.8   Wage Type

Travel expenses assigned to expense types are stored via an object called a wage type. A *wage type* is an object in which a user or the system stores amounts or units. These amounts are used in calculations, storage, reporting, and almost everywhere an amount or a unit is reported in SAP HR and SAP Payroll applications. Similar wage types are used for the Travel Expenses subcomponent as well.

Though the SAP ERP system provides more than a thousand wage types, you can also create your own custom wage types if necessary. You assign wage types to expense types via the menu path IMG • FINANCIAL ACCOUNTING • TRAVEL MANAGE-MENT • TRAVEL EXPENSES • WAGE TYPES FOR INTERFACES.

Figure 7.5 shows the assignment of an expense type to wage types. You should assign at least one wage type to an expense type. In most cases, you have to assign only one wage type to an expense type, so that all travel expenses entered for that expense type are stored in the corresponding wage type.

Travel Exp.Type	AIR	Flight
ServiceProvider		

Travel expense type attribute

Amounts are	To be reimbursed to the employee

Wage Type for Receipt : US Accounting

1st wage type	MJ30	Trav.costs/tax-exempt
2nd wage type		

Figure 7.5 Wage Type Assignment

However, you may assign a second wage type to an expense type in some scenarios. For example, if you need to split the expense amount based on taxable or non-taxable instances, or if there is a maximum amount limit on an expense type, enter a second wage type that stores the balance amount.

The wage types are associated with one or more symbolic accounts, which are discussed next.

7.1.9   Symbolic Accounts

Wage types are assigned symbolic accounts that are three characters in length. *Symbolic accounts* let you determine the accounts to which expense postings are made. We discussed the symbolic account technique in Chapter 1. All expense postings require a GL account to which the expense entry is posted. However, depending on the type of expense and on how its reimbursement or payment is done, the offsetting entry may post to a GL account or an employee account set up as a vendor or a customer account.

Keeping this in mind, it will be easier to understand the assignment of symbolic accounts to wage types as shown in Figure 7.6. Each wage type is assigned two of the following three symbolic accounts:

▶ **For expense: symbolic expense account**
This symbolic account determines the GL account to which travel expenses are posted.

▶ **For customer/vendor: first symbolic account**
This symbolic account determines the customer or the vendor account to which the offsetting entry for travel expenses is posted.

▶ **For clearing: second symbolic account**
This symbolic account determines the offsetting GL account to which the offsetting entry for travel expenses is posted.

The assignment of symbolic accounts to wage types is done using the configuration path IMG • FINANCIAL ACCOUNTING • TRAVEL MANAGEMENT • TRAVEL EXPENSES • TRANSFER TO ACCOUNTING • DEFINE ASSIGNMENT OF WAGE TYPES TO SYMBOLIC ACCOUNTS.

Symbolic Account Assignment for Financial Accounting : US Accounting

Wage ...	Key	Start Date	End Date	Symb.Ex...	W/o...	Symb.Ac...	Set ...	Wth...	2nd Sym...	W/o...	Sett
MJ10		01/01/1997	12/31/9999	+10	☐		☐	☐		☐	☐
MJ11		01/01/1997	12/31/9999	+10	☐		☐	☐		☐	☐
MJ12		01/01/1997	12/31/9999	+10	☐		☐	☐		☐	☐
MJ20		01/01/1997	12/31/9999	+20	☐		☐	☐		☐	☐
MJ21		01/01/1997	12/31/9999	+20	☐		☐	☐		☐	☐
MJ30		01/01/1997	12/31/9999	+30	☐		☐	☐		☐	☐
MJ31		01/01/1997	12/31/9999	+30	☐		☐	☐		☐	☐
MJ40		01/01/1997	12/31/9999	+40	☐		☐	☐		☐	☐
MJ50		01/01/1997	12/31/9999	+50	☐		☐	☐		☐	☐
MJ61		01/01/1997	12/31/9999	+10	☐		☐	☐	-60	☑	☐
MJ62		01/01/1997	12/31/9999	+20	☐		☐	☐	-60	☑	☐

Figure 7.6 Symbolic Account Assignment to Wage Types

The conversion of a symbolic account to an actual account is done under the same configuration menu path just mentioned but with the last node as the CONVERSION OF SYMBOLIC ACCOUNT TO EXPENSE ACCOUNT. In the next section, we will discuss how these symbolic accounts are used to determine the appropriate GL account, vendor account, or customer account.

Prior to that, let's briefly discuss another organizational unit that is relevant for travel expense reimbursement.

7.1.10 Payroll Area

Even though it is not mentioned in Figure 7.1, the *payroll area* plays a very important role while posting travel expense reimbursements. Each employee is assigned a payroll area through Infotype 0001 (see Figure 7.7). We will discuss the payroll area in more detail in Chapter 10. However, a payroll area is an organizational unit that is used to group all employees for whom payroll is run at the same time. The reason the payroll area is important for travel expenses transactions and GL account determination is that the process of settling employee trips to accounting is carried out through the corresponding assignment of the payroll area.

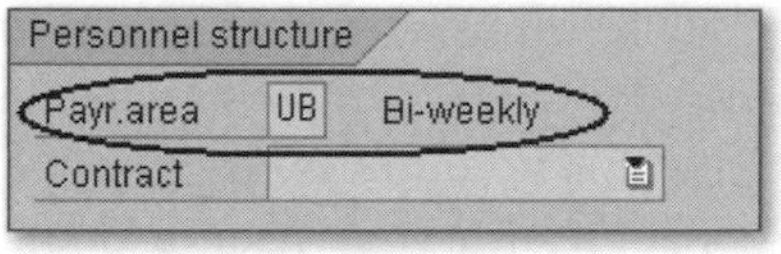

Figure 7.7 Payroll Area Assignment

In the next section, we will see how all of these objects come together for GL account determination and to process trip expense reimbursements.

7.2 General Ledger Account Determination

As we have discussed, expense details are assigned to expense types, which are assigned one or more wage types, which in turn are assigned one or more symbolic accounts. These symbolic accounts are converted to GL accounts by following the menu path IMG • FINANCIAL ACCOUNTING • TRAVEL MANAGEMENT • TRAVEL EXPENSES • TRANSFER TO ACCOUNTING • DEFINE ASSIGNMENT OF WAGE TYPES TO SYMBOLIC ACCOUNTS.

The conversion of symbolic accounts to GL accounts is carried out using the transaction key technique. Transaction group HRR (postings from travel expense accounting) groups together all transaction keys that are relevant for this configuration transaction. The following transaction keys are relevant here:

▸ **Transaction key HRT**
This transaction key is used for determination of travel expense accounts and GL accounts for posting offsetting entries.

Two rule modifiers are available for this transaction key: a debit/credit indicator and a general modifier that corresponds to symbolic accounts.

► **Transaction key HRP**
This transaction key is used for determining customer/vendor offsetting accounts.

Two rule modifiers are available for this transaction key: a debit/credit indicator and a general modifier that corresponds to symbolic accounts.

The derivation of the actual personnel account maintained as a vendor or a customer is done using a BAPI, which uses a controlled search to derive the appropriate personnel account.

After trip expenses are entered and, if applicable, approved, two processes play an important role in transferring these results to the financial accounting .The first of these processes is the settlement process, which calculates settlement results for all relevant employee trips in a given period. The settlement results are created based on the details entered in expense reports, reimbursement rates maintained in the configuration, and other criteria that influence expense reimbursement, such as maximum allowable amounts. As mentioned previously, the settlement process calculates reimbursement amounts for the trip for a given period.

After the trip results are calculated by the settlement process, the posting run interprets the settlement results and transfers these results to the financial accounting in the form of accounting documents. Depending on how these expenses are reimbursed, the posting run carries out different accounting entries. For example, expenses may be reimbursed from Accounts Payable (AP), FI-TV, and so on.

The remainder of this section describes the different business scenarios for expense reimbursements, and how different accounts are determined for each business scenario.

7.2.1   Reimbursement from Accounts Payable

This is one of the most common business scenarios. Trip expenses are entered in the Travel Expenses subcomponent, and then accounting entries are transferred to AP for further processing and payments. Under this scenario, every employee is created as a vendor in AP.

> **Note**
>
> You assign a personnel number to the corresponding vendor account using the menu path CHANGE VENDOR (TRANSACTION FK02) • COMPANY CODE DATA. Then on the ACCOUNTING INFORMATION tab in the REFERENCE DATA section, you can access the PERSONNEL NUMBER field.

SAP ERP determines the appropriate accounts in this business scenario as described in the following subsections.

Expense Accounts (HRT)

Expense amounts are posted to these accounts. Account determination takes place from the symbolic account assigned to the wage types assigned to the expense types. During symbolic account assignment, keep the following in mind:

▶ The first position indicates + (debit) or − (credit).

▶ The second and third positions indicate the symbolic account.

Employee Accounts (HRP)

Vendor accounts in AP that correspond to personnel accounts are credited with the net expense reimbursement amount. SAP ERP derives the vendor number based on the personnel number stored in the vendor master data, which in turn is derived by using the search definition specified in this configuration.

In AP, you can carry out expense reimbursement by check, direct debit, or any other payment method.

7.2.2 Reimbursement from Travel Management

In the previous business scenario, you had to transfer the expense reimbursement information to the financial accounting. However, in this business scenario, you use the Travel Expenses subcomponent to process the payments using one of the following methods: either generate a Data Medium Exchange (DME) file, or print checks for expense reimbursement. Formats of DME files are country-specific, so the individual details that are sent out to a bank will vary for each country and possibly even for different bank accounts in the same country. However, you definitely require the employee bank account to which payments are made and the house bank account from which payments are made.

Employee Bank Account

SAP ERP determines the employee bank account information from Infotype 0009 (bank details), Subtype 2 (travel expenses). Figure 7.8 shows this assignment.

Create Bank Details

Personnel No	1000000	Name	
EE group	1 Active	Personnel ar	1800
EE subgroup	Y0 Hourly Full Time	Status	
Start	01/01/2010 to	12/31/9999	

Bank details

Bank details type	Travel Expenses
Payee	Mr Payee Name
Postal Code/City	95014 Gurnee

Figure 7.8 Employee Bank Account for Travel Expenses

House Bank Account

A relevant point to consider for GL account determination is also how the house bank account is determined. If the payments are made from AP, then the house bank is determined directly from the GL account assigned to the house bank account. Refer to Chapter 5 for details on how to set up these house banks, house bank accounts, and corresponding GL accounts.

However, when you carry out a posting run for travel expenses, you may have different company codes (or even departments) that may use different bank accounts to make travel expense reimbursements.

For this purpose, SAP ERP determines the appropriate house bank and house bank account using the TRVHB feature. If required, refer to Section 7.1.2 to get an overview of how a feature is used in SAP ERP to determine the value for a parameter. This feature is maintained and can be accessed via the menu path IMG • FINANCIAL ACCOUNTING • TRAVEL MANAGEMENT • TRAVEL EXPENSES • TRANSFER TO DATA MEDIUM EXCHANGE (DME) • SET UP FEATURE FOR DETERMINING HOUSE BANK.

Accounting documents for this scenario are not immediately posted to the financial accounting, but instead when bank statement reconciliation is carried out for the house bank accounts.

7.2.3 Reimbursement from Payroll

If FI-TV is integrated with SAP HR and SAP Payroll in your SAP ERP system, then you can also choose to transfer travel expenses to SAP Payroll and make the travel reimbursements through SAP Payroll as well.

> **Note**
>
> The feature TRVPA in SAP ERP contains several trip costs parameters for FI-TV. As with any other definition of a feature, you can define this parameter determination at any level of detail as necessary. One of these parameters is the PARAMETER L+G, which controls whether and how the Travel Expenses subcomponent is integrated with SAP Payroll.

To carry out travel expense reimbursement from SAP Payroll, you have two possible options of how the expense reimbursement results are posted to the GL.

You can choose to post expense reimbursement results to the GL along with the posting of payroll results. However, in this scenario, accounting documents are posted at a summary level, so you no longer have expense reimbursement details per employee. Refer to Chapter 10 for more details about GL account determination of this type of implementation.

The other option is to post expense reimbursement at a detailed level where information per employee is retained. To make these types of reimbursement postings, use a clearing account and the following two-step process:

1. Transfer travel expenses to SAP Payroll. The clearing account is debited, and payroll accounts are credited.

2. Post travel expenses to financial accounting: The clearing account is credited, and expense accounts are debited.

The following is an explanation of how the GL account determination is carried out in that two-step process:

▶ **Payroll accounts**
Chapter 10 discusses the determination of payroll accounts in detail.

▶ **Expense accounts (HRT)**
These GL accounts are posted with the expense amounts.

▶ **Clearing accounts (HRP)**
These GL accounts are posted with the offsetting entry for expense amounts.

Account determination takes place from the symbolic account assigned to the wage types assigned to the expense types as described earlier in this chapter.

7.2.4 Reimbursement for Corporate Credit Card

In this business scenario, corporate credit cards are used to charge most travel expenses. There are different possible variations for this scenario as well. For example, a centralized travel department may use corporate credit cards to book travels, or employees may be issued credit cards by the company. Another variation is that instead of employees having to pay the credit card issuer and then request reimbursement, the company may choose to directly pay the credit card issuer.

In any case, SAP ERP provides functionality to upload daily transactional data provided by credit card issuers. This functionality is controlled by the parameter CCC in the feature TRVPA previously discussed. You carry out configuration of the feature TRVPA using the menu path IMG • FINANCIAL ACCOUNTING • TRAVEL MANAGEMENT • TRAVEL EXPENSES • DIALOG AND TRAVEL EXPENSES CONTROL • SET UP FEATURE TRVPA FOR TRAVEL EXPENSES PARAMETERS.

Depending on the level of detail available in the data received, you can assign these transactions to expense accounts or even to individual employee accounts.

> **Note**
>
> This discussion is also applicable if a similar arrangement has been made with a service provider for lodging, rental cars, or other traveling services. The service providers can send transactional detail in the required format that you can directly upload into SAP ERP.

Irrespective of which variations of this business scenario are implemented, all GL account determination refers to determination of expense accounts, clearing accounts, or employee accounts.

Expense Accounts (HRT)

We have already discussed the derivation of the GL account from the symbolic account via the expense type and wage type. There is no change in that derivation process.

However, in this case, expense types are assigned to transaction keys for *each* relevant credit card company. This assignment ensures that credit card charges are posted to the correct expense accounts. You carry out this assignment using the menu path IMG • FINANCIAL ACCOUNTING • TRAVEL MANAGEMENT • TRAVEL EXPENSES • MASTER DATA • CREDIT CARD CLEARING • DEFINE ASSIGNMENT TABLE FOR CREDIT CARD CLEARING.

Clearing Accounts (HRP)

A separate clearing account is created for each credit card provider (if there's more than one) and each service provider. These accounts are specified for symbolic account 1RR.

When transaction data from the credit card issuer is uploaded, the clearing account for the credit card issuer is credited, and the expense accounts are debited. Subsequently, when an invoice is received from the credit card issuer, debits are posted to the clearing account.

Employee Accounts

The corresponding vendor account in AP is identified and posted using the employee account determined from the credit card data.

You should note that even if employees use corporate credit cards for travel expenses, and your company makes direct payment to credit card issuers, there may still be additional reimbursable expenses incurred by the employee that you may have to reimburse using a different process. On the other hand, transactions on corporate credit cards may include non-reimbursable personal expenses. In such cases, you will also need a process in place that posts additional credits or debits to employee accounts.

In the next section, let's look at handling private expenses.

7.2.5 Handling Private Expenses

Transactional data uploaded from credit card issuers or from service providers may include private expenses that aren't allowed to be reimbursed based on corporate guidelines. You will need to handle private expenses even if trip expenses are entered manually instead of via automatic data uploads. This can be the case, for example, if expense receipts in trip expenses include any non-reimbursable expenses incurred by an employee.

Private Expenses Paid by the Company

GL account determination is done via HRT for expense accounts using symbolic accounts, as in the standard business scenario. However, a different expense type, PRBZ, ensures that a credit entry is posted to the corresponding expense accounts instead of a debit entry.

Private Expenses to Be Paid Back

Account determination is done via HRP for employee vendor accounts using symbolic accounts, as in the standard business scenario. However, a different expense type, PRIV, ensures that a debit is posted to the employee vendor account instead of a credit.

The expense types discussed previously (PRBZ and PRIV) are standard expense types provided by SAP ERP for the purpose of handling private lodging expenses. If additional expense types are required for different types of private expenses, they can be created with reference to the standard expense types discussed previously.

Finally, let's have a look at GL account determination for trip advances to employees.

7.2.6   Trip Advances to Employees

Before an approved trip, employees may be given an advance against trip expenses. You can give employee advances from the cash office or via AP. System configuration determines the treatment of cash advance posting.

In the cash advance account (HRT), all variations of the trip expense entry programs allow you to enter trip advances in a separate screen. The system creates a one-minute trip as a placeholder and posts the advance amount to this GL account.

7.3   Summary

As we have seen, there isn't much technical variation in how GL account determination is done for travel expense reimbursement. Only two transaction keys are used for GL account determination, and only a few transactions are used to assign symbolic accounts to wage types and GL accounts to symbolic accounts.

The key is to know which of the available alternatives are applicable in your situation and which accounts should be used for posting. It helps to understand the control parameters associated with the expense type and wage type to ensure that GL postings are generated as expected.

Now that we have covered the major components of SAP ERP Financials, the remainder of this guide will focus on other SAP ERP components. The next chapter discusses GL account determination for transactions in the Sales and Distribution and Purchasing functionalities of SAP ERP.

7.4   Reference

Let's take another look at the configuration transactions, tables, and structures that are relevant to the discussions in this chapter.

7.4.1   Configuration Transactions

Table 7.1 provides a list of the configuration transactions for the account determination objects that were discussed in this chapter.

Transaction Code	Description
PE03	Feature (TRVCT, TRVBH, etc.) maintenance
PRCO	Maintain trip provision variants
PR05	Trip—travel expense manager
PR02	Trip—travel calendar
PR04	Trip—weekly report
PR03	Trip advances
PRT3	Assign GL account to symbolic accounts

Table 7.1 Configuration Transactions

7.4.2   Tables and Structures

Table 7.2 contains a list of tables used to store data relevant for GL account determination discussed in this chapter.

Table /Structure	Table Description
T500P	Personnel area
T702N	Trip provision variants
T706D	Settings for trip provision variants
PA0001	Employee organizational assignment
PTRV_HEAD	General employee trip data
PTRV_SCOS	Employee trip cost assignment
T706B1	Travel expense types—per receipt
T706B1_A	Travel expense types—per diem
T702K	Service providers
T702B	Credit card transaction key to expense type assignment
T706B4	Wage type to expense type assignment
T706B4_ALTERN	Alternative wage type to expense type assignment
T706K	Initial assignment of symbolic account to wage types
T030	GL account to symbolic account assignment

Table 7.2 Tables

8 Sales and Purchasing

This chapter covers GL account determination for sales and purchasing transactions in SAP ERP. These two admittedly different functionalities are combined into a single chapter because the GL account determination techniques used in both the Sales and Distribution (SD) and Purchasing functionalities are very similar. Of course, both functionalities use different transaction codes in configuration, and most of the GL account determination for purchasing activity relates to inventory transactions, which are discussed in Chapter 9. However, you will notice that both functionalities share similar concepts, similar account determination techniques, and similar account determination objects, even though the objects may be named differently in each functionality. So for GL account determination purposes, it will make it easier to discuss and understand GL account determination for sales transactions and purchase transactions in the same chapter.

> **Note**
>
> This chapter covers GL account determination in sales transactions in detail. However, GL account determination for procurement transactions is tightly coupled with inventory transactions (Chapter 9). So you may want to use this chapter to get familiar with procurement pricing and other account assignment objects, and then read Chapter 9 for the GL account determination for inventory transactions.

Another important aspect to note is that in sales and purchasing, you also need to know, or at least be familiar with, pricing configuration when you are carrying out GL account determination configuration. For this reason, this chapter also includes details on where to find relevant pricing configuration activities. Obviously, this configuration has to be done by respective group members of your team who are responsible for SD and Materials Management (MM) configuration. Having said that, let's delve into the details.

8.1 Sales (Order-to-Cash)

For your reference, Figure 8.1 repeats the condition technique diagram from Chapter 1. The Sales and Distribution (SD) functionality in SAP ERP uses this condition technique for the GL account determination in several processes such as billing, revenue recognition, and posting accruals. If you haven't already done so, you should review and understand the condition technique overview in Chapter 1 before continuing on with this chapter.

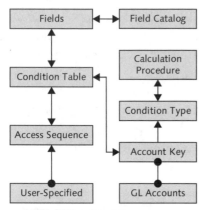

Figure 8.1 Condition Technique

Let's first start with pricing configuration in SD.

8.1.1 Pricing Configuration

In this section, we will discuss some of the pricing configuration objects that are relevant for understanding and using GL account determination for sales transactions. For SD transactions, configuration of a pricing procedure plays a crucial role in configuration of GL account determination and assignment. So let's start by discussing pricing procedures.

Pricing Procedure

A sales *pricing procedure* corresponds to a calculation procedure shown in the condition technique (refer to Figure 8.1). The primary purpose of a pricing procedure is to calculate different values such as sales price, applicable discounts, charges and fees, taxes, and so on for a sales transaction. However, a pricing procedure can also be used to calculate additional values, such as profit margin for analytical and informational purposes. In the pricing procedure, unique condition types correspond to each of the different information pieces that are assigned a value.

Determination of an applicable pricing procedure for a sales order in itself is a complex process. In SAP ERP, you can configure the pricing procedure determination based on sales areas, customer groups, document type groups, item categories, and several other characteristics that are available at the time of order processing. You can find more details on this under the configuration menu path IMG • SALES AND DISTRIBUTION • BASIC FUNCTIONS • PRICING • PRICING CONTROL • DEFINE AND ASSIGN PRICING PROCEDURES.

A pricing procedure contains one or more condition types.

Condition Types

A condition type used in a pricing procedure corresponds to a pricing element. Prices, surcharges, discounts, taxes, and freight are all examples of pricing elements that can be part of a pricing calculation for a customer. A condition type can also represent value elements that are calculated based on an order pricing, that are relevant internally only to your business, and that are never shared with your customers. Examples of these types of value elements are COGS (cost of goods sold), profit margins, sales commissions, and so on. If it is a pricing or a value element in a pricing calculation that you need to capture, then you can use a condition type for that purpose.

SAP ERP provides hundreds of standard condition types that you can use in configuring pricing procedures. Figure 8.2 shows you some of the standard condition types that are available. If required, you can configure additional condition types using IMG • SALES AND DISTRIBUTION • BASIC FUNCTIONS • PRICING • PRICING CONTROL • DEFINE CONDITION TYPES.

CTyp	Condition type	Condition class
B003	Customer Rebate	Expense reimbursement
CTXJ	Tax Jurisdict.Code	Taxes
GRWR	Statistical value	Prices
HM00	Order value	Prices
IV01	Inter-company Price	Prices
IV02	Inter-company %	Prices
K004	Material	Discount or surcharge
K005	Customer/Material	Discount or surcharge

Figure 8.2 Condition Types

A condition class shown in Figure 8.2 classifies condition types based on their purpose such as prices, taxes, discounts or surcharges, and so on. You specify an access sequence in every condition type.

Access Sequence

An access sequence in this context defines the sequence in which a pricing condition evaluates a series of tables to arrive at the required value. Access sequences used in pricing procedures refer to business scenarios such as unit pricing, rebate percentage, freight charge, commission percentage, and so on. For example, you would use a condition table containing different layers of shipping weights to arrive at a freight charge; or you may use quantity information in an order to arrive at a rebate amount or a commission amount.

> **Note**
>
> It is important to differentiate access sequences used in pricing procedure from the access sequences used in account determination. Access sequences in pricing procedures are used to determine business values; whereas access sequences discussed in the next Section are used for GL account determination.

You configure access sequences for pricing procedure conditions using IMG • Sales and Distribution • Basic Functions • Pricing • Pricing Control • Define Access Sequences.

Now let's discuss some of the technical objects involved in GL account determination for sales transactions.

8.1.2 Technical Objects

In this section, we will discuss technical objects that are relevant for GL account determination in sales transactions. *Technical objects* refers to the objects that are typically configured in SAP ERP, instead of being assigned to customer master, material master, or any other business data. Because a derivation of technical objects is done in the configuration activity, any relevant problems can usually be traced down to incorrect configuration.

Figure 8.3 shows the configuration menu area where you configure account determination for sales transactions. You will find in this figure most menu items that are discussed in this chapter with reference to sales account determination.

Although the menu path refers only to revenue accounts, you use the same configuration transaction to configure accounts for other relevant categories, such as discounts, taxes, charges, freight, duties, and so on. Similarly, as we will see later in this section, you will find configuration of other accounts such as revenue recognition also under the menu path IMG • SALES AND DISTRIBUTION • BASIC FUNCTIONS • ACCOUNT ASSIGNMENT/COSTING.

You will use most of these objects while configuring GL accounts. Also keep an eye on Figure 8.1 while reading the discussion of these objects.

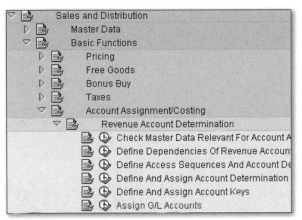

Figure 8.3 Sales Account Determination Configuration

Application

An application in SAP ERP represents a group of conditions that are used in a particular application area or a particular SAP ERP component. Examples of different application areas and components that use the condition technique, and thus an application, are SD, Purchasing, Profitability Analysis, and so on.

These values are delivered by SAP ERP. The configuration activity you are carrying out will determine which one of the application values are available. Note that each component uses only one application value in its configuration.

For the GL account determination in SD, this value is always V. An application is a required characteristic in sales GL account determination.

Field Catalog

We discussed the field catalog briefly as part of the condition technique in Chapter 1. Basically, a field catalog provides a list of valid fields that you can use as characteristics to carry out GL account determination. For example, if you want to carry out GL account determination based on a sales document type or reason code for product returns, then those fields need to be first available in the field catalog for that application before you can use them for GL account determination.

In most cases, the fields available in the field catalog of the respective application are sufficient for carrying out GL account determination. However, if necessary, you can add additional fields to the field catalog. This configuration activity is done via the menu path IMG • SALES AND DISTRIBUTION • BASIC FUNCTIONS • ACCOUNT ASSIGNMENT/COSTING • REVENUE ACCOUNT DETERMINATION • DEFINE DEPENDENCIES OF REVENUE ACCOUNT DETERMINATION • FIELD CATALOG: ALLOWED FIELDS FOR THE TABLES.

Account Determination Procedure

An account determination procedure in this context is similar to the pricing procedure discussed previously, except that the account determination procedure is used to derive GL accounts. The concept is similar to the condition technique with its associated set of condition techniques and access sequences. You must assign an account determination procedure to a billing type for the system to carry out appropriate GL account determination.

You can define and assign account determination procedures using the configuration menu path IMG • SALES AND DISTRIBUTION • BASIC FUNCTIONS • ACCOUNT ASSIGNMENT/COSTING • REVENUE ACCOUNT DETERMINATION • DEFINE AND ASSIGN ACCOUNT DETERMINATION PROCEDURES.

Account Determination Type

An account determination type in this context is a condition type that indicates whether or not the GL account determination also involves posting to objects in cost accounting. These objects, for example, are a profit center or a business area. The standard SAP ERP system provides two condition types for GL account determination for sales transactions: KOFK and KOFI. You may have additional account determination types available in your system if you have installed additional SAP ERP components such as the Point-of-Sale system, Retail Industry Solution, and so on. A condition type is a required characteristic in sales GL account determination.

You can review these condition types or create your own condition types using the configuration menu path IMG • SALES AND DISTRIBUTION • BASIC FUNCTIONS • ACCOUNT ASSIGNMENT/COSTING • REVENUE ACCOUNT DETERMINATION • DEFINE ACCESS SEQUENCES AND ACCOUNT DETERMINATION TYPES • DEFINE ACCOUNT DETERMINATION TYPES.

Access Sequence

You must also define access sequences 0for each account determination type (e.g., KOFI, KOFK, etc.). This access sequence allows SAP ERP to determine the sequence in which condition tables consisting of different fields are accessed.

The standard SAP ERP system provides access sequences KOFK and KOFI to be used with corresponding account determination types. You can create additional access sequences if necessary. You configure the access sequence for account determination types using the menu path IMG • SALES AND DISTRIBUTION • BASIC FUNCTIONS • ACCOUNT ASSIGNMENT/COSTING • REVENUE ACCOUNT DETERMINATION • DEFINE ACCESS SEQUENCES AND ACCOUNT DETERMINATION TYPES • MAINTAIN ACCESS SEQUENCES FOR ACCOUNT DETERMINATION.

Account Keys

You use account keys in sales GL account determination for different types of GL accounts such as revenue accounts, freight accounts, tax accounts, and so on. Figure 8.4 shows some of the account keys available in a standard SAP ERP system for sales transactions. SAP ERP provides close to a hundred account keys for posting different types of business postings to different GL accounts.

ActKy	Name
BCMf	Mat. in Consignment
CHB	Depreciation
ERB	Rebate sales deduct.
ERF	Freight revenue
ERL	Revenue
ERS	Sales deductions
EVV	Cash clearing
MWS	Taxes on sls/purch.

Figure 8.4 Sales Account Keys

If required, you can configure additional account keys using the menu path IMG • Sales and Distribution • Basic Functions • Account Assignment/Costing • Revenue Account Determination • Define and Assign Account Keys • Define Account Key.

While configuring pricing procedures, you assign one of these account keys to a condition type that we discussed in Section 8.1.1. You must assign at least one account key to a condition type if you want to post the value captured or calculated for that condition type to any GL account.

In the next section, we will discuss business objects.

8.1.3 Business Objects

In this section, we will discuss business objects that are relevant for GL account determination in sales transactions. Business objects are typically assigned to the customer master, material master, or any other business data. You may have to first configure valid values for these objects, but after that, the business users assign these values to the relevant master data. By extension, any errors here may be traced back to incorrect values specified in customer master data, material master data, and so on.

Sales Organization

A *sales organization* is an organizational unit that is responsible for the sale of certain products or services. Chances are that if you are reading this book, you are already familiar with the concept and configuration of the sales organization in SAP ERP. It is one of the most basic configurations you carry out while implementing an SAP ERP system. A sales organization is a required characteristic in sales GL account determination.

You define a sales organization under the IMG • Enterprise Structure • Definition • Sales and Distribution • Define, Copy, Delete, Check Sales Organization. You assign a sales organization to a company code under the IMG • Enterprise Structure • Assignment • Sales and Distribution • Assign Sales Organization to Company Code.

Chart of Accounts

In Chapter 1, we discussed the chart of accounts in great detail. Please refer to Chapter 1 if you need to get familiar with the concepts of charts of accounts. A chart of accounts is a required characteristic in sales GL account determination.

For the purposes of sales GL account determination, this chart of accounts refers to the chart of accounts assigned to the company code to which the sales organization is assigned.

Customer AAG

A *customer account assignment group* (AAG) is a two-character identifier that groups together customer accounts for the purposes of GL account determination. For example, using the customer AAG, you can differentiate revenue accounts for domestic customers, foreign customers, and customer accounts that are created for affiliate companies.

Customer AAG is an optional characteristic, but it is one of the most commonly used for sales GL account determination. You configure customer AAG values using the configuration IMG • SALES AND DISTRIBUTION • BASIC FUNCTIONS • ACCOUNT ASSIGN-MENT/COSTING • REVENUE ACCOUNT DETERMINATION • CHECK MASTER DATA RELEVANT FOR ACCOUNT ASSIGNMENT • CUSTOMERS: ACCOUNT ASSIGNMENT GROUPS.

You assign customer AAG to a customer account in the customer master using CHANGE CUSTOMER MASTER CENTRALLY (TRN. XD02) • SALES AREA DATA, then selecting the BILLING DOCUMENTS tab, and accessing the ACCT ASSGMT GROUP field in the ACCOUNTING DATA section. As you would expect, you can independently assign customer AAG to a customer account for each sales area.

Material AAG

A *material account assignment group* (AAG) is a two-character identifier that groups together materials for the purposes of GL account determination. For example, using a material account assignment group, you can differentiate revenue accounts for different product lines such as license revenue, maintenance revenue, consulting revenue, and so on.

Material AAG is also optional, but it is one of the most commonly used characteristic for sales GL account determination. You configure material AAG values using the configuration IMG • SALES AND DISTRIBUTION • BASIC FUNCTIONS • ACCOUNT ASSIGNMENT/

COSTING • REVENUE ACCOUNT DETERMINATION • CHECK MASTER DATA RELEVANT FOR ACCOUNT ASSIGNMENT • MATERIALS: ACCOUNT ASSIGNMENT GROUPS.

You assign material AAG to a material in the material master using CHANGE MATERIAL MASTER (TRN. MM02) • SALES: SALES ORGANIZATION DATA • GROUPING ITEMS SECTION • ACCT ASSIGNMENT GRP FIELD. As you would expect, you can independently assign material AAG for a material master for each sales area.

Now we are ready to discuss GL account determination. As you will see, you assign GL accounts to a combination of technical objects, business objects, and account keys. This approach allows you to specify a set of GL accounts (one for each account key) for each combination of characteristics. Let's discuss GL account determination in SD.

8.1.4 Sales-Relevant Accounts

You carry out configuration of revenue and other relevant accounts in the pricing procedure using IMG • SALES AND DISTRIBUTION • BASIC FUNCTIONS • ACCOUNT ASSIGNMENT/COSTING • REVENUE ACCOUNT DETERMINATION • ASSIGN G/L ACCOUNTS.

The first screen you will encounter when you start this configuration transaction contains a list of condition tables. This list of condition tables is derived from the access sequence configuration that we discussed in Section 8.1.2. Using different condition tables, you can first choose the combination of characteristics for which you want to maintain GL account determination.

Figure 8.5 shows a sample configuration of a sales revenue accounts. This configuration is based on a condition table that consists of characteristics customer AAG, material AAG and account key. Note that all other characteristics shown in this figure are fixed characteristics such as application, condition type, chart of accounts, and so on.

	App	CndTy.	ChAc	SOrg.	AAG	AAG	ActKy	G/L account
	V	KOFI	0010	BP01	01	01	ERL	410000
	V	KOFI	0010	BP01	01	02	ERL	410010
	V	KOFI	0010	BP01	01	03	ERL	410020

Cust.Grp/MaterialGrp/AcctKey

Figure 8.5 Sales Account Determination

The figure shows an example of account key ERL, which corresponds to sales revenue. Per this configuration, for all other characteristic values being same, the system will post to different revenue GL accounts for different material AAG values.

> **Note**
>
> Account determination figures used in this chapter are only for illustrative purpose to indicate GL account maintenance. The actual characteristic entries (key fields of the table) in your system may appear different, depending on the actual condition table that is selected for maintenance.

Let's put it all together now in the following list.

▸ When a sales transaction (e.g., a sales order, a service order or a return) is processed, the system first determines the applicable pricing procedure (Section 8.1.1).

▸ A pricing procedure consists of condition types (Section 8.1.1) that are assigned one or more account keys (Section 8.1.2).

▸ The pricing procedure uses the access sequence (Section 8.1.1) assigned to the condition types to calculate the resulting condition value using other quantities, values, and characteristics derived or calculated in the pricing procedure.

▸ At the time of billing, SAP ERP determines the account determination procedure associated with the billing type (Section 8.1.2).

▸ The account determination procedure uses condition type and access sequences to determine the condition table to use for GL account determination.

▸ The account determination procedure uses other characteristic values and the account keys to derive the GL accounts to which a condition value should be posted.

Now the significance of account keys may become clearer. For instance, in standard configuration (account keys and condition types), you assign the sales revenue accounts to account key ERL, the freight revenue accounts to account key ERF, the sales rebate accounts to account key ERB, and so on. For the purposes of sales revenue and relevant accounts, you enter the appropriate GL account in the first of the two columns in the GL account determination transaction.

Another common business process in SD is the revenue recognition process.

8.1.5   Revenue Recognition Accounts

Depending on statutory requirements, not all revenue from all types of sales trans-actions can be immediately recognized, meaning recognizing the entire revenue in the income statement for the period in which it occurred.

Let's take an example of a customer who prepays for a one-year warranty contract. In this scenario, you are required by law to distribute and recognize the revenue from that contract over a 12-month period. In accounting, this is reflected by first posting the total contract revenue to a deferred revenue account and subsequently posting a proportional amount every month from the deferred revenue account to a revenue account. Using deferred revenue is fairly common in other business transactions as well where typically revenue corresponds to a product or a service that will be delivered over an extended period of time. SAP ERP provides the neces-sary functionality that can considerably automate revenue recognition calculation and posting. The relevant configuration for the revenue recognition process is done via the menu path IMG • SALES AND DISTRIBUTION • BASIC FUNCTIONS • ACCOUNT ASSIGNMENT/COSTING • REVENUE RECOGNITION • MAINTAIN ACCOUNT DETERMINA-TION • ASSIGN G/L ACCOUNTS FOR REVENUES AND DEFERRED REVENUES.

> **Note**
>
> The concepts and interrelation of pricing configuration, technical objects, and busi-ness objects is the same for the revenue recognition process as it was for the revenue accounts process.

Figure 8.6 shows the configuration for revenue recognition account determination. The balance sheet account to which the total revenue from sales is posted initially is configured in the first white column as the deferred revenue account (01).

A	CndT	ChAc	SOrg.	ActKy	G/L Account No.		G/L Account No.	
V	KOFI	0010	3000	ERF				
V	KOFI	0010	3000	ERL				
V	KOFI	0010	3000	ERS				
V	KOFI	0010	3000	ERU	192701	(01)	883000	(02)
V	KOFI	0010	3000	EVV				

Figure 8.6   Revenue Recognition Accounts

The sales revenue account to which the recognized revenue is posted every month or periodically is configured in the second white column as the revenue account

(02). You may notice that the revenue account configured in this step is the same as the revenue account that you would have configured in Section 8.1.4 if there was no additional revenue recognition requirement.

Unbilled Receivables Account

Depending on the industry and/or statutory rules, your business may have to recognize the revenue before it is invoiced to the customer. This can be the case especially in large projects or if the product delivery is going to take a long time, for example, manufacture and delivery of an aircraft or a ship. This revenue is posted to the unbilled receivables account (NonBldRec.) (03).

You configure this account using IMG • Sales and Distribution • Basic Functions • Account Assignment/Costing • Revenue Recognition • Maintain Account Determination • Assign Account for Unbilled Receivables. Figure 8.7 shows the configuration of this GL account.

App	ChAc	Recon.acct	NonBldRec.
V	0010	140001	140010 (03)

Figure 8.7 Unbilled Receivable Account

If you have implemented and are using the automatic revenue recognition functionality in SAP ERP, then you must configure all three revenue accounts as described. There is one caveat though—the revenue recognition requirements are so complex that SAP ERP's revenue recognition program cannot support them. In such cases, you should only configure the deferred revenue account (01). Subsequently, you must post manual journal entries to recognize periodic revenue by crediting the deferred revenue account and debiting the sales revenue account. It is usually recommended to maintain a different deferred revenue account for each type of deferred revenue.

8.1.6 Accrual Accounts

Sales accrual forms a considerable part of GL account configuration in sales transactions because it provides an easier way to automate many accruals that have to be done based on sales transactions. Obviously, if an accrual requires a certain percentage of total sales value in a month, it may not be necessary to automate it. However, you may want to configure and automate any accruals that you can calculate based on another pricing element. This ensures that automatic accrual entries are posted at the same time revenue and other sales accounts are posted.

However, for SAP ERP to post accrual entries as the part of a sales transaction, you have to mark the corresponding condition type as relevant for ACCRUALS (see Figure 8.8). If necessary, refer to Section 8.1.1 to get familiar with condition types and their use in sales pricing.

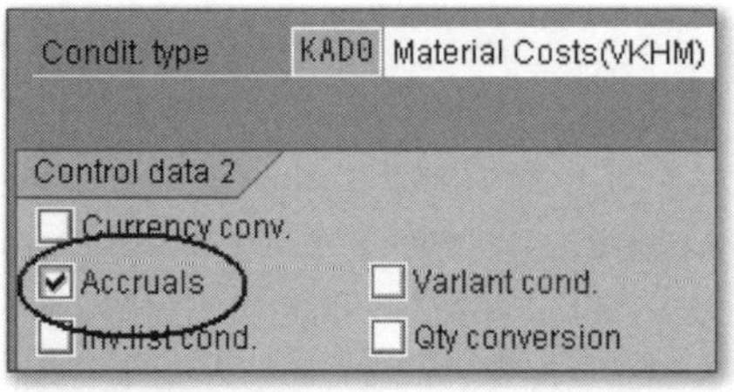

Figure 8.8 Accrual-Relevant Condition Type

For example, if sales agents are paid fixed commissions based on sales bookings, this commission liability can be accrued at the same time that other accounting entries are posted. Similarly, you can also post freight accruals or accruals for other charges by using condition types that are relevant for accruals.

Accrual accounts are maintained in the same transaction as the one used for the sales account determination discussed in Section 8.1.4. However, for the purposes of configuring accrual GL accounts, you use different condition types (that are marked for accrual relevant) and different account keys than the ones associated with sales accounts.

Figure 8.9 shows the configuration of accrual accounts. The balance sheet account to which accrued income or expense is posted is configured in the first white column as accrual accounts (01). The corresponding income or expense account (02) is configured in the second white column.

A	CndT	ChAc	SOrg	Actk	G/L Account No	G/L Account No.
V	KOFI	0010	3000	ERB		
V	KOFI	0010	3000	ERF		
V	KOFI	0010	3000	ERL	175000 (01)	800000 (02)
V	KOFI	0010	3000	ERS		
V	KOFI	0010	3000	FRU		

Figure 8.9 Accrual Accounts

8.1.7 Reconciliation Accounts

You assign a reconciliation GL account in the customer master so that all transactions posted to the Accounts Receivable (AR) subledger are automatically recorded in that GL level posting. If necessary, please review Chapter 3 for details on customer reconciliation accounts.

The reconciliation account from the customer master is used by default for all customer transactions. However, you may want to use a different reconciliation account than the one specified in the customer master. This may be the case, for example, if you are processing a special type of business transaction that needs to bypass credit limit checks. You can configure an alternate reconciliation account based on the sales document type and then configure the alternate reconciliation account as not relevant for credit checking and monitoring. Reconciliation account determination is carried out under the menu path IMG • SALES AND DISTRIBUTION • BASIC FUNCTIONS • ACCOUNT ASSIGNMENT/COSTING • RECONCILIATION ACCOUNT DETERMINATION • ASSIGN G/L ACCOUNTS.

Reconciliation account determination configuration comes with its own set of condition types and account determination objects predefined in the system. However, the concept of GL account determination remains the same.

For reconciliation account determination, the value of an application object is always VB, and the condition type provided in the standard system is KOAB. Figure 8.10 shows sample reconciliation account determination configurations. The reconciliation account is configured in the first of the two columns titled G/L ACCOUNT NO. in the corresponding transaction.

General				
App	CndTy.	ChAc	SOrg.	G/L Account No.
VB	KOAB	0010	1000	(Recon Acct)

Figure 8.10 Reconciliation Account Determination

This brings to a close our relatively long discussion about GL account determination in sales transactions. However, if you have gone through and understood this section, then the discussion about the GL account determination in purchasing transactions will be very easy.

8.2 Purchasing (Procure-to-Pay)

As discussed at the beginning of this chapter, purchasing account determination also uses the condition technique. Please refer to Figure 8.1, as it will be referenced in this discussion as well. Because we have discussed GL account determination in so much detail, in this section, we will only discuss information that is relevant and specific for purchasing transactions and configuration.

You should also read Section 8.1 even if you are only interested in GL account determination for purchasing transactions. However, the information is presented here in the same structure, so that you can easily relate the concepts in purchasing account determination to those in sales account determination.

8.2.1 Pricing Configuration

In SAP ERP, purchasing pricing is carried out using a business object called a calculation schema.

Calculation Schema

A *calculation schema* corresponds to the calculation procedure shown in Figure 8.1. A calculation schema is a framework of steps used to calculate different pricing elements in a purchasing calculation. You carry out the configuration of a calculation schema using the menu path IMG • MATERIALS MANAGEMENT • PURCHASING • CONDITIONS • DEFINE PRICE DETERMINATION PROCESS • DEFINE CALCULATION SCHEMA. Figure 8.11 shows the configuration area where you can configure a calculation schema and its components.

For the Purchasing functionality, you specify calculation schema determination for three types of business scenarios. Following are these three business scenarios and other characteristics available in the standard system that you can use to assign calculation schema:

▶ **Regular purchase orders (POs)**
You assign a calculation schema for a combination of a schema group for the purchasing organization and a schema group for the vendors.

- ▶ **Stock transport orders (STOs)**
  You assign calculation schema for a combination of a schema group for the purchasing organization, the document type, and the supplying plant in a STO.

- ▶ **Determination of market price**
  You assign calculation schema directly to each purchasing organization.

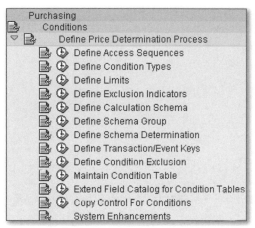

Figure 8.11 Purchase Account Determination

These configuration activities differ in terms of the objects that are available for the calculation schema determination. However, for the purposes of GL account determination, our discussion will be applicable for all three business scenarios. A calculation schema consists of one or more condition types.

Condition Types

A condition type in purchasing is similar to the condition types defined in sales. They represent different pricing elements that are either part of the vendor invoice or something that you need to calculate and report internally in your company. Prices, freight, taxes, surcharges, and similar pricing elements in procure-to-pay transactions are configured using condition types. You configure condition types for purchasing using the configuration activity IMG • MATERIALS MANAGEMENT • PURCHASING • CONDITIONS • DEFINE PRICE DETERMINATION PROCESS • DEFINE CONDITION TYPES.

SAP ERP provides close to a hundred condition types for purchasing calculation schema. Figure 8.12 shows some of these standard condition types.

CTyp	Condition type	Condition class
A001	Rebate	Expense reimbursement
A002	Material Rebate	Expense reimbursement
CUFR	Freight qty customs	Discount or surcharge
CUIN	Insurance customs	Discount or surcharge
MP01	Market Price	Prices
MWAS	Output tax manually	Taxes
MWST	Input tax	Taxes
NETP	Net Price Picking	Prices
P000	Gross Price	Prices
VKP0	Sales Price inc. Tax	Prices
VKP1	Sales Price excl.Tax	Prices
VS00	Tax trigger	Tax Classification

Figure 8.12 Purchasing Condition Types

To each condition type, you assign an access sequence.

Access Sequences

As we've discussed, an access sequence provides SAP ERP with a search strategy that the system can use to search for valid condition records for a condition type. You configure access sequences for purchasing condition types using the configuration activity IMG • MATERIALS MANAGEMENT • PURCHASING • CONDITIONS • DEFINE PRICE DETERMINATION PROCESS • DEFINE ACCESS SEQUENCES.

For example, based on material, plant, source, and destination information, you can use a tax classification access sequence to determine the taxability of a material being purchased. For another example, you can use the material information record and vendor information to determine any applicable promotional conditions for a purchasing transaction.

Now let's discuss technical objects involved in purchasing GL account determination.

8.2.2 Technical Objects

Similar to the discussion of technical objects in sales account determination, these technical objects are typically configured in SAP ERP, instead of being assigned to a vendor master, material master, or any other business data.

Application

An application in SAP ERP represents a group of conditions that are used in a particular application area or a particular SAP ERP system component. These values are delivered by SAP ERP. The configuration activity you are carrying out will determine which one of the application values is available.

For the GL account determination in the Purchasing functionality, this value is always M. An application is a required characteristic in sales GL account determination.

Field Catalog

A field catalog provides a list of valid fields that you can use as characteristics to carry out GL account determination. In most cases, fields available in the field catalog of a respective application are sufficient for carrying out GL account determination. However, if necessary, you can add additional fields to the field catalog.

This configuration activity for Purchasing is done via the menu path IMG • MATE-RIALS MANAGEMENT • PURCHASING • CONDITIONS • DEFINE PRICE DETERMINATION PROCESS • DEFINE ACCESS SEQUENCES. This configuration activity lets you add more fields to the field catalog from structures KOMG and KOMP.

Account Keys

An account key provides the same functionality as in the sales transactions. You use account keys in purchasing GL account determination for different types of GL accounts such as freight clearing, input tax, consignment payables, purchasing account, and so on.

ActKy	Name
B01	Rebates
B02	Volume rebate income
DEL	Del credere
EIN	Purchasing account
FR1	Freight clearing
FR3	Customs clearing
RUE	Prov. misc.del.costs
VST	Purchase input tax

Figure 8.13 Purchasing Account Keys

Figure 8.13 shows you some of the standard account keys available in purchase account determination. These account keys are maintained using the configuration item IMG • Materials Management • Purchasing • Conditions • Define Price Determination Process • Define Transaction/Event Keys • Trans/Event key. You have to assign at least one account key to a condition type if you want it to post to a GL account.

8.2.3   Business Objects

In this section, we will discuss business objects that are relevant for GL account determination in purchasing.

Purchasing Organization

A *purchasing organization* is an organizational unit that is responsible for the procurement of products and services. It is one of the most basic configurations you carry out while implementing an SAP ERP system. You configure a purchasing organization under IMG • Enterprise Structure • Definition • Materials Management • Maintain Purchasing Organization. You assign a purchasing organization to a company code under IMG • Enterprise Structure • Assignment • Materials Management • Assign Purchasing Organization To Company Code.

Plant

A *plant* is an organizational unit that typically refers to a facility that manufactures or stores an inventory of products. This is also one of the most basic configurations you carry out while implementing an SAP ERP system. You configure a plant under IMG • Enterprise Structure • Definition • Logistics – General • Define, Copy, Delete, Check Plant. You assign a plant to a company code under IMG • Enterprise Structure • Assignment • Logistics – General • Assign Plant to Company Code.

Chart of Accounts

In Chapter 1, we discussed the chart of accounts in great detail. Refer to Chapter 1 if you need to get familiar with this concept. A chart of accounts is a required characteristic in sales GL account determination. For the purposes of GL account determination in purchasing, this chart of accounts refers to the chart of accounts assigned to the company code to which the purchasing organization is assigned.

Account Assignment Category

The purchase account determination also utilizes the account assignment category. This one-character code determines what, if any, additional account assignment objects, such as cost center, asset, and so on, are required at the time of the PO entry. SAP ERP provides several account assignment categories to use for an asset (A), a sales order (C), a cost center (J), a network (N), a make-to-order project (Q), a WBS (work breakdown structure) element (W), and so on.

You perform the configuration of the account assignment category via the menu path IMG • MATERIALS MANAGEMENT • PURCHASING • ACCOUNT ASSIGNMENT • MAINTAIN ACCOUNT ASSIGNMENT CATEGORIES.

As shown in Figure 8.14, account assignment categories can be assigned an accounting key (ACCT MODIFICATION), which in turn is used for automatic GL account determination. The system configuration determines the combinations allowed for the PO item and account assignment categories.

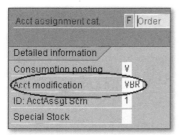

Figure 8.14 Account Assignment Categories

The next section discusses how these account assignment objects work together for purchase account determination.

8.2.4 GL Account Determination

In Purchasing and Materials Management transactions, GL account determination is dependent on many factors. Although the purchase account determination system uses the condition technique to determine the account key, assignment of GL accounts to the account key is not direct and straightforward.

For example, consider a simple transaction such as an invoice payment for a goods receipt. Where you post delivery-related unplanned cost depends on how you are valuating that particular material. If you are valuating the material using a standard price, then you post unplanned expenses to a variance account.

However, if you are valuating that material using a moving average price (MAP), then you should post the variance to an inventory account. Whether you can post the variance to an inventory account depends on whether you have enough stock in your inventory, among other factors. If you do not have enough stock, then the next question that needs to be answered is whether negative stock of that particular material is allowed in the system.

Therefore, as you can see, GL account assignment for transactions that may impact inventory cost requires a complex and detailed framework for GL account determination. Chapter 9 describes this type of GL account determination in detail. You will notice that Chapter 9 refers to the many account keys that were mentioned in this chapter.

8.3 Summary

Sales account determination primarily involves identifying the account keys associated with the condition types in the sales pricing procedures. After the account keys and their usage (revenue, differed revenue, accruals, expenses, etc.) are determined, assignment of the corresponding GL account is relatively easy.

Another piece in the sales account determination puzzle is identifying the condition table in which this GL account assignment should be done. You will need to follow the sequence of the condition tables in the configuration to determine the combination of characteristics (key fields in condition tables), and therefore the condition table in which account key and GL account assignment should be carried out.

For Purchasing and MM transactions, the derivation of the account key uses the condition technique. However, the available fields for GL account assignment and rule modifiers for each key can make GL account determination detailed and complex. For more information on this, see Chapter 9.

8.4 Reference

This section provides you with a technical reference so that you can dig deeper into the sales and purchasing topics discussed in this chapter.

8.4.1 Configuration Transactions

Table 8.1 provides a list of the configuration transactions for the account determination objects that were discussed in this chapter.

Transaction Code	Description
Sales and revenue accounts	
OV25	Maintain field catalog
V/09	Maintain condition types
V/13	Maintain condition tables
V/11	Maintain determination procedure
VKOA	Assign GL accounts
V/10	Maintain access sequences
OVUR	Unbilled receivables accounts
Purchasing accounts	
M/06	Maintain condition types
M/04	Maintain condition tables
OMFO	PO schema determination
OMFZ	STO schema determination
OMFR	Market price schema determination
M/07	Define access sequences
Reconciliation accounts	
OV60	Maintain field catalog
OV66	Maintain condition types
OV62	Maintain condition tables
OV65	Maintain determination procedure

Table 8.1 Configuration Transactions

8.4.2 Tables and Structures

Table 8.2 contains a list of the tables and structures used to store the relevant data for GL account determination as discussed in this chapter.

Table/Structure	Description
KOMCV	Allowed fields for account determination
KOMKCV	Account determination communication header
KOMPCV	Account determination communication item
MV12A	Condition generator—I/O fields
T024E	Market price calculation schema
T681A	Applications
T681F	Allowable fields per usage and application
T682	Access sequence per usage and application
T683	Pricing procedure per usage and application
T685	Condition types per usage and application
T687	Account keys per application
TMKS	PO calculation schema
TMKSU	STO calculation schema
TVRRUR	Unbilled receivables accounts

Table 8.2 Tables and Structures

Additional fields can be added to the field catalog from KOMCV, KOMKCV, and KOMPCV, which contain the fields allowed for GL account determination.

9　Inventory Transactions

This chapter covers GL account determination for inventory transactions in SAP ERP. Inventory Management (IM) is tightly integrated with other functionalities in SAP ERP, so the origin of these transactions can be in Sales and Distribution (SD), Service Management (SM), Purchasing, Production, Quality Management (QM), or any other such functionality of SAP ERP.

Before we get into the details of GL account determination in inventory transactions, let's examine some of the business-relevant factors and decisions that influence the GL account determination process. Let's begin with material valuation.

9.1　Material Valuation

You create the material master in SAP ERP for all services and products that you purchase, sell, trade, or manufacture. Depending on the material type, materials can be valuated or non-valuated. Valuated materials have monetary value assigned to their stock, whereas stock of non-valuated materials is not or cannot be assigned any monetary value. For example, inventory of raw materials (ROH) or finished goods (FERT) are almost always valuated. On the other hand, materials that are created to represent services (DIEN) are maintained as non-valuated because you can't store inventory of these types of material master. There are several points to consider with respect to material valuation.

The first point is that SAP ERP supports several combinations of configuring materials as valuated or non-valuated. The VALUE UPDATING setting in the material type configuration (see Figure 9.1) transaction controls whether materials of that material type are valuated or non-valuated. You configure material types using the menu path IMG • LOGISTICS – GENERAL • MATERIAL MASTER • BASIC SETTINGS • MATERIAL TYPES • DEFINE ATTRIBUTES OF MATERIAL TYPES.

In addition to this high-level setting that is applicable in all valuation areas, you can also choose to maintain this setting for individual valuation areas. We will further discuss valuation areas later in this chapter, but suffice it to say that the valuation area in SAP ERP represents the organizational unit at which you carry out inventory valuation. Most commonly, each plant represents a valuation area.

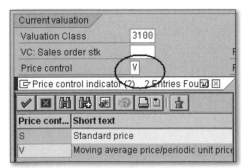

Figure 9.1 Valuation of Materials

Another constellation to consider is when material stock is earmarked for a specific sales order or a specific project in SAP ERP. For example, stocks earmarked in make-to-order or engineer-to-order scenarios represent this constellation of material valuation. In these cases, you can choose to maintain that stock as either valuated or non-valuated. In both scenarios, however, valuated stock will provide more visibility into the actual costs and values associated with the order (e.g., in the make-to-order scenario) or the project (e.g., in the engineer-to-order scenario).

9.1.1   How Materials Are Valuated

The next point to consider with respect to material valuation in SAP ERP is at what price the materials are valuated. In the material master, you can choose the price control of a material as a STANDARD PRICE or MOVING AVERAGE PRICE/PERIODIC UNIT PRICE (see Figure 9.2). You specify this control in the material master (Transaction MM02) by choosing ORGANIZATIONAL LEVEL (PLANT), selecting the COSTING 2 tab, and using the PRICE CONTROL field in the VALUATION DATA section.

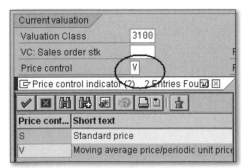

Figure 9.2 How Materials Are Valuated

In material type configuration, you specify default price control so that all materials of that material type are valuated using the same price control. However, you can also set an indicator in the material type configuration that controls whether individual materials for that material type can use a different price control than the one specified in the material type.

Let's briefly discuss the differences between valuating inventory stock using the standard price versus the moving average price (MAP). If inventory stock is valuated using a standard price, it uses a constant price maintained in the material master to valuate all goods movements for that material. Periodically, usually at least once a year, you release a new standard cost estimate that updates the standard cost for all materials in their respective material master records. All price variances are posted to price difference accounts. This may be the case, for example, if a material was procured at a different price than the standard price specified in the material master.

If inventory stock is valuated using a moving average price (MAP), then its MAP is updated based on the actual value of each goods receipt. Thus MAP keeps changing throughout the year depending on the variances in price of the material due to goods movements and available stock in the inventory (stock coverage). If there is not enough stock in the inventory, then variances in proportion to the available stock are posted to the material, therefore modifying the MAP, and remaining variances are posted to price difference accounts.

Another variation to consider is whether GL accounts need to have any controlling object assignments.

9.1.2 Controlling Object Assignments

If a GL account being posted is also set up as a cost element, then the posting transaction also makes posting to additional controlling objects. Examples of these controlling objects are cost center, internal order, project, cost object, and so on. Which controlling objects are available and posted depends on which controlling components are active and being used in SAP ERP. For example, cost center posting requires that Cost Center Accounting (CCA) is active, internal order posting requires that Internal Order Accounting (IOA) is active, and posting to a project or WBS element requires that Project Systems (PS) in is active.

SAP ERP uses different transaction keys to determine the necessary GL accounts depending on whether a business transaction has or can have Controlling (CO) account assignments.

For instance, for goods receipt from a production order, SAP ERP uses a transaction key to determine the GL accounts that may not have CO account assignment. However, when the same production order is settled, SAP ERP uses a transaction key to determine the GL accounts that may have CO account assignment.

The next section discusses account determination objects that are relevant for GL account determination in inventory transactions.

9.2 Account Determination Objects

In general, you should differentiate inventory GL accounts by at least the following three components:

▸ Stock type

▸ Geographical/manufacturing unit

▸ Transaction type

Now, let's take a closer look at these components and how they are used in GL account determination for inventory transactions in SAP ERP.

9.2.1 Stock Type

Except in rare situations, you want to separate the GL postings of different stock types to different GL accounts. For example, you don't want stock transactions for finished goods to post to the same GL accounts that are used for posting transactions for raw materials. SAP ERP provides the material type classification to help you group different types of materials. Every material created in SAP ERP is assigned a specific material type. You configure material types using IMG • LOGISTICS – GENERAL • MATERIAL MASTER • BASIC SETTINGS • MATERIAL TYPES • DEFINE ATTRIBUTES OF MATERIAL TYPES. SAP ERP provides a number of predefined material types, some of which are shown in Figure 9.3. You can create additional material types if necessary. Material types are used indirectly in GL account determination via other account determination objects that are assigned to it.

DIEN	Service
ERSA	Spare Parts
FERT	Finished Product
FGTR	Beverages
FHMI	Production Resource/Tool
FOOD	Foods (excl. perishables)
FRIP	Perishables
HALB	Semifinished Product
HAWA	Trading goods
HERS	Manufacturer Part
HIBE	Operating supplies

Figure 9.3 Material Types

9.2.2 Geographical/Manufacturing Unit

You may also want to differentiate GL accounts by geography or by the manufacturing unit in which the inventory transactions take place. Using the valuation area (the configuration menu item refers to this as the *valuation level*); you can differentiate between different geographical/manufacturing units. You can specify the valuation area at the company code level or the plant level.

> **Note**
>
> The setting for the valuation level (see Figure 9.4) is valid for an entire SAP ERP client, and once set, it cannot be changed without considerable time, effort, and (possibly) consulting expense. It is highly recommended that you set the valuation area at the plant level, even if you currently have only one company code and only one plant assigned to it.

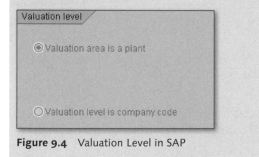

Figure 9.4 Valuation Level in SAP

The valuation area is directly used in GL account determination for inventory transactions. You specify whether your valuation level is a plant or a company code via the menu path IMG • ENTERPRISE STRUCTURE • DEFINITION • LOGISTICS – GENERAL • DEFINE VALUATION LEVEL.

9.2.3 Transaction Type

Movement types can help you in differentiating (among other things) between the type of business transactions and the type of inventories involved in the business transactions. Movement types are not directly used in GL account determination, but their attributes (in particular, account grouping) determine GL accounts that are posted. You configure movement types via the menu path IMG • MATERIALS MANAGEMENT • INVENTORY MANAGEMENT AND PHYSICAL INVENTORY • MOVEMENT TYPES • COPY, CHANGE MOVEMENT TYPES.

SAP ERP provides hundreds of movement types in the standard system. These movement types are set up with requisite configuration and links to other SAP ERP modules and components. However, if necessary, you can create additional movement types. Following is a sample list of the movement types available. This list may give you an idea of the granularity of business transactions for which different movement types are configured in SAP ERP.

- ▶ **101:** Goods receipt
- ▶ **103:** Goods receipt into blocked stock
- ▶ **105:** Goods receipt from blocked stock
- ▶ **201:** Goods issue for cost center
- ▶ **221:** Goods issue for project
- ▶ **231:** Goods issue for sales order
- ▶ **241:** Goods issue for asset

The setup and configuration of movement types is quite involved. Figure 9.5 gives you a glimpse of the various areas for which configuration settings are maintained.

All inventory related transactions in SAP ERP have associated movement types. This movement type may be manually entered, or it may be automatically derived by the SAP ERP transaction that you are using to post the corresponding business transaction.

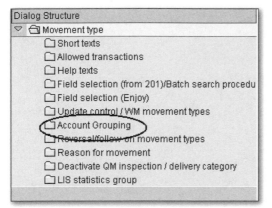

Figure 9.5 Movement Type Configuration

9.2.4 Additional Objects

It would seem that if you had these three criteria figured out—stock type, transaction type, and business unit—you could maintain GL account determination for inventory transactions (see Figure 9.6) for different combinations of these characteristics. If only things were so simple!

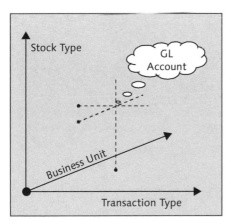

Figure 9.6 Account Determination Components

You can use additional higher-level objects in SAP ERP, which let you group together stock types, geographical/business units, and transaction types that serve the same or similar purposes. Similarly, you can use other lower-level objects to further differentiate stock types, transactions types, and business units This combination of main objects, higher-level objects, and lower-level objects gives rise to considerable flexibility as well as considerable complexity in GL account determination for inventory transactions.

Figure 9.7 shows the additional objects and their relationship with the basic objects we have already discussed.

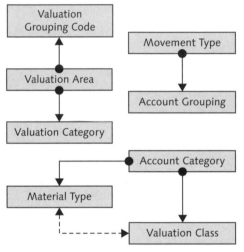

Figure 9.7 Account Determination Objects

Note

The availability and use of account grouping (lower-level object for movement types) and valuation category (lower-level object for valuation area) are conditional and are restricted by SAP ERP, so you have limited control over where and how you can use those objects.

Let's now briefly discuss these additional objects.

9.2.5 Objects for Valuation Areas

You can group multiple valuation areas into a *valuation grouping code*. As we discussed, a valuation area represents a company code or, more commonly, a plant. If you want to maintain the same GL account determination for multiple plants or company codes, you can first group them into a valuation grouping code and then assign all GL accounts to it. Without a valuation grouping code, you would have to assign all GL accounts separately for each valuation area. You assign valuation areas to valuation grouping code using IMG • Materials Management • Valuation and Account Assignment • Account Determination • Account Determination Without Wizard • Group Together Valuation Areas.

Similarly, you can use a *valuation category* to carry out GL account determination by origin of stock. This functionality is relevant if you have enabled split valuation. Split valuation allows you to valuate different stocks of the same material in the same plant differently. Take an example of a material that you typically produce in your plants but, if necessary, also procure it from external suppliers. A valuation category lets you specify the criteria according to which partial stocks are divided for the purpose valuation. You configure the split valuation and valuation category using menu path IMG • Materials Management • Valuation and Account Assignment • Split Valuation.

9.2.6 Objects for Material Types

As shown earlier in Figure 9.7, the Material Type and Valuation Class are linked in many-to-many relationships via the Account Category.

A *valuation class* lets you assign a material or a group of materials to a set of GL accounts. By separating GL account determination criteria from a material type, SAP ERP lets you assign different types of materials to the same valuation class, and similarly lets you carry out different GL account determinations for materials that belong to the same material type.

Similarly, an *account reference category* is a group of valuation classes. You can assign only one account reference category to a material type. This type of assignment allows multiple valuation classes to be used for materials with the same material type, and similarly materials belonging to different material types can use the same valuation class.

You define valuation class, account categories, and their interrelationship using the configuration transaction IMG • Materials Management • Valuation and Account Assignment • Account Determination • Account Determination Without Wizard • Define Valuation Classes.

9.2.7 Objects for Movement Types

A transaction key groups together multiple movement types depending on different types of inventory related business transactions. This definition, at least in theory, can be used to provide the same GL account determination for similar movement types (e.g., inventory increase or inventory decrease).

At the same time, you can further differentiate a transaction key, combined with the other characteristics mentioned earlier, into an *account grouping code*. Note, however, that account grouping codes are not available for all of the transaction keys; and even if account grouping codes are available, their usage or values may be restricted by SAP ERP.

You define accounting grouping codes for movement types using configuration transaction IMG • MATERIALS MANAGEMENT • VALUATION AND ACCOUNT ASSIGN- MENT • ACCOUNT DETERMINATION • ACCOUNT DETERMINATION WITHOUT WIZARD • DEFINE ACCOUNT GROUPING FOR MOVEMENT TYPES. We will discuss the configuration of account grouping codes in detail in Section 9.4.6.

For configuration and debugging purposes, fortunately, as you will soon see, not all objects are used in every GL account determination for every inventory-related transaction posted in SAP ERP.

9.2.8 Transaction Keys

At the core, all of the inventory transactions use the transaction key technique for GL account determination. However, the total number of transaction keys, account determination objects, and the possible combinations and variations of those account determination objects, makes GL account determination for inventory transactions relatively complex. SAP ERP also provides an account determination configuration wizard that you can use to carry out the configuration and simulation of account determination.

GL account configuration for inventory transactions is done through Transaction OBYC or via the menu path IMG • MATERIALS MANAGEMENT • VALUATION AND ACCOUNT ASSIGNMENT • ACCOUNT DETERMINATION • ACCOUNT DETERMINATION WITHOUT WIZARD • CONFIGURE AUTOMATIC POSTINGS • ACCOUNT ASSIGNMENT. All of the transaction keys share the same transaction group (RMK).

Figure 9.8 and Figure 9.9 show some of the available transaction keys when you start this configuration transaction.

Procedures	
Description	Transaction
Rev.from agency bus.	AG1
Sales fr.agency bus.	AG2
Exp.from agency bus.	AG3
Expense/revenue from consign.mat.consum.	AKO
Expense/revenue from stock transfer	AUM
Subsequent settlement of provisions	BO1
Subsequent settlement of revenues	BO2
Provision differences	BO3
Inventory posting	BSD
Change in stock account	BSV
Inventory posting	BSX
Revaluation of other consumables	COC
Del credere	DEL
Materials management small differences	DIF
Purchase account	EIN
Purchase offsetting account	EKG
Freight clearing	FR1
Freight provisions	FR2
Customs clearing	FR3
Customs provisions	FR4
Purchasing freight account	FRE

Figure 9.8 RMK Transaction Keys (1)

Procedures	
Description	Transaction
Offsetting entry for inventory posting	GBB
Account-assigned purchase order	KBS
MM Exchange Rate Differences	KDG
Materials management exch.rate diffs	KDM
MM exchange rate rounding differences	KDR
Material ledger frm low.levels E/R diff.	KDV
Consignment payables	KON
Price diff. offset. entry (cost object)	KTR
Accruals and defer.acct(material ledger)	LKW
Price Differences from W/Off WIP	PRA
Differences (AVR Price)	PRC
Cost (price) differences	PRD
Price Differences (Mat. Ledger, AVR)	PRG
Price differences (cost object hierarc.)	PRK
Price Diff. from WIP Written Off (Mat.)	PRM
Product cost collector price differences	PRP
Prod.cost coll.price diff. offsett.entry	PRQ
Material ledger fr.low.levels price dif.	PRV
Cost (price) differences (mater.ledger)	PRY
Expense/revenue from revaluation	RAP
Inv.reductions from log.inv.verification	RKA
Neutral provisions	RUE

Figure 9.9 RMK Transaction Keys (2)

Each transaction key has one or more account modifiers associated with it. At the end of this chapter, you will find a matrix of the transaction keys and corresponding account modifiers that are available in the standard SAP ERP system.

Note that the following explanation references a single GL account and multiple GL accounts interchangeably. This is because the number of GL accounts configured for a transaction key depends on the number of account modifiers used for a transaction key and their valid number of combinations. Also, any reference to invoice posting refers to an invoice posted against a purchase order in Logistics via Logistics Invoice Verification (LIV).

In the next section, we will discuss several transaction keys displayed in Figure 9.8 and Figure 9.9.

9.3 General Ledger Account Determination—Procurement

Inventory accounts, the goods receipt/invoice receipt (GR/IR) clearing account, and purchasing tax are some of the topics covered in this section.

9.3.1 Inventory Accounts (BSX)

These accounts represent the monetary value of stock owned by the company. These are the balance sheet inventory accounts. To determine these GL accounts, SAP ERP transactions use the BSX (inventory posting) transaction key. Figure 9.10 shows the GL account configuration for transaction key BSX.

Because this is the first transaction key we are discussing for inventory transactions, let's consider Figure 9.10 in some detail. First thing to note is that all of the GL accounts in Figure 9.10 are configured for the combination of chart of accounts INT and the transaction key BSX. For that specific combination, different GL accounts are configured for every valuation class for a valuation grouping code.

Now you may be able to appreciate how useful valuation grouping code can be. In this example, you can assign this valuation grouping code to all valuation areas (plants or company codes) in your system, and they all will use the same GL accounts that are specified here for their inventory transactions. If one company requires a different set of GL accounts for the BSX transaction key, you can simply assign it a different valuation grouping code and correspondingly maintain a different set of GL accounts in this configuration.

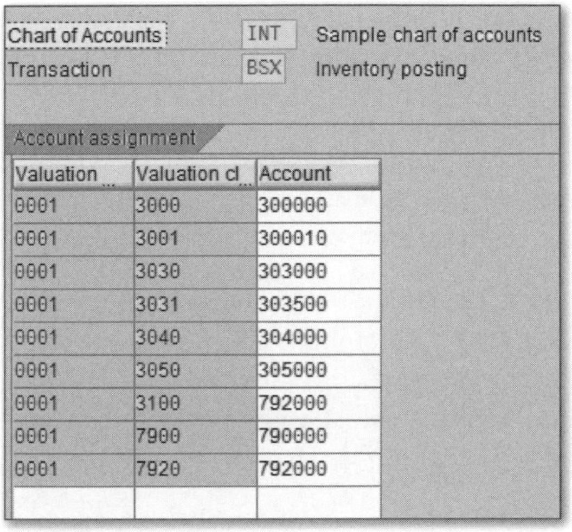

Chart of Accounts: INT Sample chart of accounts
Transaction: BSX Inventory posting

Account assignment

Valuation ...	Valuation cl...	Account
0001	3000	300000
0001	3001	300010
0001	3030	303000
0001	3031	303500
0001	3040	304000
0001	3050	305000
0001	3100	792000
0001	7900	790000
0001	7920	792000

Figure 9.10 Transaction Key BSX

As we've discussed before, valuation classes usually correspond to different material types presented in the inventory section of your balance sheet. So these valuation classes can represent raw materials, work in progress, finished goods, trading goods, and so on. Any increase/decrease in inventory stock due to GR/IR is reflected by a debit/credit posting to these accounts. For example, the loading opening inventory balance for materials will debit these GL accounts, and transactions for issuing raw materials to the production order will credit the GL account assigned to the valuation class maintained in the raw material master record.

All transaction keys discussed in this chapter follow similar configuration. The only difference is in what types of characteristics (account modifiers) are available in place of the valuation grouping code and the valuation class displayed in Figure 9.10. The matrix at the end of this chapter lists all account modifiers available for the different transaction keys relevant for inventory transactions.

9.3.2 GR/IR Clearing Account (WRX)

The WRX (GR/IR clearing account) transaction key is used for determining GR/IR clearing accounts. GL accounts defined for this transaction key act as a clearing account between goods receipts and invoice receipts in a regular procure-to-pay business process.

At the time of a goods receipt, the GL account maintained for this transaction key receives a credit posting, while the corresponding offsetting debit entry is posted to the inventory account determined via transaction key BSX.

Similarly, at the time of invoice receipt from a vendor, the GL account maintained for this transaction key receives a debit posting, while an offsetting credit entry is posted to the vendor's Accounts Payable (AP) account.

Analysis of this account at any given time can provide information about goods received but not invoiced and goods invoiced but not received. In particular, this account is used to make accrual entries at month-end. Typically, you maintain only one GL account, a balance sheet account, for each valuation grouping code. However, account modifiers available for this transaction key let you specify separate GL accounts at a very detailed level.

9.3.3   Purchasing Tax (VST)

The VST (purchase input tax) transaction key is used to determine GL accounts to post (input) tax from purchasing transactions. Usually, this tax is included on the invoice received from the vendor. The general modifier for this transaction key refers to the tax code, which in turn enables posting to different GL accounts for different purchasing tax codes. Of course, you need to weigh the efforts versus the benefits of using different GL accounts for different tax codes, especially considering that the standard SAP ERP system provides several reports that can give you transactional details by tax codes. Typically, it is sufficient to maintain just one GL account for each valuation grouping code.

For details about if and how the Purchasing functionality links to this transaction key (called an account key in Purchasing), see Chapter 4.

9.3.4   Planned and Unplanned Delivery Costs

Most procurement transactions involve paying freight and possibly even customs duty. If these costs on purchases can be planned or known ahead of time, these are entered as the planned costs on the purchase order.

Planned Costs (FR1, FR3)

The FR1 and FR3 transaction keys are used to determine GL accounts that act as clearing accounts for freight charges and customs duty, respectively. At the time of goods receipt, GL accounts maintained under the FR1 and FR3 transaction keys are posted (credited) with freight and customs duty, respectively. Subsequently, when you post corresponding invoices from vendors, these accounts are posted (debited) with clearing entries.

Typically, it is sufficient to configure one GL account for each valuation grouping code. This GL account is always a balance sheet account.

Provision for Planned Costs (FR2, FR4)

The FR2 (freight provisions) and FR4 (customs provisions) transaction keys are used as provision accounts for planned costs. For better liquidity management and cash flow planning, you can make a provision for planned delivery costs when the purchase order is placed.

If a condition type in pricing (see Chapter 8) is marked as provision-relevant, then provision entries for freight charges and customs duty are posted to the GL accounts maintained under FR2 and FR4, respectively. For this business purpose also, it is sufficient to maintain one GL account for each valuation grouping code.

Additional Costs (RUE)

In addition to the freight and customs duty charges just discussed, there may be additional types of delivery costs on a purchase order. You can create provision for other delivery costs using the RUE (neutral provisions) transaction key.

Of course, as is the case with provision accounts for freight and customs duty, the condition type associated with these delivery costs should also be marked as provision-relevant in the system configuration.

Unplanned Costs (UPF)

Even if delivery costs were planned, additional delivery costs may have incurred that were not originally planned. These unplanned delivery costs can be entered when you enter the invoice details in purchasing. The UPF (unplanned delivery costs) transaction key is used to determine GL accounts to which these unplanned delivery costs are posted. In this case also, typically maintaining one GL account for each valuation grouping code is sufficient.

You may have noticed that for most account keys mentioned in the planned and unplanned delivery costs section, it is common to maintain only one GL account for each valuation grouping code. This is the case even though account modifiers available for these transaction keys let you configure GL accounts at a fairly detailed level.

Now let's look at the GL accounts used for posting price variances.

9.3.5   Price Variance Accounts

There can be several reasons for price variances in procurement. For materials valuated at a standard price, price variances can occur because of, for example, goods receipt against a purchase order where the purchase order price is different from the standard price or because of an invoice receipt where the invoice price is different from the purchase order price and/or standard price.

For materials valuated at the MAP, if there is enough stock in inventory, any price variances are absorbed on the inventory stock, and the material's MAP is recalculated. However, if there is not enough stock in inventory, price variance postings may occur. These variances can also occur for materials that are produced in house.

The transaction key used for posting these entries is PRD (offsetting entry for inventory posting). This transaction key has the following account grouping codes that let you separate out GL accounts to which price variances are posted based on the type of business transaction: blank (GR and IR against purchase orders), PRF (GR against production orders and production order settlement), PRA (goods issues and other movement), and PRU (for transfer postings). Figure 9.11 shows a sample configuration of this transaction key with a couple of account grouping codes.

It is possible to configure different price variance GL accounts for each valuation class, that is, material type. However, in the sample configuration provided in the standard SAP ERP system, this transaction key is assigned only two GL accounts: one for debit price variances and another one for credit price variances.

Transaction		PRD	Cost (price) differences	
Account assignment				
Valuation	General m	Valuation cl	Account	
0001		3050	4402001	
0001		7900	4402001	
0001		7920	4402001	
0001		7925	4402001	
0001	PRA	3050	4402001	
0001	PRA	7900	4402001	
0001	PRA	7920	4402001	
0001	PRA	7925	4402001	
0001	PRF	3050	4705007	
0001	PRF	7900	4705007	
0001	PRF	7920	4705007	
0001	PRF	7925	4705007	

Figure 9.11 Transaction Key PRD

9.3.6 Other Differences in Logistics Invoice Verification

In the Logistics Invoice Verification (LIV) process, you may encounter other differences that you have to post to different GL accounts. Any differences between the invoice price and the purchase order price at the time of the LIV can be handled as explained in the subsections that follow.

Difference Write-Off (DIF)

If you choose to write off any small differences between debit and credit balances at the time of invoice posting, then you have to maintain tolerance limits. The concept of tolerance limits in these transactions is not very different from the tolerance limits defined for AR and AP transactions. As long as these differences are within the tolerance limits, SAP ERP posts them to GL accounts determined using transaction key DIF (MM small differences).

Invoice Reduction (RKA)

Invoice differences can be acceptable for small, infrequent variances. However, if invoices from a vendor are consistently overpriced, you can use the invoice-reduction functionality.

This functionality automatically reduces the payable amount and posts it to a clearing account. This clearing account is determined using transaction key RKA (invoice reductions from LIV).

Subsequently, postings in this clearing account can be used to generate vendor credit memo postings. This is also one of those transaction keys, for which specifying one GL account per valuation grouping code is sufficient.

In the next subsection, we will discuss GL account determination for foreign currency transactions.

9.3.7 Foreign Currency transactions

In today's interconnected world of global business, it isn't uncommon to have some or all of your procurement done from other countries. This gives rise to scenarios where there can be exchange rate differences during the different stages in the procure-to-pay cycle.

Exchange Rate Difference (KDM)

At the time of posting a goods receipt, the material price is compared with the corresponding invoice price (if the invoice is already received) or the corresponding purchase order price. Any differences in price that can be attributed to an exchange rate difference are posted to the GL accounts determined by using transaction key KDM (MM exchange rate difference).

Rounding Differences (KDR)

Any rounding differences due to exchange rate conversion and calculation are posted to GL accounts determined by using transaction key KDR (MM exchange rate rounding differences).

Let's continue with discussing GL account determination for other types of inventory transactions.

9.3.8 Differences in Stock Transfer (AUM)

If stock transfer occurs between two plants or materials that have different prices, the difference in price is posted using transaction key AUM (expense/revenue from stock transfer). Of course, this requires that the receiving material or the material in the receiving plant is maintained using a standard price control.

If the receiving material is valuated at the MAP, the difference is absorbed on the existing inventory of stock and is posted to corresponding inventory accounts.

9.3.9 Consignment Process

In this section, we will only focus on the consignment process as it relates to the procure-to-pay cycle. For the GL account determination for the consignment process in the order-to-cash cycle, you use condition techniques as discussed in Chapter 8.

Consignment processing involves a vendor providing and storing goods on your premises. However, you own the stock and pay for it only when you withdraw a necessary quantity from the consignment stock stored on your premises. The vendor regularly replenishes the consignment stock so that you always have sufficient stock available when you need it. This procurement process is also applicable for materials that are delivered via a pipeline (e.g., oil, water, etc.).

Consignment Payables (KON)

GL accounts maintained under this transaction key act as clearing accounts between two business transactions: withdrawal from consignment stock for your usage and settlement (i.e., invoicing) of consignment stock. Transaction key KON (consignment payables) is used for this GL account determination. These accounts act similarly to regular GR/IR accounts maintained under the transaction key WRX.

You use account grouping codes (general modifier) to specify different GL accounts for consignment materials and pipeline materials. To configure this scenario, you must maintain account grouping codes as blank and PIP, for regular materials and for pipeline materials, respectively.

Price Difference (AKO)

When the consignment stock is withdrawn, SAP ERP uses the price maintained in the corresponding purchasing info record. However, if consignment stock is valuated at a standard price, there may be price differences similar to price differences that arise in regular business transactions. Transaction key AKO (expense/revenue from consignment material consumption) is used to determine GL accounts to which such price differences are posted.

9.3.10 Subcontracting Process

Another variation of a procurement process is a subcontracting order. In a typical and rather simplistic subcontracting scenario, this is what occurs:

1. You provide component materials to a subcontracting vendor.

2. The subcontracting vendor performs the ordered services.

3. The vendor delivers the final product to you.

4. The vendor invoices you for the service.

Following are the different processes and corresponding GL account determination in the subcontracting process.

Consumption of Raw Materials (GBB)

The consumption of component materials is posted when the goods receipt of the final product from the subcontracting vendor is posted. This entry is posted as a credit to the component materials inventory accounts (determined via BSX) and as a debit to the goods consumption of component materials.

The following transaction key and account grouping combinations are used to determine the GL accounts to which a debit entry is posted for goods consumption:

▸ **Transaction key**
  GBB (offsetting entry for inventory posting).

▸ **Account grouping**
  VBO (goods consumption for subcontracting).

In Section 9.4.5, we will discuss transaction key GBB in considerable detail.

Goods Receipt of Final Product (BSX, BSV)

Goods receipt of the final product generates a debit posting to the corresponding inventory accounts (determined via BSX) and a credit posting to the change in stock account. Transaction key BSV (change in stock account) is used to determine the GL account to which a credit entry is posted for goods receipt of the final product.

Subcontracting Variances (FRL, FRN)

At the time of the goods receipt, the subcontracting vendor may report any variances in the component materials consumed. Any such variances, along with the offsetting entry for the services, are posted to the GL account determined using transaction key FRL (external activity).

Similarly, when a subcontracting vendor sends an invoice, there may be a variance in costs. These costs are posted to the GL account determined using transaction key FRN (incidental costs of external activities).

In the next section, we will discuss GL account determination for the volume rebate agreements.

9.3.11 Volume Rebate Arrangements (BO1—BO3)

Vendor rebate agreements refer to the vendor arrangements where you receive volume rebates based on the quantities purchased. Typically, these rebates are not part of regular vendor invoices. Instead, you settle these rebates only if your business with the vendor reaches a certain volume. These rebate agreements can be as simple as buying certain quantities of one material, or they can be complex agreements requiring certain quantities or monetary business for a predefined combination of product purchases.

It is possible to handle this entire process in SAP ERP by configuring rebate arrangements for the procure-to-pay cycle. You carry out the configuration for rebate agreements using the menu area IMG • MATERIALS MANAGEMENT • PURCHASING • SUBSEQUENT (END-OF-PERIOD REBATE) SETTLEMENT • AGREEMENTS.

You can post a provisional entry for accrued income for the rebate if you have marked the rebate arrangement pricing condition in the purchase order calculation schema as provision-relevant. The provision amount is posted to GL accounts determined using transaction key BO1 (subsequent settlement of provisions).

When you carry out the interim or final rebate settlement process, the revenue account posting is made to GL accounts that are determined using transaction key BO2 (subsequent settlement of revenues).

Lastly, there may be differences between the actual rebate income and the accrued rebate at the time of invoicing. Any such provision differences are posted to GL accounts determined using transaction key BO3 (provision differences).

In this section, we have discussed several transaction keys that relate to the procurement process and inventory transactions. In the next section, we will discuss revaluation and other types of inventory transactions.

9.4 General Ledger Account Determination—Revaluation and Other Accounts

This section discusses various transaction keys used to determine GL accounts for the revaluation processes. You may run inventory revaluation for a variety of reasons. Some examples of these requirements are you may run the revaluation process when material prices have changed in the material master and you want to revalue inventory transactions that are already posted; you may run revaluation process because you carry stock inventory in a country that has high inflation; and so on.

Let's look at some of these scenarios and the corresponding GL account determination.

9.4.1 Revaluation Revenue/Expense (UMB)

Consider a business scenario where you've updated the standard price of a material in the current period, and then you post a transaction to the previous period at the previous price. This type of business transaction can give rise to price differences (gain or loss) because of the difference in the previous price and the current price. For such scenarios, transaction key UMB (gain/loss from revaluation) is used to determine the GL accounts to post any gain or loss calculated due to this process,

9.4.2 Work in Process Revaluation

If Material Ledger is active in your SAP ERP system, you can choose to revalue your work in process (WIP) inventory. In such a scenario, you should make note of the following transaction keys.

If the WIP has already been reduced due to the delivery of products to a warehouse, the corresponding price variances are backed out. Next, variances corresponding to components and activities, as applicable, are posted to relevant accounts.

Transaction keys PRM (represents written off price differences from WIP: material) and PRA (represents written off price differences from WIP: activities) are used to determine the GL accounts to which the variance back-out is posted for components and activities are made.

Transaction keys WPM (WIP from price differences: material) and WPA (WIP from price differences: activities) help determine the GL accounts to which the total price differences for components and activities are posted.

9.4.3 Revaluation for Inflation

These transaction keys are relevant if there are any requirements for business or statutory purposes to revalue inventory due to inflation. The revaluation process uses the market price and/or inflation index maintained in SAP ERP.

The goods issue revaluation process compares the price in the goods issue with the newly calculated inflation-adjusted price to determine any differences. Transaction key WGI is used to determine the GL accounts to post inventory adjustments.

Stock transfers are handled differently when the goods issue revaluation process is run. In the receiving plant, the process calculates the price differences and posts inventory adjustments to the GL accounts determined using transaction key WGR (wrongly valued GR).

9.4.4 Cost Object Hierarchy Settlement

In product costing, you can use cost object hierarchies to collect actual costs that cannot be assigned directly to individual cost collectors or manufacturing orders.

There are two alternatives to process costs that are collected at the top node of a cost object hierarchy. You can distribute the collected costs to lower nodes in the hierarchy and subsequently settle the costs from lower nodes, or you can settle the costs directly from the top node in a cost object hierarchy. Regardless of whether you settle costs from a top-level node or a lower-level node of a cost object hierarchy, you have to configure GL accounts to settle these costs.

Transaction key PRK (price differences) provides the GL accounts to which costs from the highest node of the cost object hierarchy is settled.

Transaction key KTR (price differences offsetting entry) provides the GL accounts to post the offsetting entries to the settlement done to PRK.

Finally, let's look at one of the most important transaction keys in the GL account determination for inventory transactions: the transaction key used to determine GL accounts for offsetting entry for inventory postings.

9.4.5 Inventory Offsetting Accounts (GBB)

As you can imagine, there are many different business scenarios that post to inventory accounts that you would want to post to different GL accounts as well. For example, the initial upload of opening stock balances will debit the inventory accounts, and goods receipt from a production order will also debit the inventory accounts.

Obviously, in both cases, you would prefer to use different GL accounts to post offsetting entries. SAP ERP provides transaction key GBB (offsetting entry for inventory posting) where you can configure different GL accounts for offsetting entries in different business transactions.

This transaction key makes extensive use of account grouping codes to differentiate business transactions. Following is a list of the most commonly used account grouping codes and corresponding business scenarios; these account grouping codes determine offsetting accounts:

- **BSA**
  Used for posting initial opening stock balances.

- **AUF**
  Used for posting goods receipt from a production order, and for order settlement purposes if GL accounts for account grouping code AUA are not configured.

- **AUA**
  Used when a production order is settled to financial accounting.

- **VQP**
  Used when a sample goods issue to Quality Management (QM) is posted without account assignment.

- **VQY**
  Used when a sample goods issue to QM is posted with account assignment.

▶ **VBR**

Used when an internal goods issue (e.g., for a cost center) occurs, or as a consumption account in a collective order settlement in production.

▶ **VAX**

Used when a goods issue from a valuated sales order stock is made, that is, the sales order item does not carry costs and revenues.

▶ **VAY**

Used when a goods issue from a non-valuated sales order stock is made, that is, the sales order item carries costs and revenues.

▶ **VNG**

Used when inventory stock or material quantities are scrapped.

▶ **ZOB**

Used when a goods receipt without reference to a purchase order is posted, that is, when the SAP Purchasing functionality is not active or not used.

▶ **ZOF**

Used when a goods receipt without reference to a production order is posted, that is, when the SAP PP is not active or not used.

As mentioned earlier, you can create your own account grouping codes for this transaction key. In the next section, let's briefly discuss the configuration of new account grouping codes.

9.4.6 Account Grouping Codes

To define additional account grouping codes for the transaction key GBB, you use the configuration Transaction OMWN, which is available at IMG • MATERIALS MANAGEMENT • VALUATION AND ACCOUNT ASSIGNMENT • ACCOUNT DETERMINATION • ACCOUNT DETERMINATION WITHOUT WIZARD • DEFINE ACCOUNT GROUPING FOR MOVEMENT TYPES.

Figure 9.12 shows an example of account grouping code configuration. This transaction is used to specify additional account grouping codes for GL account determination. Table 9.1 describes different columns in this configuration screen.

MvT	S	Val.Up	Qty up	Mvt	Cns	Val.strng	Cn	TEKey	Acct modif	C
101		☑	☑	B	A	WE06	1	KBS		☑
101		☑	☑	B	A	WE06	3	KDM	ERA	☐
101		☑	☑	B	V	WE06	1	KBS		☑
101		☑	☑	B	V	WE06	3	KDM	ERA	☐
101		☑	☑	F		WF01	2	GBB	AUF	☑
101		☑	☑	F		WF01	3	PRD	PRF	☐
101	E	☑	☑	B		WE01	3	PRD		☐
101	E	☑	☑	B		WE01	4	KDM	ERN	☐
101	E	☑	☑	B	E	WE06	1	KBS		☑
101	E	☑	☑	B	E	WE06	3	KDM	ERA	☐
101	E	☑	☑	B	P	WE06	1	KBS		☑
101	E	☑	☑	B	P	WE06	3	KDM	ERA	☐
101	E	☑	☑	B	V	WE06	1	KBS		☑
101	E	☑	☑	B	V	WE06	2	WRX		☑
101	E	☑	☑	F		WF01	2	GBB	AUF	☑
101	E	☑	☑	F		WF01	3	PRD	PRF	☐
101	K	☑	☑	B	V	WE06	1	KBS		☑
101	K	☑	☑	B	V	WE06	2	WRX		☑

Figure 9.12 Configuring Account Grouping Codes

Configuration Column	Purpose and Usage
Movement type	This is a classification key that determines the type of material movements (movements types were discussed in Section 9.2.3).
Special stock indicator	This indicator lets you manage inventory of the same stock separately for different reasons.
	Examples of special stock indicators are customer stock, project stock, consignment stock for customer or for vendor, pipeline material, and so on.
Value update	This setting indicates that material is managed on a value basis (valuation was discussed in Section 9.1).
Quantity update	This setting indicates that material is managed on a quantity basis.
	We haven't discussed this business requirement in detail, but it is similar to managing stock by value basis, except in this case, it is the material quantity that is updated or not updated.

Table 9.1 Account Grouping Key Configuration Details

Configuration Column	Purpose and Usage
Movement indicator	This indicator signifies the type of document that constitutes the basis for this material movement.
	Examples of movement indicators are goods movement without reference, for purchase order, for production order, and so on.
Consumption posting indicator	This indicator specifies whether and where the goods movement makes the consumption posting.
	Examples of this indicator are posting to consumption account, an asset, a sales order, a project, or no consumption posting.
Posting string for value (value string)	A value string indicates the business event that characterizes the value determination for that business transaction.
	SAP ERP provides more than 100 value strings for different basic events. You can find these values in Table T156W.
Counter	This counter uniquely identifies the key values of this configuration transaction.
Transaction key	This is the transaction key we have been discussing all along in this chapter.
Account modifier	This is the field where you specify account modifier codes for the combination of key values in that configuration row.
Check account assignment	If this indicator is set, the system uses the account assignment specified on the item screen, if available.
	If the account assignment is not available on the item screen, or if this indicator is not set, the system uses automatic account determination as discussed in this chapter.

Table 9.1 Account Grouping Key Configuration Details (Cont.)

As is evident, the characteristics available for configuring account grouping codes let you configure GL account determination as detailed as necessary.

9.5   Summary

Inventory transactions and their GL account determination are extremely complex. The information discussed in this chapter covered some of the most basic business transactions.

For GL account determination, it is critical that you are aware of the transaction key or keys that SAP ERP uses for a business transaction. In some cases, this information is easily available, and there are a plethora of references. However, in other cases you will need to do considerable research or have the prerequisite experience to identify those transaction keys.

Account modifiers associated with transaction keys provide invaluable functionality to control GL account postings as per the business requirement. You can choose to make account determination as simple as possible (one account for one transaction key), or you can create an elaborate GL account assignment to assist in reporting.

The configuration of transaction key GBB provides you with very a powerful functionality. That is, you can create your own account grouping codes. Because account groupings and movement types are linked, you can really fine-tune GL account determination to your requirements.

Chapter 10 explains GL account determination for payroll transactions, a subject that is at least as complex as this one, if not more so.

9.6   Reference

This section provides a technical reference for the GL account determination for inventory transactions.

9.6.1   Configuration Transactions

Table 9.2 provides a list of the configuration transactions for the account determination objects discussed in this chapter.

Transaction Code	Description
OBYC	Maintain account determination

Table 9.2   Configuration Transactions

Transaction Code	Description
OMJJ	Customize movement types
OMS2	Maintain material type
OMSI	Define valuation class
OMSK	Maintain and assign account category reference to material type, valuation class
OMWD	Assign valuation area
OMWM	Maintain valuation grouping code
OX14	Maintain valuation level

Table 9.2 Configuration Transactions (Cont.)

9.6.2 Tables and Structures

Table 9.3 contains a list of the tables and structures used to store data relevant for the GL account determination discussed in this chapter.

Table/Structure	Description
BEWC	Split valuation configuration
ICURM	Valuation control
MBEW	Material valuation
T001K	Valuation area
T025	Valuation classes
T025K	Account category reference
T030	Standard accounts table
T030A	Assign transaction key to transaction group
T030R	Account determination rules
T030X	Transaction group
T156M	Quantity strings
T156SC	Quantity/value string determination—client-dependent

Table 9.3 Tables and Structures

Table/Structure	Description
T156SY	Quantity/value string determination—client-independent
T156W	Value strings
T156X	Account grouping code
T163K	Valuation grouping code

Table 9.3 Tables and Structures (Cont.)

9.6.3 Enhancements

Table 9.4 provides a list of the enhancements that can be used to influence GL account determination in inventory transactions that were discussed in this chapter.

Enhancement	Description
SRVESKN	Set account assignment in service line
SRVKNTTP	Setting account assignment category
LIFO0040	User interfaces for last in first out (LIFO) valuation
NIWE0000	Change quantities within scope of balance sheet valuation
NIWE0001	Lowest value determination based on market prices
NIWE0002	Lowest value determination by range of coverage/movement
NIWE0003	Loss-free valuation
MM08R002	User exit for tolerance checks
RMVKON00	For settling consignment liabilities
LMR1M001	User exits in LIV
LMR1M002	Account grouping for GR/IR account reconciliation

Table 9.4 Enhancements

9.6.4 Account Modifier Matrix

Figure 9.13 shows the available account modifiers for the transaction keys. An X indicates that an account modifier is available. A shaded box indicates that the selection is not modifiable.

T.Key	Acct Grp	Description	Dr/Cr	Val. Mod.	Val. Class	Gen Mod
AKO		Consignment price diff	X	X	X	X
AUM		Exp/Rev from Stk Trf	X	X	X	X
BO1		Vendor rbt - prov.settle.	X	X		
BO2		Vendor rbt - rev.settle.	X	X		
BO3		Vendor rbt - prov. diff	X	X		
BSD		B/S reval - inv posting	X	X	X	X
BSV		Change in stock acct	X	X	X	
BSX		Inventory posting	X	X	X	
DIF		MM small differences	X			
FR1		Freight clearing	X	X	X	
FR2		Freight provisions	X	X	X	
FR3		Customs clearing	X	X	X	
FR4		Customs provisions	X	X	X	
FRL		External activity	X	X	X	
FRN		Incidental costs	X	X	X	
GBB	AUA	Prod order settlement	X	X	X	X
GBB	AUF	Prod order GR	X	X	X	X
GBB	BSA	Initial/ opening stock	X	X	X	X
GBB	VAX	GI to sales-not cost elem	X	X	X	X
GBB	VAY	GI to sales-cost elem	X	X	X	X
GBB	VBO	Stk consum in Sub-contr	X	X	X	X
GBB	VBR	Internal goods issue	X	X	X	X
GBB	VKA	GI to sale instead of BSX	X	X	X	X
GBB	VKP	GI to proj instead of BSX	X	X	X	X
GBB	VNG	Stock scrap	X	X	X	X
GBB	VQP	GI to QM - not cost elem	X	X	X	X
GBB	VQY	GI to QM - cost elem	X	X	X	X
GBB	ZOB	G/R w/o purch order	X	X	X	X
GBB	ZOF	GR w/o prod order	X	X	X	X
KDM		MM exchg rate diff	X	X	X	X
KDR		MM exchg rate rounding	X			
KON		Consignment Liab	X	X	X	X
KON	PIP	Pipeline Liab	X	X	X	X
KTR		Cost object - price diff off	X			
PRA		WIP price diff - act off	X	X		
PRC		Price diff - VAR	X	X	X	
PRD		Price Var - Purch GR	X	X	X	X
PRD	PRA	Price Var - Goods Issue	X	X	X	X
PRD	PRF	Price Var - Prod GR	X	X	X	X
PRD	PRU	Price Var - Trf Posting	X	X	X	X
PRK		Cost object - price diff	X			
PRM		WIP price diff - mat off	X	X	X	
RKA		Inv. reduction from LIV	X			
RUE		Provision for del costs	X	X	X	
UMB		Revaluation gain/loss	X	X	X	X
UMD		B/S reval - gain/loss	X	X	X	X
UPF		Unplanned del costs				
VST		Purchasing tax	X	X	X	X
WGI		Wrongly valued GI	X	X	X	
WGR		Wrongly valued GR	X	X	X	
WPA		WIP price diff - act	X	X		
WPM		WIP price diff - mat	X	X	X	
WRX		GR/IR clearing	X	X	X	X

Figure 9.13 Account Grouping Matrix

10   Payroll Transactions

In this chapter, we will discuss GL account determination for payroll transactions. Payroll processing in SAP ERP provides comprehensive functionality that encompasses wages, incentive payments, payroll tax calculations, garnishment, bonuses, leave accounting, and a large number of relevant functionalities. Obviously, these functionalities vary from country to country because these requirements are governed by the statutory, tax, and employment laws of each country. SAP ERP provides payroll drivers or calculation templates for more than 35 countries that take into account the local requirements of the respective country. Thankfully, the GL account determination technique used in payroll transactions for all of these types of calculations is the same, so that we can discuss GL account determination independent of any country localization.

Even though detailed requirements may be different, the functionalities just mentioned are commonly used in the payroll processing of almost all countries. In addition, each country typically has its unique localization requirements that also require GL account assignment. However, the technique and account determination objects used for GL account determination for these unique localization requirements are similar to those discussed in this chapter.

> **Note**
>
> The examples and screen shots in this chapter refer to SAP ERP's functionality for United States payroll processing. Also, whenever we refer to a localized version, we are referring to the U.S. edition, unless noted otherwise.

Some of the concepts and components used in SAP Human Resources (HR) and payroll processing are discussed here. Some of the concepts and account determination objects discussed in Chapter 7 provide good introduction to the GL account determination discussed in this chapter. So if you haven't already done so, you might want to review Chapter 7 first. Nevertheless, let's go through some of the high-level concepts and account determination objects.

10.1 Account Determination Objects

Most of the account determination objects discussed in this section fall into the area of SAP HR and Payroll processing. However, considering the tight integration of SAP components, it is imperative that while configuring these objects, due attention is given to their impact on GL account determination. For example, several infotypes that have to be separated for the purpose of payroll analysis and reporting may post to the same GL account. Similarly, the necessity of having to post to different GL accounts may manifest itself into having to configure additional infotypes. Let us start with the discussion of infotypes.

10.1.1 Infotype

An *infotype* is a set of relevant data grouped together. All of an employee's data is maintained using different infotypes. So, an employee's contact information is stored in one infotype, while his or her organizational assignment (company code, employee group, cost center, etc.) is stored in another. For the purposes of payroll transactions, different infotypes store relevant information for basic pay, worker's compensation, payroll taxes, employee loans, recurring deductions, and multitudes of other data for every employee. The standard SAP ERP system provides more than 700 infotypes, including country-specific infotypes, for storing wide a variety of employee-related data.

Figure 10.1 shows a small sample of these infotypes. You can review infotypes via the menu path IMG • PERSONNEL MANAGEMENT • PERSONNEL ADMINISTRATION • CUSTOMIZING PROCEDURES • INFOTYPES • INFOTYPES.

IType	Infotype text
0000	Actions
0001	Organizational Assignment
0007	Planned Working Time
0008	Basic Pay
0016	Contract Elements
0022	Education
0023	Other/Previous Employers
0081	Military Service
0145	Personnel Tax Status JP
0429	Position in PS
0495	Retirement Benefits/Death Gratuity
0552	Time Specification/Employ. Period
0623	Career History (Public Sector BE)
2001	Absences

Figure 10.1 Standard Infotypes

Another concept unique to SAP HR and Payroll applications is called a feature.

10.1.2 Feature

A decision tree technique called *feature* is used in HR and Payroll to determine default values or to control process flow. We discussed this technique in Chapter 7. The benefit of this technique is that it allows one branch of the decision tree (at any level) to be as deep as required without impacting the depth of other branches of the decision tree. Payroll uses a large number of predefined features to derive requisite data values or characteristic values for different calculations.

Following is a list of some of the features used in payroll accounting to give you an idea of the wide range of processing in which features are used:

▸ **MOLGA:** Is payroll active?

▸ **ABKRS:** Default value for payroll area.

▸ **BETAX:** Closing payroll period of actual tax period.

▸ **NLSIM:** Determine payroll program variant for simulation.

▸ **DTXED:** Assignment of external data to payroll area.

▸ **CEDME:** Payroll management for extra monthly payment.

▸ **ADRUN:** Periods with a special payroll run.

▸ **FMODE:** Payroll offset modifier for cost accounting.

▸ **OTSEL:** Select data for payroll outsourcing.

▸ **PU137:** Manual checks for off-cycle payroll.

For the features that are available for user configuration, you will find transactions for feature maintenance in the corresponding sections of the payroll component's configuration guide. Alternately, you can also use Transaction PE03 to review and maintain features.

Another important object in payroll calculations is a wage type.

10.1.3 Wage Type

As you might imagine, payroll calculations require numerous amounts and numbers to be stored, calculated, evaluated, added, subtracted, and processed in general.

Each such piece of information is stored in a *wage type*. A wage type has numerous attributes that control how the value contained in the wage type is/can be manipulated. Following are some of the attributes of a wage type:

▶ Whether a wage type is a deduction wage type

▶ The minimum and maximum permissible values for this wage type

▶ Whether the amount entered in the wage type should be taken into account in basic pay total

▶ Whether the amount and/or number unit must be maintained for this wage type

▶ Rounding rules for the wage type values

▶ Whether the value in the wage type can be overwritten

These attributes not only control the type of value stored in the wage type, but they also determine whether and how this value is posted to financial accounting.

The standard SAP ERP system provides a large number of wage types, some of which are shown in Figure 10.2. You can check wage type settings via the menu path IMG • PAYROLL: USA • BASIC SETTINGS • ENVIRONMENT FOR MAINTAINING WAGE TYPES • CHECK WAGE TYPE ATTRIBUTES.

```
Wage types

A15X    Fellowship Adjustment
M002    Payscale Salary
M003    Pay Period Salary
M004    Pension/Retiree Pay
M021    Tip income
M032    Gross up result-reg meth
M101    Merit bonus - regular
M102    Merit bonus - special run
M112    Commission
M113    Severance pay
M114    Uniform allowance
M115    Equipment allowance
M116    Car allowance
M117    Premium pay (% of gross)
```

Figure 10.2 Wage Types

Let's now discuss another important object: a payroll schema.

10.1.4 Payroll Schema

The payroll processing workflow is controlled through a *payroll schema*. You maintain a payroll schema using a configurable tool. This tool lets you control the sequence and content of code snippets that are to be executed. A payroll schema resembles pseudo-code or the sequence of activities that consist of function modules, rules, operations, and parameters.

Figure 10.3 shows part of a payroll schema (QP00) delivered in the standard SAP ERP system for the U.S. PS (public sector). As you can see in this figure, the first column represents sequential numbers in which the commands entered in the second column (e.g., BLOCK, COPY, IF, etc.) are processed. These commands carry out corresponding tasks on the results of the payroll schema entered as one of its four variables (PAR1, PAR2, etc.). And the TEXT field provides a meaningful explanation of the task that is performed in that step.

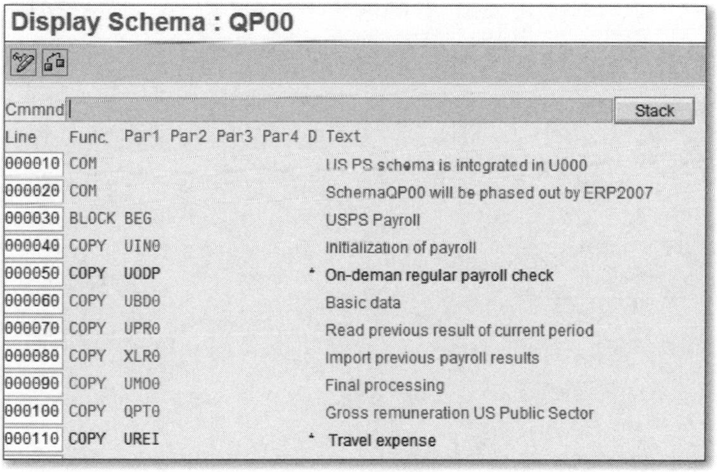

Figure 10.3 Payroll Schema QP00

You will find transactions for payroll schema maintenance in the Payroll configuration guide under the respective Payroll components. Alternately, you can use Transaction PE01 to maintain the payroll schema.

For the purposes of GL account determination, you should keep in mind that the code in a payroll schema may manipulate or influence the wage type in payroll results, which may impact GL account determination.

Payroll transactions in SAP ERP use a combination of the symbolic account technique and the transaction key technique for account determination. Figure 10.4 shows account determination objects that participate in GL account determination.

Let's first discuss the payroll components.

10.1.5 Payroll Components

In Figure 10.4, the PAYROLL COMPONENTS descriptor is used as a generic identifier for any functionality that is part of or that impacts payroll result calculations. Some examples of payroll components are basic pay, attendance or absence information, incentives, deductions, taxes, garnishments, and so on. Each of these components has a corresponding configuration IMG under the menu path IMG • PAYROLL • PAYROLL: USA.

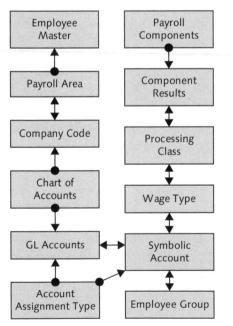

Figure 10.4 Payroll Transactions

Each payroll component uses a different set of infotypes, wage types, calculation results, and rules. However, at the end, every component must still produce a component result in a consistent format that can be used in the payroll calculation process.

For instance, the employee absence component uses specific rules to valuate different types of absence (e.g., sick leave, training, personal time off, etc.) and assigns the resulting values to wage types. The payroll component dealing with tax goes through a multitude of rules and calculations. The result of this process may have values from taxable, non-taxable, taxable but not taxed, and so on. Finally, this end result gets assigned to a wage type. The payroll component dealing with deductions checks for any mandatory deductions as well as any optional deductions (e.g., union dues) to calculate different deductions and assign them to the corresponding wage types.

This means the payroll process requires a framework that helps it determine which wage types can be used for what type of processing, and also what types of processing are allowed on what types of wage types. This is where the processing class comes into the picture.

10.1.6 Processing Class

In different payroll components, wage types are assigned to one or more processing classes. For example, processing class 5 (create net remuneration and total expenditure) is assigned to deductions wage types, and tax wage types are associated with five processing classes that correspond to different tax attributes of a wage type.

A processing class specification consists of multiple values. In the wage type assignment, you select one value from the list of allowed values. Subsequently, during payroll processing, you can use that value to calculate processing results.

Figure 10.5 displays some of the available processing classes for a U.S. payroll, and Figure 10.6 shows individual values for processing class 68, which is PAYMENT TYPE FOR TAX CALCULATION.

PCl	Description
30	Cumulation update
48	Automatic special payment
50	Deduction/donation processing
64	Alternate formula indicator
68	Payment type for tax calculation
71	Wage type tax classification
72	Employer / employee tax
76	Special payroll run
78	Third-party Remittance

Figure 10.5 Processing Class (U.S.)

	Specifications for Processing Class	
	Spec	Name
	1	Regular payment
	2	Supplemental payment
	3	Cumulative payment
	4	Vacation payment
	5	Perform gross-up using regular method
	6	Perform gross-up using supplemental method

Figure 10.6 Processing Class Values (68)

For example, if you have configured several wage types for different types of payments, to each one you assign a value from 1 to 4 for processing class 68. You can put the logic in the payroll calculation so that depending on the wage type value for processing class 68, you use the amount associated with a wage type for tax calculation on regular payment, supplemental payment, vacation payment, and so on.

You configure the processing class via the menu path IMG • PAYROLL: USA • BASIC SETTINGS • ENVIRONMENT FOR MAINTAINING WAGE TYPES • PROCESSING CLASSES AND EVALUATION CLASSES • MAINTAIN PROCESSING CLASSES AND THEIR SPECIFICATIONS. SAP ERP provides close to 50 processing classes that are relevant for different payroll processes and components.

However, the individual assignment of a wage type to the corresponding processing class values is done in the configuration IMG of the respective payroll components. For example, you assign processing class values to deductions wage types using the configuration menu path IMG • PAYROLL: USA • DEDUCTIONS • ASSIGN PROCESSING CLASSES TO WAGE TYPES. Whereas you maintain tax-relevant processing class values for wage types using IMG • PAYROLL: USA • TAX • TAX-RELATED WAGE TYPES • MAINTAIN TAX-RELATED PROCESSING CLASSES.

Payroll calculations refer to the specific processing class value associated with a wage type to determine whether and how to process amounts contained in that wage type. We can continue to explore other nitty-gritties of payroll calculations, and discuss the different objects that influence payroll calculations, and possibly GL account determination as well. This is because payroll calculations are highly complex, and there are many other objects such as evaluation classes, cumulation wage types, rules, and operations that influence payroll calculation. However, because the primary focus of this book is GL account determination, let's continue our discussion of another account determination object payroll area.

10.1.7 Payroll Area

A *payroll area* in SAP ERP is one of the objects in the personal structure from an administrative perspective. A payroll area groups all those employees together for whom payroll processing is carried out at the same time. For example, full-time employees that are paid a monthly salary are assigned to one payroll area, whereas all temporary workers are assigned to another payroll area for their weekly payments. The periodic payroll process is run per payroll area. So a payroll area not only determines the number of employees for whom a payroll accounting run is performed but also the specific payroll dates and other details such as when the last payroll run for that payroll area was performed, the date for the next payroll run, and so on.

You define valid payroll areas using IMG • Personnel Management • Personnel Administration • Organizational Data • Organizational Assignment • Create Payroll Area. You assign the payroll area to an employee master in Infotype 0001 (organization assignment).

You use the feature ABKRS to determine the default payroll area. This default value is proposed at the time of creating an employee master. You maintain feature ABKRS using IMG • Personnel Management • Personnel Administration • Organizational Data • Organizational Assignment • Check Default Payroll Area.

The default ABKRS feature in the standard SAP ERP system lets you determine the default payroll area based on country, employee group, and employee subgroup. Of course, you can modify this feature to add other available characteristics for determining the default payroll area.

Finally, let's discuss symbolic accounts and the role they play in GL account determination.

10.1.8 Symbolic Accounts

We discussed in Section 10.1.3 what a wage type represents in the context of payroll transactions. For the purpose of GL account determination, you assign one or more *symbolic accounts* to these wage types. We discussed in Chapter 1 the symbolic account technique where you assign symbolic accounts to a combination of characteristics; and then use additional logic to determine the actual GL account from the symbolic account.

You define symbolic accounts for payroll processing under the configuration menu path IMG • PAYROLL: USA • POSTING TO FINANCIAL ACCOUNTING • ACTIVITIES IN THE HR-SYSTEM • EMPLOYEE GROUPING AND SYMBOLIC ACCOUNTS • DEFINE SYMBOLIC ACCOUNTS.

Figure 10.7 displays a sample list of symbolic accounts. You will notice that two attributes of symbolic accounts that are shown in Figure 10.7 are also account determination objects, as shown earlier in Figure 10.4. These two attributes are employee grouping (shown in the figure as column EG) and account assignment type (column AATYPE). Let's discuss these attributes in little more detail.

SymAc	Description of the symbolic	AATyp	EG-...
1100	Wages and salaries	C	☑
1110	Direct labor costs	C	☑
1190	Other Wage and Salary Exp	C	☑
1210	Overtime	C	☑
1220	Shift bonus	C	☑
1221	Work center bonus	C	☑
1230	Remuneration for idle time	C	☑
1250	Reimbursements, condition	C	☐
1260	Special payments	C	☐
1270	Expenses	C	☐
1271	Travel Expenses	C	☐
1320	ER taxes	C	☐

Figure 10.7 Symbolic Accounts

Employee Grouping

This is a binary value field associated with a symbolic account. If selected, this field indicates that the GL account assignment to a symbolic account can vary based on employee grouping values. If the field is not selected, employee grouping values are not taken into account in GL account determination.

We have discussed several times in other chapters how account modifiers provide lower level classification of a transaction key and thereby enable configuration and derivation of multiple GL accounts for a transaction key. Similarly, in this case, you can consider employee grouping as providing you with additional criteria that allows you to assign multiple GL accounts for the same symbolic account.

You derive valid employee grouping values using feature PPMOD. You configure this feature using the menu path IMG • PAYROLL: USA • POSTING TO FINANCIAL ACCOUNTING • ACTIVITIES IN THE HR-SYSTEM • EMPLOYEE GROUPING AND SYMBOLIC ACCOUNTS • DEFINE EMPLOYEE GROUPING/ACCOUNT ASSIGNMENT.

In this configuration activity, you first define valid values for employee grouping and account assignment. Next you configure the feature PPMOD to derive valid employee groupings for GL account determination.

Account Assignment Type

Account assignment type is the second attribute of a symbolic account. It is assigned one of the predefined values that control the type of account that can be assigned to it. Figure 10.8 shows a list of valid values for the account assignment type field.

AAT	Name
C	Posting to expense account
CN	Posting to expense account(w/o quantity)
D	Posting to personal customer accounts
DF	Posting to fixed customers
E0	expense not relevant for cost accounting
F	Posting to balance sheet account
FE	Post to Bal.Sheet Acc., Evaluate C1/C0
FL	Posting to check RA balance
FO	Posting to bal.sheet acc. in O-per.only
K	Post to personal vendor accounts
KF	Posting to fixed vendor accounts
L	Posting to customer per loan
Q	Posting to bal.sheet acc. with pers.no.
R	Posting to expense account (for R/2)

Figure 10.8 Account Assignment Type

The symbolic account, using these two attributes, provides a link between the wage types in payroll processing and the GL accounts in SAP ERP Financials.

Now we are ready to discuss GL account determination by putting together everything that we've discussed so far in this chapter.

10.2 General Ledger Account Determination

The account assignment types listed in Figure 10.8 are grouped under different transaction keys. Figure 10.9 shows these transaction keys and their corresponding account modifiers.

Figure 10.9 shows the availability of the following account modifiers:

- ▶ DR/CR: Debit/credit
- ▶ EMP.GRP: Employee grouping
- ▶ SYM.ACCT: Symbolic account
- ▶ GEN MOD: General modifier

T.Key	Description	Dr/Cr	Emp. Grp	Sym.Acct	Gen Mod
HRF	Financial accounts	X	X	X	
HRC	Expense accounts	X	X	X	X
HRA	Technical accounts				X
HRD	Customer accounts	X	X	X	
HRK	Vendor accounts	X	X	X	

Figure 10.9 Account Modifiers for HR Transaction Keys

In Figure 10.9, an X at the intersection of a transaction key and an account modifier indicates that the particular account modifier is available for that particular transaction key. If the background of that intersection is shaded, it means that the availability of that particular account modifier cannot be changed.

This GL account configuration can be reached by following the menu path IMG • PAYROLL: USA • POSTING TO FINANCIAL ACCOUNTING • ACTIVITIES IN THE AC-SYSTEM • ACCOUNT ASSIGNMENT. Let's look at these transaction keys in detail.

10.2.1 General Ledger Accounts

A typical payroll run generates numerous postings that post to balance sheet accounts and income statement accounts, as described here:

▸ Balance sheet accounts, such as payables, receivables, accruals, and so on, are defined under transaction key HRF (financial accounts).

▸ Income statement accounts for payroll expenses are defined under transaction key HRC (expense accounts). Figure 10.10 shows an example of an account assignment for income statement accounts.

Chart	INT	Sample chart of accou
Transact	HRC	HR postings, expense

Account assignment

Symb: acct	Emp grp	Account
1100	1	420000
1100	2	430000
1110	1	420000
1190	1	431900
1190	2	430900
1240		449000
1250		449000

Figure 10.10 General Ledger Account Assignment

If you use account assignment type F (posting to the balance sheet account), it indicates the account assignment of the regular balance sheet account.

Similarly, you can indicate that the account assignment should be of the income statement type by using account assignment type C (posting to the expense account).

Two other account assignment types allow you to control additional information included in these postings:

▸ **Account assignment type Q (posting to balance sheet with personnel number)**
This is used if you would like to include an employee personnel number in posting to the balance sheet account.

Posting with a personnel number can be useful if, for example, you are posting employee advances. Posting with a personnel number to such balance sheet accounts assists you in carrying out reconciliation or automatic clearing in SAP ERP Financials.

▶ **Account assignment type CN (posting to expense account w/o quantity)**
   This is used if the expense postings are to be made without quantity information. Quantity in this case can be, for example, the number of hours worked in a shift or the number of days worked by a temporary employee.

In the next section, we will discuss customer/vendor accounts.

10.2.2 Customer/Vendor Accounts

A payroll run typically also posts to a number of different customer accounts and vendor accounts. For the purpose of this posting, the payroll process uses the account determination specified under the transaction key HRD for customer accounts, and the transaction key HRK for vendor accounts.

Examples of these types of accounts are government authorities, third-party service providers such as vendors that provide health insurance, or even employee accounts that are set up as customer accounts or vendor accounts in accounting. There are two approaches to this type of account determination.

One approach is to assign the actual customer account or vendor account number to a symbolic account. For this approach, you can use account assignment type DF (posting to fixed customers) and account assignment type KF (posting to fixed vendors).

However, not all account assignments yield to such simplistic and direct assignment; for example, it is difficult to carry out such direct assignment for postings that are to be made to employee accounts. It is just not practical to assign every single personnel number using this approach.

SAP ERP provides account assignment type D (posting to personnel customer accounts) or account assignment type K (posting to personnel vendor accounts) so that you can post to customer or vendor accounts using a personnel number.

These two account assignment types indicate that you can obtain the personnel number from a field in the customer or the vendor master. The field that carries the personnel number is indicated by the ACCOUNT value in the configuration.

You should note that even though a field called PERSONNEL NUMBER is available in both the customer master and vendor master; it is also possible to maintain an HR personnel number in other fields in the master data. Figure 10.11 shows the

ACCOUNT value to be assigned to a symbolic account, depending on the master data field used to maintain the personnel number.

Field used	Account
Personnel number	*0002
Search term	*0001
Telephone 2	*0003
Data line	*0004
Teletex number	*0005

Figure 10.11 Partner Account Assignment

10.2.3 Technical Accounts

If a document posted to SAP ERP Financials must be split into more than one document, then the configuration for transaction key HRA, determines which GL account is used for balancing the individual document. There are two possibilities depending on the reason a document is being split.

If the document split is required because of document size (e.g., the number of line items exceeds the specified number), then SAP ERP uses the GL account assigned to general modifier 1002 to balance the document.

A document split may also be required if postings have to be made across company codes, or there are multiple posting dates. For such a split, SAP ERP uses the GL account assigned to general modifier 1001 to balance the document.

The parameters that impact these postings are configured via the menu path IMG • PAYROLL: USA • POSTING TO FINANCIAL ACCOUNTING • ACTIVITIES IN THE HR-SYSTEM • CREATE POSTING VARIANTS. Figure 10.12 displays the parameters associated with the POSTING VARIANT configuration.

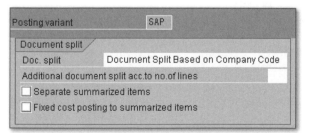

Figure 10.12 Document Split Parameters

10.2.4 Symbolic Account Derivation

Irrespective of the account assignment type, the way that symbolic accounts are assigned to wage types remains the same. This configuration is done via the menu path IMG • PAYROLL: USA • POSTING TO FINANCIAL ACCOUNTING • ACTIVITIES IN THE HR-SYSTEM • WAGE TYPE MAINTENANCE • DEFINE WAGE TYPE POSTING ATTRIBUTE.

Figure 10.13 shows the assignment of symbolic account 3110 (ADVANCES) for WAGE TYPE MJ90 (ADVANCE).

Wage Type		MJ90	Advance		
End Date		12/31/9999			
Posting a Wage Type					
No	V	SymAc	ProcessTyp	AA	Description
1	+	3110	Normal processing	Q	Advances

Figure 10.13 Symbolic Accounts, Example 1

The V column indicates what sign (+ or –) of the calculated result is posted as a debit entry. In the example, a positive result is posted as a debit entry to symbolic account 3110. Of course, the reverse sign is posted as a credit entry.

You can use the processing type (PROCESS TYP) field values to assign different symbolic accounts to actual postings (FI) and to cost planning (CO). However, in all other cases, you will keep this field as NORMAL PROCESSING.

Wage Type		/406	TX ER Medicare Tax		
Posting a Wage Type					
No	V	ProcessTyp	SymAc	AA...	Description
1	+	Normal processing	1320	C	ER taxes
4	-	Normal processing	2222	F	FICA Taxes (US)
9	+	Month end accruals	1320	C	ER taxes
10	-	Month end accruals	3320	F	Accruals Adjustment

Figure 10.14 Symbolic Accounts, Example 2

The assignment of symbolic accounts to wage types is not always as simple as shown in Figure 10.13. Consider the example illustrated in Figure 10.14. It shows the symbolic account assignment to the MEDICARE TAX wage type. During NORMAL PROCESSING, this assignment carries out a debit posting to the Medicare tax expense

(No. 1) and a credit posting to the tax payable account for government (No. 4). Notice how the usage of a + or a – sign achieves this result. Similarly, additional symbolic account assignments ensure accrual adjustments during month-end processing.

10.3   Other Transactions

In Section 10.2, we discussed standard account determination in payroll processing. Now we will discuss account determination for a few other scenarios in payroll processing.

10.3.1   Month-End Accruals

Consider a business scenario where a business uses different posting periods for payroll processing and for financial books. In such a scenario, you have to make accrual entries at month-end to take into consideration payroll postings.

For example, let's say your entire company or one of the locations in your company processes bi-weekly payroll, whereas the financial posting periods in your company correspond to calendar months. This can be the case where the company's fiscal year is the same as the calendar year, and most of the company is paid on a monthly payroll, but workers at one of the plant locations are paid bi-weekly. Invariably, in this case, there will be payroll periods that span across two financial posting periods. However, when payroll results from such payroll periods are transferred to FI, corresponding accounting entries will be posted in only one (later) posting period.

To ensure that payroll postings that correspond to both the posting periods in SAP ERP Financials are accounted accurately, you have to carry out additional configuration that automatically posts the necessary accrual entries in SAP ERP Financials.

SAP ERP determines whether and how to post accrual entries by comparing the dates specified in the Payroll configuration (see Figure 10.15). As you can see, you specify three dates under this section for every payroll period: posting date, closing date, and latest document creation date.

▸ A posting date is the date when accounting entries for a payroll period are posted in the GL. Typically, this is last day of the period or check date, such as the 1st and 15th of every month.

▶ A closing date specifies the month-end closing date for each pay period. This is the date by which accrual entries should be posted in the GL for the corresponding accounting period. You make this specification for each company code.

▶ A latest document creation date is the date by which all relevant documents should be created for a pay period. This date helps you take into account mailing times so that recipients receive payroll checks by intended dates.

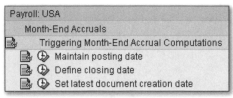

Figure 10.15 Accrual Date Specification

SAP ERP goes through the following calculations to determine whether to post accrual entries for a payroll period.

Assuming that the next payroll period corresponds to two posting periods, SAP ERP checks the latest document creation date (LDCD) and the closing date of the next payroll period, during the current payroll period processing.

If the LDCD is after the closing date for the next payroll period, the posting period in SAP ERP Financials might be closed when payroll processing for the next payroll period is carried out. In this case, SAP ERP uses payroll postings from the current period to estimate the accruals to be made for the current posting period in SAP ERP Financials.

However, if the LDCD is before the closing date for the next payroll period, the posting period in SAP ERP Financials will be open when payroll processing for the next payroll period is carried out. In this case, accruals are posted to the current posting period based on actual postings when payroll processing is done for the next payroll period.

SAP ERP can determine a split of amounts between two posting periods based on calendar days, workdays, or working hours. This setup is carried out in the personnel calculation schema UT00 via the menu path IMG • PAYROLL: USA • MONTH-END ACCRUALS • BASIS FOR COMPUTATIONS • SETUP COMPUTATION OF PART AMOUNTS BELONGING TO EACH PERIOD.

For GL account determination, you should ensure that relevant wage types are assigned symbolic accounts and that the assignment has the process type, month-end accruals.

Before concluding the discussion in this chapter, let's briefly discuss bank account determination in payroll processing.

10.3.2 Bank Account Determination

More often than not, payable entries from payroll processing are first posted to Accounts Payable (AP). Examples of such payments include payments made to third-party service providers, government authorities, and so on. Subsequently, the outgoing payment process in AP settles this liability by making payments just like any other payment run. For these types of payments, the house bank determination configured for AP can be used to determine which bank account the payments are made from. More often than not, companies use separate bank accounts and separate payment methods to uniquely identify payroll payments. So, you can easily configure the house banks from which payroll payments should be made.

However, if you want to send out payment information from the payroll subcomponent, then you have to specify which bank accounts should be used for making payments. The DTAKT feature is used to carry out this determination for sending bank accounts. This feature can be configured via the menu path IMG • PAYROLL: USA • ELECTRONIC FUND TRANSFER (EFT) • DIRECT DEPOSIT/DATA MEDIUM EXCHANGE • PRELIMINARY PROGRAMS • DETERMINE SENDING BANKS.

You should note that in this bank, account determination refers to the bank accounts from which outgoing payroll payments are made. The receiving bank account details are maintained either in the corresponding employee master data or in the corresponding business partner data.

10.4 Summary

As already discussed, payroll calculation is an extremely complex subject. However, from an account determination perspective, it follows a consistent technique. The setup for account determination in payroll processing requires a collaborative effort from the SAP ERP Financials and Payroll implementation teams.

There are other components in SAP Payroll that impact finance postings. For instance, in retroactive payroll calculation, payroll results in past periods are recalculated due to employee master data changes that are effective retroactively.

Or consider the special adjustments made to employee payroll data by using Infotype 0221, which forces the recalculation of payroll results. We did not discuss these functions in detail because they all follow the same account determination techniques described in this chapter for normal payroll processing.

Other payroll components deal with third-party remittance, remittance to tax authorities, or payroll outsourcing. All of these scenarios have different subsequent processing or preliminary processing of payroll data. However, it is important to note that account determination for all of these scenarios is similar to the process described in this chapter.

10.5   Reference

This section provides a list of the configuration transactions and tables and structures corresponding to the payroll transactions we have discussed in this chapter.

10.5.1   Configuration Transactions

Table 10.1 provides a list of the configuration transactions for the account determination objects discussed in this chapter.

Transaction Code	Description
PE01	Maintain schema
PE02	Maintain rule
PE03	Maintain feature
OH02	Wage type posting attributes
OBYG	Assign financial accounts
OBYE	Assign expense accounts
OBYL	Assign technical accounts

Table 10.1   Configuration Transactions

Transaction Code	Description
OBYT	Assign customer accounts
OBYU	Assign vendor accounts
OBYE	Assign accrual expense accounts
OG00	Overview of GL account assignment

Table 10.1 Configuration Transactions (Cont.)

In addition, Transaction PC00_M99_DLGA20 displays details about the wage type, processing class, and so on, and Transaction PC00_M99_DKON displays details about the wage type and GL account assignment.

10.5.2 Tables and Structures

Table 10.2 contains a list of the tables and structures used to store data relevant for the GL account determination discussed in this chapter.

Table/Structure	Description
T030	GL account assignment
T511	Wage types
T52D1	Processing classes
T52D2	Values for processing classes
T52E2	Posting variants
T52EK	Symbolic accounts
T52EL	Wage type posting attributes
T52EM	Employee grouping values
T549A	Payroll areas
T549S	Payroll period date specification

Table 10.2 Tables and Structures

10.6 Conclusion

We are now at the end of this Essentials guide. You may have expected a silver bullet that points you toward a specific screen among the hundreds of configuration transactions, which would help you immediately identify why your SAP ERP transaction is posting to the wrong GL account. Unfortunately, there is no such silver bullet—nothing that works for everyone in all scenarios.

In relatively simple implementations, it is enough if you are familiar with GL account determination techniques and configuration transactions that are applicable in your specific scenario.

However, as the complexity of business requirements and implementation increases, you must also become familiar with modifications that are available or that are being used in your specific scenario. As discussed in Chapter 1, many forms of modifications can and do impact GL account determination.

This guide provides you with a conceptual understanding of GL account determination based on a sound theoretical discussion. How you use the information in this guide depends on your specific and individual tasks.

Obviously, the way you would use this guide in your business requirement analysis will be quite different from the manner in which you might use it to assist in troubleshooting a problem.

If you are using the information to assist you in gathering business requirements for an SAP ERP component, you will want to understand how GL account determination works in that component, how standard SAP ERP functionality meets your requirements, and what, if any, additional available modifications can be utilized to meet your specific business requirements.

On the other hand, if you are using the information in this guide to troubleshoot a GL account determination problem, then you will want to identify account determination objects and their values as they are applicable in your scenario. You can then use the technical reference sections to identify the configuration transactions or the tables to help you in your error analysis.

Appendices

A   Field Status Group

A *field status group* lets you group GL accounts based on the type of accounts and the level of details you want to capture in corresponding GL postings. At the minimum, you will find that your GL accounts are grouped into two field status groups: balance sheet accounts and income statement accounts. However, you may find SAP ERP implementations that have GL accounts grouped into several different field status groups such as material accounts, fixed asset accounts, clearing accounts, receivable accounts, revenue accounts, personnel accounts, tax accounts and so on. In fact, the standard SAP ERP template provides more than 40 field status groups for GL accounts.

One of the reasons field status groups are important for the GL account determination is that even if GL account configuration is appropriate, you will run into posting errors if the field status group settings are incorrect. So in this appendix, let's go through the settings for a field status group.

A.1   An Overview

Figure A.1 shows how field status groups fit among the other account determination objects.

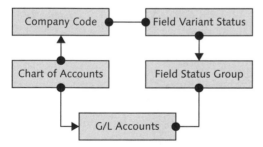

Figure A.1   Field Status Group Derivation

Company code, chart of accounts, and GL accounts are self-explanatory, and we have discussed them numerous times throughout this book. So let's focus on the two other objects in Figure A.1.

A.1.1 Field Status Variant

A *field status variant* helps you group together field status groups, so that you can assign them to a company code. The advantage of a field status variant is that it lets you assign the same set of field status groups across multiple company codes, thereby avoiding repetitive configuration.

You define field status variants using the configuration path IMG • FINANCIAL ACCOUNTING • GENERAL LEDGER ACCOUNTING • BUSINESS TRANSACTIONS • G/L ACCOUNT POSTING • MAKE AND CHECK DOCUMENT SETTINGS • DEFINE FIELD STATUS VARIANT. As Figure A.2 shows, a field status variant consists of a four-character code and corresponding description.

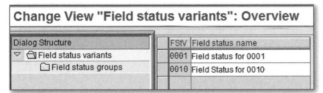

Figure A.2 Define Field Status Variant

You assign one of these field status variants to a company code using the configuration menu path IMG • FINANCIAL ACCOUNTING • GENERAL LEDGER ACCOUNTING • BUSINESS TRANSACTIONS • G/L ACCOUNT POSTING • MAKE AND CHECK DOCUMENT SETTINGS • ASSIGN COMPANY CODE TO FIELD STATUS VARIANTS.

A field status variant groups together several field status groups.

A.1.2 Field Status Group

As we've already discussed, a *field status group* lets you group GL accounts based on the type of postings and the status of different field values in the posting. You use the same menu path to configure field status groups as for field status variants. In Figure A.2, you configure field status groups by clicking on the FIELD STATUS GROUPS node after selecting a field status variant.

Table A.1 shows a partial list of field status groups available in a standard SAP ERP system.

Field Status Group	Description
G001	General (with text, assignment)
G003	Material consumption accounts
G004	Cost accounts
G005	Bank accounts (obligatory value date)
G006	Material accounts
G007	Asset accts (without accumulated depreciation)
G008	Assets area clearing accounts
G009	Bank accounts (obligatory due date)
G012	Receivables/payables clearing
G013	General (obligatory text)
G023	Plant maintenance accounts
G025	Inventory adjustment accounts
G026	Accounts for down payments made
G029	Revenue accounts
G030	Change in stock accounts
G031	Accounts for down payments received
G032	Bank accounts (obligatory value/due dates)
G033	Cost accounts for external services
G036	Revenue accts (with cost center)
G039	Accounts for payments on account made for assets
G040	Personnel clearing accounts
G041	Tax office clearing accounts
G045	Goods/invoice received clearing accounts
G049	Manufacturing costs accounts

Table A.1 Field Status Groups

Now let's look at how to configure a field status group.

A.2 Field Status Group Configuration

In a nutshell, a field status group consists of several groups of fields, and you can set status of each field as either SUPPRESS, REQ. ENTRY (required entry), or OPT. ENTRY (optional entry).

Table A.2 shows the list of field groups available for each field status group.

Field Group	Description
General data	Contains fields such as assignment, line item text, and reference specifications 1, 2, and 3.
Additional account assignments	One of the most important field groups that contains additional account assignments that provide links to other modules and subcomponents of SAP ERP. Check this one for any problems with postings that involve cost center, profit center, internal order, asset number, production order, and similar objects.
Materials management	Consists of inventory, purchase order, and goods movement fields, among others.
Payment transactions	An important field group for all cash management transaction postings. This group consists of important fields such as due date, value date, payment terms, reason code, and so on.
Asset Accounting	Consists of three fields related to asset accounting: asset retirement, asset number, and asset subnumber.
Taxes	Contains fields that correspond to withholding tax, European (EC) tax, and income tax.
Foreign payments	Contains fields related to customs data and supplying country.
Consolidation	Relevant if you are using the consolidation module. This field group consists of only one field: consolidation transaction type.

Table A.2 Field Groups

Field Group	Description
Real estate management	Consists of fields relevant for the real estate or the extended real estate component in SAP ERP.
Financial assets management	Consists of fields relevant for financial asset management.

Table A.2 Field Groups (Cont.)

As you can see in Table A.2, the last four field groups are highly specific, and they are relevant only if you are using specific SAP components or functionalities. Otherwise, primarily, your focus will be on field groups such as general data, additional account assignments, materials management, and payment transactions.

Figure A.3 shows an example of individual field setting for fields contained in the ADDITIONAL ACCOUNT ASSIGNMENTS field group for MATERIAL CONSUMPTION ACCOUNTS.

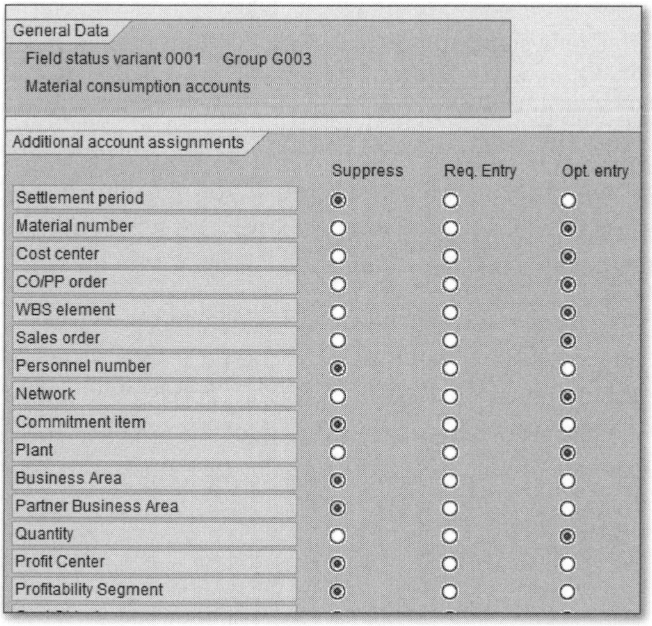

Figure A.3 Field Status Group Configuration

As you would expect for material consumption accounts, fields related to plant, cost centers, and special stock (for a sales order or for a project) are enabled for optional entry, whereas revenue-related fields are suppressed from entry.

> **Note**
>
> Even though technically it is possible to configure and use field status groups that differentiate and group GL accounts based on minute differences, it is usually sufficient to use a handful of field status groups. You may be able to use other SAP ERP functionalities to meet your business requirements.

However, you may want to consider other functionalities in SAP ERP before creating and using large number of field status groups. Consider an example in which you are planning to configure two field status groups that are exactly the same, except that one of them has Cost Center as a required field. You may be able to fulfill this business requirement by configuring one field status group in which the Cost Center field is an optional entry, and then using validations to make sure that Cost Center is a required field for a selected group of accounts.

You may also want to note that field status groups are especially important if most of the transactions posted to associated GL accounts are automatically generated in other SAP ERP modules. For example, most of the material consumption postings (Figure A.3) are generated automatically in SAP ERP. However, if field settings were not correctly done, you will notice the problems only when you start processing transactions in the system. Thankfully, however, after the problems are identified, it is fairly easy to correct them with field status groups.

SAP ERP provides several customizing and consulting notes related to field status variants. Mostly they provide solutions to commonly encountered transactional problems in processing withholding tax (SAP Note 1626838), goods movements (SAP Note 9281), down payment processing in sales (SAP Note 213526), manual bank statement (SAP Note 136936), and cross-company sales (SAP Note 39254).

B   Validations and Substitutions

Validations and substitutions functionality in SAP ERP provide you with an ability to validate or substitute data at the time of posting a document. It is important to note that validations and substitutions are triggered regardless of whether the document is entered manually (e.g., manual journal entry) or automatically generated from a different SAP component (e.g., AR invoice).

You can configure validations and substitutions on a large number of fields in an accounting document. So in addition to GL accounts, the discussion in this appendix is also valid for validations and substitutions for other accounting objects such as a cost center, a profit center, and so on. Let's start our discussion with details of accounting document validations.

B.1   Validations

The main components of a validation are a prerequisite condition and a validation check. If a document meets the prerequisite conditions but does not pass validation checks, then the validation fails, and it issues a validation message.

In this section, we will start with the configuration details of an accounting document validation, and then we will discuss its components, followed by its potential usage in the GL account determination.

B.1.1   Validation Configuration

You configure accounting document validations using the menu path IMG • FINANCIAL ACCOUNTING • FINANCIAL ACCOUNTING GLOBAL SETTINGS • DOCUMENT • LINE ITEM • DEFINE VALIDATIONS FOR POSTING.

You should note the following points about accounting document validations.

▸ You assign validations to a company code for different call-up points. Call-up points indicate the point in transaction processing when corresponding validations are carried out. SAP ERP provides the following call-up points:

- ▸ 0001: Document header

- ▸ 0002: Line item

- ▸ 0003: Complete document

You should select a call-up point that is appropriate for your validation checks. For example, a validation for a cost center or a profit center should be configured at the document line item level.

- ▸ Because there are only three call-up points, you can assign only three validation rules to a company code—one at each call-up point.

  This means that a validation definition should consist of all checks you want to carry out at a particular call-up point; even though those individual checks may not be related to each other. You can achieve this by specifying multiple steps in a validation (more details about this later in this appendix).

- ▸ For each call-up point validation for a company code, you can choose whether that validation is inactive, always active, or active for all instances except batch input.

Figure B.1 shows an example of an accounting document validation.

| Validation name | COSTCEN | Cost Center Validation |
| Validation step | 001 | Ccrtr Validation for line item |

Prerequisite
```
BSEG-HKONT IN GLHKNTR
```

Check
```
BSEG-KOSTL IN GLKOSTLR
```

Message (Output if prerequisite is met and check is NOT fulfilled)
⚠ Only Cost center starting with '62' allowed
Message number ZZ   600

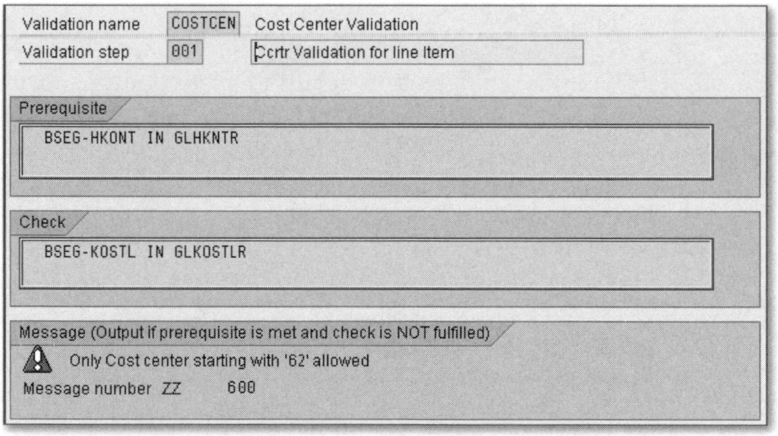

Figure B.1 An Accounting Document Validation

Let's look at each of the components of a validation.

B.1.2   Validation Components

Please refer to Figure B.1 while going through the discussion in this section. Different components of a validation are a validation step, a prerequisite, a validation check, and a message.

Validation Step

A *validation step* is a sequential step number assigned to a validation rule. As we already discussed, you can only assign one validation rule to a company code at each call-up point. By using validation checks, you can carry out multiple, possibly unrelated, validations for an accounting document posted to a company code using a single validation rule. In the example shown in Figure B.1, the details are for VALIDATION STEP "001".

All validation rules are processed sequentially in increasing order of validation step number.

Prerequisite

A *prerequisite* consists of a logical condition consisting of fields from an accounting document. A prerequisite allows you to make sure that your validation is not executed for all accounting documents posted to a company code. You can use any field values from accounting document tables, system field values, a user exit, or a constant or a set of values in the prerequisite condition definition. In the example shown in Figure B.1, a PREREQUISITE condition checks whether the GL account in an accounting document line item is part of R&D GL accounts specified in the set GLHKNTR.

A validation check is processed only if the prerequisite condition is met. Otherwise, that validation step has no effect on document processing.

Validation Check

A *validation check* consists of a logical condition that validates fields of an accounting document. You can use any field values from accounting document tables, system field values, a user exit, or a constant or a set of values in the validation check. In Figure B.1, a validation CHECK is used to check whether the cost center in the accounting document line item is part of the R&D cost center specified in the set GLKOSTLR. In the example, the message is issued as an error message.

Depending on the results of a validation check, an accounting document is considered to have passed or failed a validation step. If an accounting document passes a validation check, the validation process continues to the next validation step. If an accounting document fails a validation check, a validation message is issued.

Validation Message

A *validation message* consists of a text message and a message type that indicates whether the message should be issued as an information message, a warning message, an error message, or an abort or a cancel message. You choose the message type depending on the severity of the validation you want to carry out.

If a validation message is issued as an error or an abort message, the process of posting the accounting document stops, and you have to fix the problem before continuing further. Otherwise, you can click on corresponding entries

Now let's now see how you can use a validation check for an accounting document.

B.1.3   Usage

More typically, validations on accounting documents use GL accounts as one of the parameters to validate something else, rather than validate GL accounts themselves. This is because in most cases, these GL accounts come from automatic account configuration. So if there is something wrong, you should fix it in the appropriate configuration transactions. In the instances where a GL account is entered manually, you use transaction authorizations to make sure that only someone responsible in the accounting department is able to manually post to GL accounts.

However, it is very common to use accounting document validations to validate other fields on the accounting document. For example, you may put validations in place that for a certain range of GL accounts, the accounting document being validated contains a cost center, an internal order, a trading partner ID, an asset number, or some similar fields.

> **Note**
>
> In place of using field status groups, you can use these validations to validate required entries in certain fields of an accounting document. This can bring down the total number of field status groups you need to configuration and maintain.

Now, let's look at the concept of accounting document substitutions.

B.2   Substitutions

The main components of a substitution are a prerequisite condition and one or more substitutions. If a document meets the prerequisite conditions, the system substitutes field values as defined in the substitution.

In this section, we will start with configuration details of an accounting document substitution, and then we will discuss its components, followed by its potential usage in the GL account determination.

B.2.1   Substitution Configuration

You configure accounting document substitutions using the menu path IMG • FINANCIAL ACCOUNTING • FINANCIAL ACCOUNTING GLOBAL SETTINGS • DOCUMENT • LINE ITEM • DEFINE SUBSTITUTION IN ACCOUNTING DOCUMENTS.

You should note the following points about accounting document substitutions:

▶ You assign substitutions to a company code for different call up points. Call up points indicate the point in the transaction processing when corresponding substitutions are carried out. SAP ERP provides the following call-up points

  ▶ 0001: Document header

  ▶ 0002: Line item

  ▶ 0003: Complete document

  ▶ 0006: Cost of Sale Accounting

  You should select a call-up point that is appropriate for your substitution checks. For example, a substitution for a GL account, a cost center, or a profit center should be configured at the document line item level.

▶ Because there are only four call-up points, you can assign only up to four substitution rules to a company code—one at each call-up point.

  This means that a substitution definition should consist of all substitutions that you want to carry out at a particular call-up point; even though those individual substitutions may not be related to each other. You can achieve this by specifying multiple steps in a substitution. See more details later in this appendix.

▶ For each call-up point substitution for a company code, you can choose whether that substitution is inactive, always active, or active for all instances except batch input.

Figure B.2 shows an example of an accounting document substitution.

```
Substitution      FISUBLI  Cost of sales accounting
Step              001      Account Substitution

Prerequisite
    SYST-TCODE = 'FB05' AND
    BSEG-HKONT = '0000011002'


Substitutions (if prerequisite is met)
    Field                   is substituted by
    G/L                     Constant value      0000011003
```

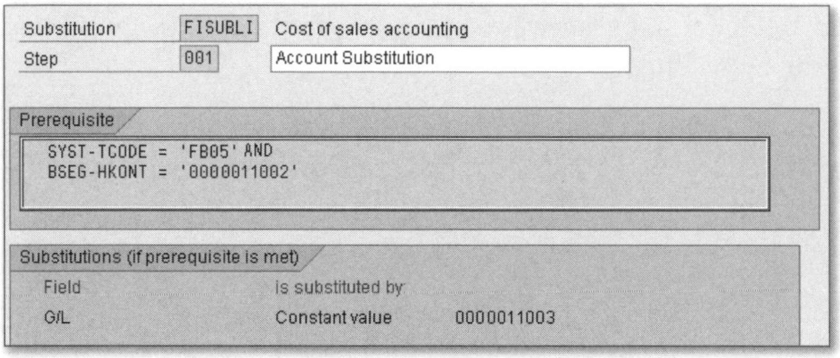

Figure B.2 An Accounting Document Substitution

Let's look at each of the components of a substitution.

B.2.2 Substitution Components

Please refer to Figure B.2 while going through the discussion in this section. Different components of a substitution are a substitution step, a prerequisite, and one or more substitutions.

Substitution Step

A *substitution step* is a sequential step number assigned to a substitution rule. As we already discussed, you can only assign one substitution rule to a company code at each call-up point. By using substitution checks, you can carry out multiple, possibly unrelated, substitutions for an accounting document posted to a company code using a single substitution rule. In the example shown in Figure B.2, the details are for substitution STEP "001".

All substitution rules are processed sequentially in increasing order of substitution step number.

Prerequisite

Similar to the definition in a validation, a prerequisite for substitution consists of a logical condition consisting of fields from an accounting document. A prerequisite allows you to make sure that your substitution is not executed for all accounting documents posted to a company code. You can use any field values from accounting document tables, system field values, a user exit, or a constant or a set of values in the prerequisite condition definition. In the example shown in Figure B.2, a PREREQUISITE condition checks whether the GL account in an accounting document line item is "1102" and whether the accounting document was posted using Transaction FB05.

All substitutions are processed only if the prerequisite condition is met. Otherwise, that substitution step has no effect on document processing.

Substitutions

A substitution consists of a substitution rule for an accounting document field. A substitution step consists of one or more substitutions. You have three options in which you can determine the value that will be substituted ("to value"). The substituted value can either be a constant, a result of a user exit, or a value from another field in that accounting document. In Figure B.2, the substituted value is a constant. So, effectively, if an accounting document was posted using Transaction FB05, and it contained GL account "1102", this substitution step will replace it with GL account "1103".

Let's now see how you can use substitutions for an accounting document.

B.2.3 Usage

Substitutions provide an excellent opportunity to augment GL account determination configuration transactions in SAP ERP. As you may have already noticed, GL account determination configuration can become quite complex for certain components in SAP ERP. Not only that, sometimes just to determine a different GL account, you may have to do extensive configuration of additional account determination objects, which may not be practical or possible. Instead, you can use substitutions to derive a different GL account. Having said that, substitutions are equally used in the scenarios where depending on the GL account in a document line item, other fields in the document line item are substituted.

This brings us to the end of Appendix B. One final note: Because it is possible to substitute a GL account at the time of posting an accounting document, it is imperative that you should be familiar with active substitution rules in your system, especially those that are used to substitute GL accounts.

C   The Author

Manish Patel is a senior SAP professional with almost 15 years of experience in the IT industry. After graduating from Bombay University, Manish worked at an Indian software company on various financials projects in Asia Pacific. During his tenure at this company, he gained experience as a finance lead responsible for implementing the company's indigenously developed ERP system. After building a solid foundation in the various areas of software development and project management, he started his career as an SAP consultant. Over the last ten years, he has worked on a variety of SAP projects in a number of different industries. He has also conducted several successful SAP trainings at SAP America locations. This breadth of assignments has honed his abilities to successfully perform different roles in an SAP project ranging from system configuration to project management. He is currently working as a Senior SAP Solutions Consultant in Northern California.

Manish is also the author of other best-selling SAP books published through SAP PRESS. *Discover SAP ERP Financials* provides useful information to project managers and decision makers on the functionality available in more than 20 SAP ERP Financials components. *Maximizing SAP ERP Financials Accounts Receivable* provides very detailed functional and technical explanation and reference to the project team involved in implementing Accounts Receivable functionality.

Manish enjoys working through the challenges and complexities that are inherent in an implementation of such an enterprise-wide system. He understands that experiences and aftereffects of such implementations can range from justifiably thrilling to maddeningly frustrating. So, he thrives in contributing to help ease the transition of SAP users into the new, integrated world of SAP. This book is an attempt to ease such transitions.

Index

Shows how to use production variance
analysis in SAP Controlling (CO)

Helps identify breakdown points in
your company's performance and tells
how these processes can be improved

Details how to make production
processes more efficient to positively
impact your bottom line

John Jordan

Production Variance Analysis
in SAP Controlling

This book presents a detailed explanation of how production variance
analysis works in Controlling and focuses on the SAP processes and
reports that assist with all phases of the Controlling process. It explains
Controlling concepts from a simple and easy-to-understand level, while
also containing master data and configuration setup requirements.
Each chapter deals with a major sub-component of variance analysis
and includes real-life examples and case study scenarios.

292 pp., 2. edition 2011, 69,95 Euro / US$ 84.95
ISBN 978-1-59229-381-0

Learn how Product Costing works and integrates with other modules

Master integrated planning, product cost planning, manufacturing methods, reporting, and more

Understand how to reduce long run times during month-end processing

John Jordan

Product Cost Controlling with SAP

This comprehensive resource is for anyone with an interest in the integrated areas of product costing. You'll learn how overhead costs flow from financial postings to cost centers and then on to manufacturing orders. In addition, you'll master the material ledger, transfer pricing, reporting, and discover how to address common problem areas, including month-end processing, long run times, and message and variance analysis. This new edition includes updated content on cost object hierarchies and engineer-to-order, as well as new case studies and real-world examples.

approx. 635 pp., 2. edition, 79,95 Euro / US$ 79.95
ISBN 978-1-59229-399-5, Dec 2011

>> www.sap-press.com

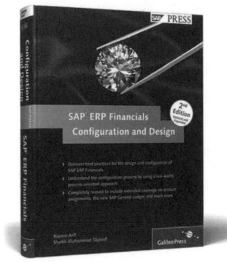

Discover best practices for the design and configuration of SAP ERP Financials

Understand the configuration process by using a real-world, project-implementation approach

Completely revised to include real-world examples and extended coverage on account assignments, the new SAP General Ledger, and much more

Naeem Arif, Sheikh Tauseef

SAP ERP Financials: Configuration and Design

Master the issues involved in designing and configuring an SAP ERP Financials implementation using this overview guide. This is an invaluable reference that covers what you need for the configuration and design process, the enterprise structure, reporting, data migration, Accounts Payable and Receivables, Financials integration with other modules, and all other critical areas of SAP ERP Financials. This new edition is updated for SAP ERP 6.0, Enhancement Package 4.

664 pp., 2. edition 2011, 79,95 Euro / US$ 79.95
ISBN 978-1-59229-393-3

>> www.sap-press.com

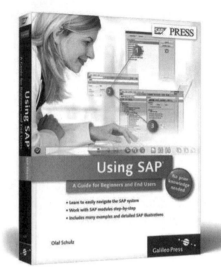

Learn to easily navigate the SAP system

Work with SAP modules step-by-step

Includes many examples and detailed SAP illustrations

Olaf Schulz

Using SAP:
A Guide for Beginners and End Users

This book helps end users and beginners get started in SAP ERP and provides readers with the basic knowledge they need for their daily work. Readers will get to know the essentials of working with the SAP system, learn about the SAP systems' structures and functions, and discover how SAP connects to critical business processes. Whether this book is used as an exercise book or as a reference book, readers will find what they need to help them become more comfortable with SAP ERP.

388 pp., 39,95 Euro / US$ 39.95
ISBN 978-1-59229-408-4

>> www.sap-press.com